ORDINARY
HEROES

118

ORDINARY HEROES

UNTOLD STORIES FROM THE FALKLANDS CAMPAIGN

CHRISTOPHER HILTON

FOREWORD BY MAJOR GENERAL JULIAN THOMPSON

The History Press

Front Cover Photograph: Royal Marines wait to go on patrol from Ajax Bay during the Falklands Conflict in 1982. (© Adrian Brown / Alamy)

First published 2012

The History Press
The Mill, Brimscombe Port
Stroud, Gloucestershire, GL5 2QG
www.thehistorypress.co.uk

© Christopher Hilton, 2012

British Library Cataloguing in Publication Data.
A catalogue record for this book is available from the British Library.

ISBN 978 0 7524 5714 7

Typesetting and origination by The History Press
Printed in Great Britain
Manufacturing managed by Jellyfish Print Solutions Ltd

CONTENTS

FOREWORD

BY MAJOR GENERAL JULIAN THOMPSON, CB, OBE

One of the enduring myths of the Falklands War is that of under-age Argentine soldiers being committed to an unequal battle; the implication being that the British servicemen were so much older, and hence better. That is why the Argentines were defeated. It is, of course, a face-saving myth propagated to explain why they lost, and reminds one of the age-old childish gripe 'it isn't fair'. In fact, no Argentine soldier was conscripted before his 18th birthday, and many were well over 18 because they were not plucked off the street the moment they reached that age, but drafted in batches. So by the time an Argentine soldier was shipped to the Falklands, having completed training, he was around 18½ years old. At least one of the regiments who served in the Falklands was made up of Argentine conscripts who had had their service extended for the operation and were over 19½.

Yes, the British were better, but not because they were older – we shall return to that. The two youngest British soldiers to be killed were just 17. Several British marines and paratroopers celebrated their 17th birthday on the journey south. Every single one was a volunteer, along with the rest of his comrades.

This book is special because it consists exclusively of contributions by men who were the equivalent of private soldiers at the time – ordinary seamen, marines and the like. Not one of them was even as elevated as a lance-corporal. This is important because the popular image of the

7

armed services is of a pyramid. At the top is the general or admiral sitting on a base consisting of myriad junior folk. In reality, one should view the armed services as a collection of inverted pyramids, each point being an individual without whom the battle would not be won: a sailor, marine or soldier. The best-laid plans and the cleverest generals and admirals are not sufficient by themselves. They need people to win the battle for them. This book contains accounts by those that did just that. They won it because they were better, not because they were British and not Argentine. They were professionals, better trained and hence better motivated. I was once asked why we won. I said there were three reasons: training, training and training.

All of the British servicemen who took part in the Falklands War were thrown in at the deep end, metaphorically speaking. There were no plans to retake the Falkland Islands in the event of an Argentine invasion. There were two reasons for this: first, the British Government, and the Foreign & Commonwealth Office in particular, believed that the Argentines were bluffing and would not invade; and second, about six months before the proverbial hit the fan the Ministry of Defence had come to the conclusion that retaking the islands was impossible. This is well documented in the British official history of the war.

When the Argentines did invade, the box marked 'Mission Impossible' was opened and the British armed forces were invited to see if they could prove this assumption was incorrect. The task was only possible because of the professionalism, skill and courage of the people who appear in the pages of this book, and thousands more like them.

Readers today may wonder at the differences between the conditions in which this war was fought and today's conflicts. There were no emails or mobile telephones. Mark Hiscutt of HMS *Sheffield* had to write to his fiancée: 'Not coming home. Cancel the wedding. Lots of love. Mark.' He was not allowed to say why his ship was suddenly not going back to England from Gibraltar but steaming off 180 degrees in the other direction. He was not alone: there were thousands like him. Once deployed no-one could communicate with home other than by mail. As the Task Force approached the Falklands, mail for home was often deliberately delayed to ensure that no secrets were inadvertently betrayed – the alternative being to censor letters.

The handling of the media was poor. The news about the *Sheffield* being hit was on the TV well before any next of kin were informed. This was not an isolated case. Newspapers and mail arrived episodically. There was no satellite TV. Everyone down south lived in a bubble, cut off from the outside world.

If you were in a ship you might be drier and better fed than your opposite number ashore, but your end could be swift, violent and while it lasted extremely unpleasant: cut off alone in a burning compartment, or battened down below in a sinking ship, with no chance of getting out. When ships were hit, casualties were usually heavy; many dead, many with horrific burns.

A marine or soldier ashore faced cold, injuries, hunger, fatigue and broken bones caused by the unforgiving weather and terrain, all without the enemy lifting a finger. He would be invited to assault the enemy, and patrol, often at night. Having eventually arrived on his objective, he might be shelled for several days and nights, existing on short rations because his rucksack had not arrived, shivering in the cold because his sleeping bag was in his rucksack, and glad of captured Argentine blankets. The helicopters were too busy carrying ammunition. Soldiers in rear areas were subject to the attentions of the Argentine air force, and lived in holes like their fellows nearer the enemy. Napoleon knew what he was talking about when he said 'the first quality of a soldier is fortitude in enduring fatigue and hardship: bravery but the second.'

Nobody knew when it would end. There was no tour length as in Afghanistan, Iraq or Northern Ireland. It would end when it ended.

One of the greatest remedies in time of danger and doubt is humour. The British services are renowned for their 'black' humour. David Buey, on being picked out of the water by HMS *Alacrity* after the *Atlantic Conveyor* was hit, asked a sailor how Tottenham Hotspur had got on in the Cup Final against Queen's Park Rangers. 'If I'd known you were a Tottenham fan, I would have thrown you back,' replied the *Alacrity* sailor.

Some of the contributors are suffering from, or have experienced, Post-Traumatic Stress Disorder (PTSD). This is a condition about which too little is known even today. At the time of the Falklands War, thirty years ago, a great deal less was known about it, or, more correctly, a great deal that had been learned in the Second World War and Korea had been forgotten. In the 1970s and early 1980s PTSD was popularly thought to be something that happened to Americans in Vietnam. The British forces medical services were apparently unaware of the work being done in Australia on their veterans returning from Vietnam; and, if they were, they were not interested – nothing was done. There were no arrangements in place to cope with PTSD at the time of the Falklands War. Now service people returning from a war zone are put through a period of 'decompression'; then there was no such thing, except by chance. Those that came back in ships together with their mates on a voyage that averaged three weeks were better off than those who were evacuated by air from Montevideo, having been taken there by hospital tender from the battle area. Those that came back with strangers, and flew part of the way, to be decanted straight into the midst of their families, were more prone to PTSD. They suffered, as did their families.

Fortunately, a British psychiatrist, Surgeon Commander Morgan O'Connell, RN, who had accompanied the medical teams in SS *Canberra*, understood what was happening, and did something about it. He started treating Royal Navy personnel who showed symptoms of PTSD, and the Royal Navy became the first British service to recognise it as a condition and treat it. The others have now followed suit.

The war in the South Atlantic was short, but bloody. The fighting at sea and ashore had much in common with the Second World War experience. Some of the technology was different, but watching the ships in San Carlos Water repelling Argentine air attacks day after day reminded me of accounts I had read of the Royal Navy fighting it out toe-to-toe with the Luftwaffe off Crete only forty years before. Young marines and soldiers not only closed with the enemy, but endured prolonged artillery and mortar bombardments, as well as being on the receiving end of enemy air attacks – this last is something that no British service person has experienced since.

These, and much else besides, are the subject of this book: the authentic voice of the point of the pyramid.

INTRODUCTION

E very man in this book is a volunteer twice. Each volunteered to join the British services, which is what took them to the Falkland conflict with Argentina thirty years ago, and each has volunteered to describe what happened to them when they got there, with, just as important, what has happened to them since.

I want to set out the book's framework immediately. I did not know any of these men and I did not select them. Through various organisations (which will be fully credited in a moment) the word went out that a book was in the making, it would consist almost entirely of memories, and the volunteers selected themselves by coming forward. There was a condition: none of them could have had a rank at the time of the conflict, so that even lance-corporals were excluded.

One volunteer, Paratrooper Dave Brown, had reservations about this: 'A lot of the navy people were junior ranks. A lot of times there were lance-corporals leading section attacks at Goose Green.' Brown felt the exclusion should be everyone above sergeant, because otherwise 'they miss out in telling their bit'.

If this was a history of the conflict, Brown would be right. It isn't. It is the very personal stories of ten men who were all of modest background, and who were young, who mostly left school early and were at the very lowest strata of the services. None could give any man an order, only obey the orders given to them. That is why there are no lance-corporals (and no disrespect whatever is intended).

From the obedience, the lowest – outnumbered and trapped in the unavoidable confusions of such an enterprise – won a war at a windswept, treeless, frozen place 8,000 miles from home which they had never heard of before. You can argue, and must argue, that a military victory is a tight-knit team effort, and each varied – very, very varied – component essential. In this, you cannot fail to argue that brilliant generals and brilliant technology come to depend, down all the centuries, on the quality of the men in the boots with simple weapons, what they can do and what they will do.

This book is about what they did.

The fact that they were *un*selected makes them representative in a bigger way: what happened to ordinary blokes.

Nationalism and chauvinism can lead straight to triumphalism. It's easy to get there, and particularly easy with a conflict which was so precisely defined between right and wrong: Argentina invaded and occupied a British colony, full of people who'd lived there for a couple of centuries and didn't want Argentina in any guise. If you live in Falkirk or Folkestone, imagine waking up having been 'liberated' by a Spanish-speaking army and you get the idea.

You will be finding very little triumphalism, but a profound sense of satisfaction at a job well done, against the odds in every sense; terrible fear and authentic bravery; great gales of gallows humour; grief etched into the sadness of ultimate sacrifice; and pity for the Argentine conscripts who, taken prisoner en masse, would be better treated by the British soldiers than their own officers. As one of the volunteers puts it, 'in the end you looked at them and thought they were human beings just like you.' Every volunteer came back wiser, or, as another put it, 'I went as a 19-year-old and came back as a 29-year-old several weeks later'.

Each volunteer was interviewed on the telephone, and for a reason. At a physical meeting the writer will be unable (trust me, I know) to resist setting the scene in florid detail, describing the look and mannerisms of the interviewee, catching and reporting their gestures. I didn't want any of that. I wanted them unadorned, revealing themselves through their words alone, not through my descriptions and interpretations. What you will be reading is *exactly* what came down the phone, so that you will be as close to it as I was. At strategic places, words of explanation and background have been added, but not much more.

Each interview was, by its nature, a self-contained story with its own insights; each was strong enough to demand its own chapter, and the order of the chapters is the order in which the interviews were done. Cumulatively they demonstrate what the most ordinary of British people can achieve, and if their discipline and purpose stands in direct contrast to so much ill-discipline in today's society by people of the same age and background, isn't that interesting?

Most of the volunteers have paid a price, although they were completely unaware of that at the time. The price was called Post-Traumatic Stress Disorder, and it can devastate lives. Each volunteer has coped – or tried to cope – with it, and I offer sincerest thanks to them for their extraordinary candour in describing what they have endured. Part Two, where the PTSD is recounted, does not make happy reading, although, now that the condition is recognised, hope is threaded through. Several of the volunteers said quietly that if their words comfort others – *you are not alone* – or if their words point out that professional help is at hand, their descriptions will have been worthwhile.

One man has been selected, and here I must declare an interest. I worked for the *Daily Express*, and so did reporter Bob McGowan, who covered the war for the newspaper. McGowan co-authored his own book, *Don't Cry for Me, Sargeant-Major*, with Jeremy Hands, which has been much praised since it first appeared shortly after the war – and a sequel in 1989, *Try Not to Laugh, Sergeant-Major*. McGowan, a razor-sharp news reporter, and Hands caught the chaotic humanity spread before them. I asked McGowan to reflect on how ordinary servicemen coped, and he has captured that with touching (and highly amusing) insights.

I offer thanks to Gordon Smith of www.naval-history.net for allowing me to quote. The website is a superb resource.

I am particularly grateful to Neil J. Kitchener of Cardiff & Vale NHS Trust Laision Psychiatry for all his help; to Jane Adams, secretary of South Atlantic Medal Association; and to Alex Bifulco, press officer of the RAF Association. I don't need to thank the ten volunteers here. Just read on, and you'll understand the depth of my gratitude to them all.

PART ONE

1

ALL AT SEA

It seemed a most trivial thing. On 20 December 1981 an Argentine scrap metal merchant, Constantino Davidoff, landed on South Georgia, an island lost in the cold waters of the southern Atlantic. With the South Sandwich Islands, which lay some 300 miles further on, it represented, literally and figuratively, the end of the British Empire.

South Georgia has been described as 'breathtakingly beautiful and a sight on an early spring day not easily forgotten'. It has also been described as:

long and narrow, shaped like a huge, curved, fractured and savaged whale bone, some 170 kilometres long and varying from 2 to 40 kilometres wide. Two mountain ranges (Allardyce and Salvesen) provide its spine, rising to 2,934 metres at Mount Paget's peak (eleven peaks exceed 2,000 metres). Huge glaciers, ice caps and snowfields cover about 75% of the island in the austral summer (November to January); in winter (July to September) a snow blanket reaches the sea. The island then drops some 4,000 metres to the sea floor.[1]

On a global scale, *anything* which happened there would be a most trivial thing.

South Georgia had no native population, but it did have a small number of residents, including staff from the British Antarctic Survey, which had scientific bases at Bird Island in the far north. The residents would see, among other things, a lot of elephant seals, fur seals and king penguins. The capital, Grytviken, was no more than a few buildings huddled between the ocean and the stark, immense Allardyce Range rising behind.

Davidoff landed without permission at Leith Harbour, a derelict whaling station 15 miles north of Grytviken. Thereby lies a tale, because he had, he would insist, tried to get permission from the British and even 'signed a deal worth $270,000 [£180,000] with the Scottish owners' of the station to take the scrap away.[2]

Word reached the British Antarctic Survey base at Grytviken, but, when they got to Leith Harbour, they found Davidoff had gone. They also found that he had left a message, in chalk, announcing that South Georgia belonged to Argentina, which had laid claim to them since 1927. Argentina had trained more covetous eyes on the Falkland Islands, which had many more inhabitants amongst the seals, penguins and particularly sheep. The Falklands, a British colony since 1833 and some 800 miles to the north-east, had always been claimed by Argentina and they even had a Spanish name, the Islas Malvinas. With South Georgia and the South Sandwich Islands they formed a community composed of small, distant parts.

Two days after Davidoff's landing, Lieutenant General Leopoldo Galtieri seized power in Argentina using that country's traditional method of transferring power: a military coup. Davidoff's landing still seemed a most trivial thing, in total no more than a fleeting visit by a scrap-metal dealer who scented scrap on South Georgia and left some mindless graffiti on his way out. It had, of course, nothing to do with Galtieri.

Mark Hiscutt, a 21-year-old gunner – or missile man, as they're known – from Farnborough had joined HMS *Sheffield*, a Type 42 destroyer, in March, and since November had been in the Gulf. In the New Year, *Sheffield* would take part in Exercise SPRING TRAIN, but Hiscutt would be home by 8 May. He had to be. It was his wedding day. 'I had a fair idea where the Falklands were, yes, I knew they weren't north of Scotland' – which many in the services did not know.

Brian Bilverstone, a 20-year-old radio operator on HMS *Herald*, an ocean survey ship, was in the Middle East on a seven-month trip. Watch duty tended to be quiet. There were four teleprinters in a bank, one permanently on, the other three on standby. One was invariably enough because the *Herald* rarely received more than thirty messages a day. Bilverstone would spend time listening to the teleprinter chattering away – or more likely hearing silence. He 'didn't have a clue' where the Falklands were: 'We thought it was Scotland.'

On 9 January 1982 the British Ambassador in the Argentine capital, Buenos Aires, lodged a formal protest about Davidoff's landing. Three days later the Argentinian Joint Armed Forces Committee began plans to invade the Falklands. Galtieri, now ruling through a *junta*, inherited a country destroyed by financial problems and traumatised by fighting a 'dirty' internal war against all manner of perceived opponents. He was not popular, but a solution lay to hand: the Islas Malvinas. Their value was entirely symbolic, but, to the destroyed and traumatised, *hugely* symbolic. Just as importantly, they were defended by only a symbolic force of sixty-eight Royal Marines and HMS *Endurance*, an Antarctic patrol vessel which 'maintained Britain's presence around the Falkland Islands and supported the British Antarctic Survey'.[3] The *Endurance* was to be decommissioned as an economic measure which British Prime Minister Margaret Thatcher announced on 9 February. Galtieri could be forgiven for reading this as a withdrawal, opening the islands to him.

Steve Wilkinson, a 21-year-old marine engineer from Chesterfield, was on HMS *Exeter*, another Type 42 destroyer, halfway through a three-month tour of the West Indies doing guard duty. 'It was very nice and pleasant. The locals were very friendly and there were were quite a few barbeques and parties to be had.' He 'didn't know where the Falklands were. It was very sketchy because it's like the Shetlands and the Orkneys. It's just another bunch of islands, but because the UK had sovereignty on all sorts of bits and pieces, unless you were a geographical whizz you didn't necessarily know.'

In New York, the British and the Argentinians met to discuss the sovereignty of the islands. As February melted in to March these talks were described as 'cordial and positive'. Potentially, if a formula could be worked out, two problems would be solved: the Falklands were only 300 miles from Argentina and, in all practical terms, it made more sense to have a working relationship than rely on Britain 8,000 miles away; and Galtieri could pose as the man who reclaimed the Malvinas. There was a problem, however: other British politicians and diplomats who'd tried these negotiations had encountered opposition – sometimes ferocious – within Britain, and Galtieri was a career soldier.

David Buey was a 20-year-old mechanic with the Fleet Air Arm working on helicopters. His squadron was based at Royal Naval Air Station Yeovilton, in Somerset, and he might have expected to be going on a tour of Northern Ireland. It was a front-line squadron and had been there before. The Falklands were something else. 'Very few people did know where the Falklands were, I think.'

Mario Reid, a 20-year-old from Huntingdon, was a sapper with 9 Parachute Squadron of the Royal Engineers, the Parachute Regiment's attached combat engineering unit. He was a fit young man who'd joined the engineers but volunteered, or been volunteered for, para training. 'I didn't mind.' He was in barracks at Aldershot and had no idea where the Falklands were. 'No, of course not. Most people thought they were in Scotland.'

A day after the meeting in New York the Argentinian foreign minister dismissed all talk of the 'cordial and positive' talks and threatened that if Britain did not relinquish sovereignty then the Argentinians would use 'other methods'. It wasn't looking trivial any more and, for those who could read the currents, a general and a *junta* which could not back down and survive were locking themselves in against a woman who could not back down and survive. Moreover, for Galtieri the word survival might involve physical dimensions; for Thatcher it would only mean her career as prime minister would be over, perhaps very quickly.

On 3 March in London a Member of Parliament asked if all precautions were being taken to defend the Falklands, and didn't get a clear reply. Two days later the British Foreign Secretary reportedly refused to send a submarine to patrol the Falklands. A day after that, a Hercules aeroplane run by LADE, a branch of the Argentine military, landed at Port Stanley airport claiming a fuel leak. LADE had a man there and he gave the senior officers on the plane a tour of the area. Two days later

Thatcher asked for plans to be drawn up in the event of an Argentinian blockade or even full-scale invasion.

On 19 March Davidoff and forty workmen returned to South Georgia and did not seek permission. In response, HMS *Endurance* and twenty-two Royal Marines were despatched from the Falklands.

Dave Brown, a 20-year-old born in Glasgow and now with 2nd Battalion the Parachute Regiment 'was up at home in Leeds for the weekend, Easter leave. My plan of action was watching Leeds v Liverpool at Elland Road and then travelling over to see my sister in Holland, who was just about to have her first baby. Unfortunately we got called back. I managed to stay over for the Leeds game – which I think we lost, by the way – and then I phoned my mate up who was on guard duty because obviously nobody had mobiles in those days. I did not know where the Falklands were. I don't think 80%, 90% of the lads did.'

On 3 April the Argentinians put significant forces ashore on South Georgia and, although the marines resisted and caused considerable damage, they could not withstand the numbers put against them.

By then Argentina had invaded the Falklands, too. The images of surrender exercised a profound impact on ordinary British people, who knew that regular British people like themselves, in distant Port Stanley and the sheep stations scattered across the two islands – East and West Falkland – were now being ruled by a military *junta* with a lot of blood on its hands against a constant backdrop of a lot of mothers marching in Buenos Aires for their disappeared sons.

Thatcher was fighting for her political life, while Galtieri saluted adoring, chanting multitudes.

The British Parliament authorised the sending of a Task Force and almost immediately the first RAF planes were heading towards Ascension Island, a British dependent territory since 1653, almost 2,000 miles from Angola and 1,500 from Brazil. Within a short while the airport on this tropical volcanic island became the busiest in the world. Ascension would be a forward base where supplies could be flown for when the Task Force arrived.

By now all manner of diplomacy was going on. With American President Ronald Reagan's approval, Secretary of State Alexander Haig would shuttle from London to Buenos Aires and back trying to find common ground.

Jimmy O'Connell was a 22-year-old paratrooper from Liverpool who'd just come back from Northern Ireland: 'I went on Easter leave. I didn't know where the Falklands were. I don't think anyone knew. We thought they were in Scotland – some people were saying Scotland. Truthfully, I had never heard of them.'

Graeme Golightly was a 19-year-old marine from Knowsley in Merseyside, based in Seaton Barracks, Plymouth. 'We were in Altcar, a weapons range in Southport. We'd just gone up for some weapon training.' Now they were recalled to Seaton Barracks 'to get our spearhead kit all ready for whatever was going to be happening. Truthfully, no, I did not know where the Falklands were.'

The Task Force, which would have to operate at that range of 8,000 miles, comprised the navy's four remaining major surface ships: the aircraft carriers *Hermes* and *Invincible*, and the assault ships *Fearless* and *Intrepid*. Half the nuclear submarine fleet went. Eight destroyers went: one Type 82, *Bristol*; two 'County' Class, *Antrim* and *Glamorgan*; five Type 42s, *Cardiff*, *Coventry*, *Exeter* – which had Stephen Wilkinson on – *Glasgow* and *Sheffield* – which had Mark Hiscutt on. There were fifteen frigates: *Brilliant* – which had William Field on – and *Broadsword* (Type 22s); *Active, Alacrity, Ambuscade, Antelope, Ardent, Arrow* and *Avenger* (Type 21s); *Andromeda, Argonaut, Minerva, Penelope* (Leander class); and *Plymouth* and *Yarmouth* (Rothesay class).[4]

There were survey ships being used as hospitals, including HMS *Herald*. There were Merchant Navy cargo vessels and a North Sea ferry, the *Norland* – which had Dave Brown on. Ocean liners were requisitioned as gigantic troop transporters: the *QE2* – which had Mario Reid on – and the *Canberra* – which had Jimmy O'Connell and Graeme Golightly on. And there were auxiliary ships like the *Fort Austin* – which had David Buey on.

On 25 April South Georgia was recaptured by the Royal Marines.

The British Government declared a 200-nautical-mile Exclusion Zone round the Falklands a day later. On 29 April the Task Force arrived at the Exclusion Zone and on 2 May the Argentinian cruiser *General Belgrano* was sunk by the Royal Navy submarine HMS *Conqueror*, killing 323, although it was outside the Exclusion Zone.

Up until this moment there had been a general assumption, not least among the young men in the Task Force, that a shooting war was unthinkable. The diplomats and politicians would find the common ground after all this military posturing and everyone would go home. After the *Belgrano*, they all sensed a shooting war had begun.

They were right.

Notes

1. www.sgisland.gs
2. news.bbc.co.uk/2/hi/programmes/from_our_own.../8599404.stm
3. www.chdt.org.uk/.../Falklands
4. Type 42: guided-missile destroyer; Type 21: general-purpose escort frigate from the 1970s to the 1990s; Type 22: specialist anti-submarine warfare frigate; *Rothesay* class: modified Type 12 frigates named after seaside towns.

2

THE MISSILE MAN

I went inside the ship twice, the first time with my mate *Bones*, and while we were down there we didn't have breathing apparatus. All we had was our gas masks. Part of your training is that you never wear a gas mask in a smoke-filled environment – it's not built for it – but that's all we had. It was that or nothing.

Mark Hiscutt's father was in the army, 'so we moved around a lot and we ended up living in Farnborough in Hampshire. I joined the Sea Cadets and I thought *this looks good*. I didn't want to join the army because I didn't want my father saying, "Well, it wasn't like that in my days" – that's natural. I do it to my mate's son! – so I chose the navy. I was born in 1960 and I was sixteen and a half when I joined up.

'I was a typical boy. I played football for the school and various clubs, I was in the Sea Cadets. We visited a lot of countries, we holidayed in Italy, driving down and back. It wasn't the case for me that I was going into the services because of an unhappy childhood – I'd had a good childhood. I think I wanted to join the navy because of the Sea Cadets.

'At my interview in 1976 I said I didn't want to join the army because of the reason about dad and, secondly, I didn't want to go to Northern Ireland. Then it was pointed out to me that there were matelots in Northern Ireland, which I didn't know. I joined up in 1977. I did my basic training at HMS *Raleigh* and HMS *Cambridge* because I was a gunnery rate – missile man, as they call them. They are the ones who fire the guns, in my day four-and-half-inch guns, all metric now.'

Raleigh, the navy says, is the:

premier training establishment in the South West where all ratings joining the service receive the first phase of their naval training. The 9-week phase one training course is designed to be challenging, exciting, maritime in its focus and relevant to the operational environment individuals will find themselves in. It aims to develop individuals as part of a team, inculcate naval ethos and a sense of being part of the naval family.[1]

Cambridge, at the former Wembury Point Holiday Camp south-east of Plymouth, was 'to provide live firing practice with conventional weapons for officers and ratings qualifying in gunnery'.[2]

Hiscutt joined HMS *Sheffield* in March 1981. The *Sheffield*, built at Barrow, was a guided-misile destroyer which had been commissioned in 1975. She had a complement of 287, was 410 feet long, 47 feet wide and could do a maximum 30 knots.

Hiscutt explains that 'you had 20mm close-range weapons, that sort of thing. The four and a half is the one at the very front so if you think about a Type 42 destroyer, it's that gun there. I don't know exactly how fast it fired but it was pretty fast and it had a range of a couple of miles. It could knock an aircraft out and be used as naval gunfire support, which is laying rounds down against enemy targets on land, so it was a versatile and important gun. I was in the gun bay. The gun we had on the *Sheffield* was a Mark 8, an automatic loader. There was nobody in the turret. During action stations there were four or five of us in the gun bay and we kept loading the rounds which went up into the turret.'

The *Sheffield* was 'away on deployment in the Gulf from November 1981 to March 1982 when we started Exercise SPRING TRAIN in, I think, April. We were roughly six days from home when we were turned around. We were part of SPRING TRAIN and the idea was that we were going to do a Sea Dart firing[3] – because we had the missile on the front – and during it we did the firing. We got 100% because we hit the target and we were getting quite happy because we were nearly coming home, too, and I was quite happy because I was going to get married. We knew things were bubbling down south [in the South Atlantic] because we were hearing it on the radio, but we thought they wouldn't send us because we'd been away for six months.'

On 2 April *Sheffield* was ordered to stand by for deployment to the Falklands. That day warships of the First Flotilla, under Rear Admiral Sandy Woodward, were in Gibraltar for SPRING TRAIN.

'On the way back we stopped off at Gibraltar,' Hiscutt says. 'One morning we were woken up and told that First Lieutenant Mike Norman would make an announcement to ship's company. He said we were going to be turned round to go down south. At the time they did something called "sons at sea" so some of the lads had their sons on board – we had been on our way home – and it was a way of keeping the family together. They'd flown down to Gibraltar and, in fact, Mike Norman's son must have been about 13 or 14 because he was in our mess with me. I had a fair idea where the Falklands were, yes, I knew they weren't north of Scotland.

'We were told mail would be closing on board quite soon so we could write a quick letter home. As with everything, we weren't allowed to say what we were doing, where we were going or anything like that. I got a piece of paper and wrote on there to my fiancée: *Not coming home. Cancel the wedding. Lots of love, Mark.* We should have been married on 8 May.

'When the Task Force was being *prepped*, the ships that were part of the exercise became the advance party as such. When we left we refuelled with a Royal Fleet Auxillary ship which had been round the Gulf with us so it was nice that we said goodbye to them. As we broke away from the refuelling they played *Don't Cry For Me, Argentina* and that was quite … funny.

'There was nothing in the press about us on our way down, all quiet. Eventually something hit the papers – it was a small bit, Kirsty said, but I think that was when we got to Ascension Island and we were waiting for the rest of the Task Force to join us.'

The *Antrim, Glamorgan, Coventry, Glasgow, Brilliant, Arrow, Plymouth* and *Sheffield* reached Ascension on 10 April. A vast quantity of stores had been flown to the island, some not appropriate for a war zone, and a degree of chaos reigned. The official report says the procedure was to load what were considered 'useful items' and 'ignore the rest. The stores situation ashore contributed to *Sheffield*'s decision not to take advantage of this further opportunity to offload personal possessions, valuables and inflammables.'[4]

'Ascension was surreal,' Hiscutt says. 'We were busy because we were now *prepping* the ship for war. We were getting more ammo on board because [in exercises] you have practice rounds and but you get rid of them for the proper rounds. We were painting everything grey. Because the Argentinians had two Type 42 destroyers they'd bought from the British they had the same look as the *Sheffield*. The *Sheffield* had something called "ears" on its funnel – they were extra vents on top of the funnel. No other 42 in the fleet had them, but the two Argentinian ships did. So that people could identify our 42 from their 42s we painted a black stripe from the top of the funnel down to the waterline on both sides.

'Because we had been away for six months people were sending things home, like presents they'd bought, and I remember saying to one bloke, "You are tempting fate." I didn't send anything home because I thought we would be going home and nothing would happen.

'A lot of the journalists went down with the troops on the *QE2* and they had a nice time, but we were on a warship. I must say we did think about it and when we were at Ascension Island – or on the way down to Ascension Island – the gunnery officer called all the gunnery rates together down the mess and we were talking about what had to be done. Someone said, "Where's the Falklands?" We had the game of Risk, a board game where you have countries and armies, and the more countries you get the more armies you get. Someone opened that up and said, "Well, there's the Falklands. If we attack Argentina we get two extra armies!"

'I think there was an underlying understanding of the seriousness, because we had a job to do, but you never thought it would happen to us. I was getting letters from my sister, who is four years younger than me, and I wrote a letter back saying, "Don't worry, we are well protected and nothing can happen to us".'

The official report says:

Preparations for War – Stores

Ships of the Task Force were paired off, *Sheffield* with *Active*, for stores transfer. This involved *Sheffield* receiving a large quantity of such stores and ammunition as might be useful in a war situation, in particular 4.5-inch ammunition, chaff rockets, and some medical stores, together with food and miscellaneous items, including canteen stores, of which the ship was short following her Indian Ocean deploymant. [Hiscutt says 'we were getting food on board and it was all Argentinian beef. It *was* surreal eating that.'] The ammunition then carried exceeded outfit, possibly by as much as 100% in some categories. However, it was all stowed in magazines, although inevitably not in approved stowage. For example 4.5-inch ammunition was stowed on the deck in the 4.5-inch Magazine and also in the Air Weapons Magazine adjacent to the Hangar. Back-loading to *Active* of unwanted stores was restricted to defective items and empties; it did not include furniture or furnishings, possessions or inflammables.

Preparations for War – Material

Material preparations were in accordance with Ships War Orders … and included the removal of pictures, taking up of carpets below 1 Deck, and stowing away of loose fittings. … Some material preparations were significant, also, from the point of view of increasing the Ship's Company's awareness of the reality of the threat. For example *Sheffield* issued, at an early stage, their Atropine and other prophylactics[5] for use in the event of chemical attack.

On 14 April *Brilliant*, *Glasgow*, *Sheffield*, *Coventry* and *Arrow* left Ascension.
 'When we sailed south from Ascension we got our rules of engagement because apparently there was an Argentinian aircraft out looking for the Task Force,' Hiscutt says. 'We never saw it.
 'The first of May was a few weeks away and we knew that if nothing happened by then hostilities would start because we understood that

that was an ultimatum. We knew things were getting serious because the *Antrim* and *Yarmouth* were sent to South Georgia to take that back. That's when we knew. We were getting quite a lot of information, we were being kept up to date.

'On the first of May we went to action stations early in the morning. The ship was somewhere off the Falklands by then. We hadn't seen the islands because the *Sheffield* didn't get close enough. We were right out on the edge acting as the first line of defence for the aircraft carriers. Then, as you came in, you got other ships so if the attackers got past us they had to get through the second wave before they got to the carriers. The carriers were the things that we had to protect.

'So we were out there and the Harriers were going in, dropping bombs. Part of my problem is I can't remember much between the 1st of May and the 4th of May. People have told me we had air attacks. I can't remember that. Some things I must have blocked out. I do remember one occasion before the 4th of May we got told to brace because they thought an Exocet had been launched at us. I was in the gun bay surrounded by all the ammo and I went and stood behind the live rounds thinking, *I'm not going to be injured, if I'm going to go, I want to go in one bit.*

'I knew what an Exocet was. The British navy has them so we knew about them anyway. If I remember rightly, the *Antrim* – one of the destroyers that was with us – had Exocets on board as well.[6]

'If you read the Board of Inquiry about the *Sheffield* it says our *ops* officers were more concerned about shells being dropped from the air rather than missiles. The concern was aircraft because all we had was a four-and-a-half-inch gun. Close range we had machine guns and that was it, really, so if fighter planes came in close we were kind of sitting ducks. That's why we were worried about aircraft. Anyway, we stayed out there.

'When the *General Belgrano* was sunk we were informed of it through the broadcast in the evening. We said a prayer for the sailors. They're sailors just like us and our problem isn't with them. They were doing their job and it was either them or us. When we had the prayer said we thought about them. That's when we really knew it was getting serious.

'On the fourth of May the *Sheffield* was at defence watches: half the ship's company on watch, the other half were turned in. At midday I went on watch – midday – and I went into the gun bay. There were three of us in there. Because nothing was happening we weren't at action stations, the air-raid warning was low – the threat was low – so we were just sat in there talking. I took a cushion with me because it's a bare metal floor. When we went to action stations I put it out of the way but we knew there would be periods of us sitting around doing nothing. We weren't allowed to leave the gun bay because when you go in you shut the doors behind you.'

Two Super Étendards,[7] armed with Exocets, had taken off from the Rio Grande Naval Air Base and were approaching. The Exocets were launched from about 6 miles away. The *Sheffield* had an old radar system, Type 965, and it picked up *something* – might have been the enemy, might have been a Harrier, might even have been a helicopter.

'We're sat in there and a warning came across the radio saying, "Guns stand to." We got up and got ready then we heard, "Alarm, aircraft" – aircraft were coming in.'

On the bridge, when the Exocets were about a mile away, they were identified as missiles. They took five seconds to reach *Sheffield*.

'Next thing we knew there was a *whoosh* going down the starboard side of the ship. I heard it. The ship kind of rocked. I didn't hear any bang because I was in an enclosed compartment.'

One Exocet struck amidships about 8 feet above the waterline, bored into the main engine compartment and the missile's own fuel caused a fire. The other Exocet passed harmlessly by and went into the sea.

'Some of the lighting went out and there were people shouting over the intercom. My mate *Bones*, who I was run ashore with when I met my wife, came running in and said, "What's going on?" We said, "Not too sure but we've lost power to the gun." He went up forward and got power back to the gun, came back in and when the door was open we could see there was smoke and blokes were standing round outside the gun bay. They were making their way to the fo'castle through an escape hatch.'

The official inquiry stated that the missile gouged a hole 15 feet by 4 feet in the *Sheffield*'s side, causing:

widespread minor shock damage, typically the buckling of doors and collapse of ladders ... Large fires broke out immediately. The overwhelming initial impression is of the very rapid spread of acrid black smoke through the centre section of the ship and upward, as far as the Bridge. This smoke very quickly forced evacuation of the Machinery Control Rod, Main Communications Office, HQ1 and the Bridge, followed after a few minutes by the Ops Room ... Missile propellant and burning Dieso [diesel oil] ... were the main sources of this smoke, which was responsible for the early and almost complete loss of the ship's fighting capability. Smoke clearance was unsuccessful forward and only partially successful aft.

The Firemain was breached at impact. Pressure was lost immediately and never restored ... Fire fighting was largely restricted to external boundary cooling, using portable pumps and buckets, and this had little or no effect on the fires raging within the ship.

Hiscutt remembers: 'The power had gone again. I remember looking out through the gun-bay doors and having a pair of eyes peering up at me. It was one of the blokes from the operations room. It wasn't until 2005 when I was down at the Falklands that I remembered that person's name. All I remembered before was the eyes. He was an able seaman, radar.

'You think, *Christ, what's going on?* We closed the door and eventually we were allowed to leave the gun bay. I think we were the last ones to leave the inside of the ship. When we went onto the fo'castle it was covered with men just sitting down because the helicopters were coming in and lifting casualties off. Once the casualties went we were detailed to go and start fighting the fire. We lost our firemain because that had been breached in a couple of places and the only way we could get water was by using pumps to suck it out of the sea. Unfortunately on the Type 42 it was stored on the quarter deck and we weren't able to reach ours because we couldn't get through the smoke. We were waiting for the other ships to supply them to us.

'We were using buckets and string and bits of rope, throwing them over the side and using the water to try and do some cooling. You could see the steam coming off the fo'castle steel.'

The official inquiry states: 'The fires gained quickly, soon embracing most of H, J and K Sections … and subsequently spreading forward and aft. Re-entry attempts were made … These were well briefed, determined attacks by men wearing fearnought suits and BA, but all wore beaten back by heat and smoke.'

Hiscutt says, 'I went inside the ship twice. The first time I went down with my mate *Bones* and while we were down there we didn't have breathing apparatus. All we had was our gas masks. Part of your training is that you never wear a gas mask in a smoke-filled environment – it's not built for it – but that's all we had. It was that or nothing. *Bones* said to me, "*Ginge*" – my nickname – "Have you seen Number One?" You have laundrymen on board, and Number Two, but Number One is the boss. [The first lieutenant is responsible to the captain for the crew's domestic matters. He is sometimes known as 'Jimmy the One' or simply 'Number One'.]

'I said no I hadn't seen Number One and we went looking for him. We looked around and couldn't find him. *Bones* said, "Not feeling too well *Ginge*, better make our way out" and as he was climbing up the ladder he collapsed. *Bones* is 6 foot 6, pretty strong guy and he was my mate. I was 21, I was fit but I was a skinny little runt, no meat on me at all. I wasn't very strong. I was having to hold him up on the ladder because if I'd let go he would have fallen a deck below.

'I had to get my gas mask off to shout for someone to pull him up. The last time I saw him he was having fits on the fo'castle, he was shaking like he was having a fit. This was purely the smoke. He had to be revived a couple of times before he was airlifted off onto the *Hermes*. I came out and said, "Has anybody seen Number One?" and they said no. A petty officer said, "I'm going down to have a look for him." I said I'd go down with him. I'd only been down a couple of minutes when I started feeling ill. I had to get out. I was sat down in the fresh air for a period of time with the vicar, then I started helping to fight the fire again.'

At 2.26 the *Yarmouth* heard *Sheffield* might have been hit by an Exocet. Two minutes later the *Yarmouth* and *Arrow* were ordered to get to the *Sheffield* at full speed. Three minutes after that the Exocet strike was confirmed to *Yarmouth*.

'While we were fighting this fire we had *Yarmouth* on one side spraying water and HMS *Arrow*, a Type 21 frigate, on the port side feeding
us equipment and spraying water on that side of the ship. It was very
reassuring in a way, knowing they were there. They were alongside us
during the six hours we fought the fire and the *Yarmouth* actually fired
her mortars because, as an old type frigate, she had mortars: someone had
seen traces of torpedos. Nobody has verified there was a submarine in
the area but people who were down on the back end said they saw traces.
So she went off looking for this sub and then came back.'

The official inquiry states:

> Much external assistance was provided. To port, *Arrow* did an excel-
> lent job of boundary cooling, supplying hoses and general support.
> Conditions for *Yarmouth*, to starboard, were less easy. Both ships' efforts
> were bedevilled by frequent spurious submarine and torpedo alarms.

At 5.26 lines were passed from the *Yarmouth* to the *Sheffield* because the
fire was now visibly out of any sort of control. At 5.45 there was no
choice but to abandon ship.[8]

Twenty officers and ratings died. The official inquiry states: 'Some
personnel, in the Galley area, were killed on impact. Others were asphyx-
iated, later, either attempting to escape, re-entering the ship or staying at
their quarters to try and restore the ship's fighting capability.'

Hiscutt says that, 'we fought the fire for between four and six hours
before [the skipper] Sam Salt[9] made the decision to abandon ship. The
way that happened was *Arrow* came along our port side and we jumped
on board from our flight desk on to the side of their ship. It came up so
close you could jump across. I think at the most the gap would have been
about 4 feet and it was straight across, but you had to time it: if you imagine ships stationary in the water but bobbing up and down, you mis-time
it, you go down between the two ships and you'll be crushed. There were
blokes on the other side, anyway, to catch us.

'We were put down in one of their mess decks and in the one where
I was they wanted to close the hatch to keep the ship watertight. We

threatened to throttle the bloke if he closed that hatch. We wanted that hatch open. For us it was so important because the hatch was a means of escape: the mess decks were below the water line. If you were on the *Sheffield* by the magazine, where the shells are, you were way below the water line. You are in there and, if there is a hole in the ship, people really shouldn't open the hatch to let you out. You're expendable, you're cannon fodder – because the ship must be kept afloat otherwise everything goes. It's a very hard thing but obviously true. It's something you didn't think about – well I never did when I joined up, anyway. We always joked about it on board, joked about life expectancy in a war zone, but nobody thought it would ever happen.

'Anyway, the captain of the *Arrow* relented in the end and said yes, so there we were sitting on the *Arrow*. In each junior rates' mess you had able seamen and seamen, which was my rank. In the navy you were entitled to three cans of beer per man per day if you were over the age of 18. In each mess there was a locker where your beer would be kept; we found it, broke into it and we shared their beer amongst us. Next thing one of the senior rates handed down a pint mug full of rum and we passed that around.

'They came out of action stations and we spent the night on board there. I was being pretty sick, coughing up all the muck and stuff that I'd inhaled from a lot of fumes. Every time I blew my nose it was black with what I was bringing up.

'The next morning we were taken off and put onto the *Fort Austin*, a store ship, and we were actually allocated *cabins* because civilian ships don't have mess decks like we do in the navy. It was two or three men to a cabin and we were allocated a cabin to share with the ship's company. I was sharing with a young airman, an aircraft handler, a civilian. He was telling me how much extra he was getting for being in a war zone and I thought *Christ*.

'We had a meeting, if you want to call it that, in the *bar* because once again it was a civilian ship and so it had a bar. The ship's company met in there and we were told this would be our action stations – this is where we'd come. We said, "No, we won't." It was too far inside the ship. So they said, "OK, what we'll do is go the next level up." That was still inside the ship, but we actually went to action stations in this area, where the fork lifts drive to move all the stores round. We were standing there and without any warning they fired three-inch rockets which have chaff in them, the bits of tinfoil to put off radar and so on. They fired their rockets but they didn't tell us and I haven't ever seen so many people hit the deck so hard. You can imagine what our bottoms were doing at the time.

'We said, "We want to be on the upper deck" and in the end our action stations was the dining hall on the upper deck.

'The job during the day was to make sure the bar was full of beer ready for the evening. We were allowed to send a telegram home – one telegram – and I had to make a choice: do I send it to my father, who was my next of kin, or Kirsty, my wife-to-be? I sent it to Kirsty: *I am alive and well and OK and let dad know.*

'My father was sitting at home – my mother died in 1980 – with my little sister and they were watching ITV. Kirsty was in Weymouth in her bedroom writing me a letter. One of the neighbours came knocking on my dad's door and said, "Have you seen the news?" Dad said, "No." The neighbour said, "The *Sheffield's* been hit." Dad put the news on and it was announced then. That's the first they heard.

'My mother-in-law ran up to the bedroom and told Kirsty, but she wasn't allowed to phone the military information telephone numbers because she wasn't my next of kin. My father was. My dad phoned up and heard, "Your son's name is not on the survivors list. Phone back in a couple of hours." He did phone back and they said, "No. Someone will be coming to see you tomorrow." My dad, being ex-military, knew what that meant. He phoned again at 6 o'clock in the morning and was told, "Yes, he's on the survivors list but we don't know what injuries he has." It wasn't until they got my telegram saying I was fine that they knew I had no injuries. Before that, all they'd known was that I was alive.

'We were getting drunk every night on the *Austin* because that's what we did. During the day we were just doing things, but there was not much we could do. In the evenings, when there was no air threat, we went down the bar.

'Eventually we were put onto a tanker, which had been refuelling the ships. This was a civilian ship that had been requisitioned by the MoD. It was owned by BP and it was named the *British Esk*. This little vessel had a crew of about forty and you then put 200 of us on board. We were sleeping on campbeds, in passageways, anywhere we could. The food was rationed. I think there were three or four sittings for each meal. Flushing the toilets was using sea water. Showers, you were allowed one a week or something. We got to do some work on there to keep us busy, helping to clean the ship down and that sort of thing. When they refuelled a warship, which was going down, we got involved in that because we were happier doing something than sitting around.

'The only other thing we had to do was write out statements of what we did and they were being typed up ready for the Board of Inquiry. We arrived at Ascension Island and were offloaded there. The last time we were together as a ship's company was on Ascension at an open-air cinema where Sam Salt addressed us. We were told he had been told we were not allowed to go home in what we were wearing, we had to go home in brand new uniforms. We went through some boxes and picked up new action working dress, which we call Number 8s. It wasn't proper uniform, it was working dress. We were given a canvas bag to put our belongings in so when we walked off the plane we all wore Number 8s. I had a t-shirt underneath!

'We flew in two waves from Ascension to Brize Norton. The first flight had everybody who lives up north on it plus Sam Salt and a few of the other officers, because they were required to make press statements when they got back. The second wave was everybody else – those who lived down south. When we landed we were met by the families. They were informed (from what I've heard) that they were not allowed to run out onto the tarmac to meet us, they had to stay indoors and wait for us to come in. Well, that didn't happen. My little sister came running up to me followed by Kirsty and my dad was there so it was nice. My father brought me some clothes up but unfortunately they didn't fit me so I was still wearing my Number 8s. I was a single man of course and the *Sheffield* was my home. That's where all my clothes were, everything. When I got home I didn't have anything.

'I got home and the rest of my family were there to welcome me in – and the local press. It was pretty funny because people were asking what happened and I didn't go into a lot of detail. My father didn't know that I helped *Bones* out.

'People were leaving the house and one of my sisters said, "It's like rats leaving a sinking ship" then she thought *I shouldn't have said that*. I said, "Don't worry," because we were seeing the funny side of things. It was black humour. Those words didn't worry me – it's just the way you deal with it. It's like the police, ambulance and fire services deal with it.

'I didn't see what happened to the *Sheffield*. When we jumped was the last I saw of her. We were told when she sank. We were on the *Fort Austin* and Sam Salt was on the *Hermes*. The *Sheffield* was being towed to South Georgia by the *Yarmouth*. The seas got high and they had to slip the tow and she just rolled over. It was a sad day because the *Sheffield* was more than my second home. It's hard to describe.

'We [the ship's company] had been together for six months. We'd been through the Gulf and we'd had some really good times so when we heard the *Sheffield* had gone – yes, it was a ship but it was more than that to me. The *Sheffield* was what was keeping us all together, because, unlike the army where they move regiments around, they don't do that in the navy. So the last time we were together was Ascension Island. After that we were scattered through the Fleet.

'It's hard, because then you can't really talk to people. Some of them didn't know what you were talking about if they hadn't been down there, and some didn't want to know. You didn't even talk really to blokes who you'd served on the *Sheffield* with.

'Every evening we got an update and that was the worst bit about coming home because you were out of that line of communication and you didn't know what was going on. Whereas down there you knew what was going on.

'I did get married. We set the date of 19 June and we were putting a guest list together. I consciously didn't invite anybody from the *Sheffield* because I thought they'd want to be with their families, so I didn't invite my mate *Bones* (and he hasn't let me forget it, either).

'We got married and we went on honeymoon. We stayed at an hotel in Taunton and the day after the wedding *Bones* turned up at dad's. *Bones* was a biker. He rode into the estate where my father lived, him and twenty other blokes on these big motorbikes, and you can imagine what my dad thought. It wasn't a Hell's Angels chapter but it was that type. Because my father didn't know about *Bones* – I hadn't told him – when he saw these motorbikes pull up outside the house and saw this big guy in leathers knocking on the door he was a bit … worried. He opened the door and *Bones* said, "Is *Ginge* in?" My dad said, "No, he got married yesterday." And *Bones* burst out crying. My dad invited him in and *Bones* told my dad what I'd done, because *Bones* reckons I saved his life. I didn't. I just held him up.

'I didn't see *Bones* again until the end of 1982, when we worked together for a short time and then we lost contact because he left the navy. He was due to come out anyway. I never stopped thinking about him and Kirsty knew him as well because he was there when I met her. Then – I think it was 1997 – Kirsty did an article for a magazine because Kirsty suffered from anorexia. *Bones* was in bed with his then wife and said, "That's *Ginge!*" He told his wife all about me, she got in touch with the magazine, who got in touch with Kirsty. We got together. He's now godfather to one of my children.

'I have six children: David, Gemma, Tony, Melanie, Mark and Corby. I had a vasectomy after number five and seven years later it reversed itself. The kids were playing around with names, one said, "Corby" and that's how it came about. I was number four of five children. It's strange because my wife is number four of five as well. I think being part of a large family was a good thing.

'We renewed our wedding vows a couple of years ago and *Bones* was there for it. He has never been out of my mind and he is someone that I hold very, very close to me.

'If people hear me talking on the phone to any of my mates from the *Sheffield* the thing that we always end with is "I love you." There is that bond between us and I'm not embarrassed to say it.'

Notes

1. www.royalnavy.mod.uk
2. www.arrse.co.uk/wiki/HMS_Cambridge
3. Sea Dart: a British surface-to-air missile system.
4. www.mod.uk/.../LossOfHmsSheffieldBoardOfInquiry.htm
5. Prophylactics: used to prevent something or protect from it, especially disease.
6. Exocet: a French missile in several variants for attacking warships, capable of being launched from ships, submarines, helicopters and planes. It had a range of 70km (43 miles), later extended to 180km (110 miles), and used radar late in its flight to lock onto a target. During the Falklands conflict it achieved an almost mythical status as a terrible killer of ships against which there seemed little or no defence.
7. Super Étendard: French fighter plane which came into service in 1978 and was first used in anger in the Falklands. In 1981 Argentina obtained five of them – and five Exocets.
8. www.twogreens.co.uk/navy/FALKLANDS/falklands.html
9. James Frederick Thomas George Salt, always known as Sam (1940–2009), commanded the *Sheffield*, the first British warship to be sunk since the Second War. He subsequently became Assistant Chief of Staff (Operations) before taking senior positions in industry.

3

THE RADIO OPERATOR

We spent a lot of time hiding amongst icebergs and that can be quite scary when you think about how big they are. There were four floating around in a rough rectangle and we were literally in the middle of them. When you're in a ship with only one screw, that's fairly deep in the water because she's laden, and not very manoeuvrable, it's a bit of a worry.

Brian Bilverstone was born in 1961 in Stratford in London and 'as long as I can remember I had this fantasy about being a sailor. I say fantasy because obviously the reality is rather different. My father joined the Royal Navy during the Second World War, mum was a Wren and I suppose that was part of it. I've always had my face in books about the days of sail and all that sort of thing, always had that interest and I still do. For as long as I can remember I wanted to be a sailor and it was always Royal Navy. I don't know why but it always was.

'I was 16 when I joined and initially I started on a long-term reserve engagement, which was twenty-two years – the equivalent of three lifetimes at that age! Eventually I did five so I came out in 1983. I was a radio operator trained at HMS *Raleigh* and HMS *Mercury*.

'My first ship was HMS *Scylla*. It has been mis-spelt and mis-pronounced down the years like you wouldn't believe. She was a broad-beam *Leander*-class frigate.'

The *Scylla*, built at Devonport, was launched in 1968 and would have a lively career, involving a collision with a ferry, an excursion into two Cod Wars with Iceland and being rammed by an Icelandic gunboat. She took part in the Queen's Silver Jubilee celebrations and was involved in humanitarian relief to the Cayman Islands after a hurricane, but was being modernised during the Falklands War and so missed it. She was having Exocets fitted ...

Bilverstone 'served in her for eighteen months. I joined her as a radio operator second class and got my qualifications as a class one. That's as far as I went in that ship because I was drafted off. I went back to HMS *Mercury* as ship's company for six months. HMS *Mercury* is a training establishment so you have trainees – who, as the name suggests, are undergoing training – and then ship's company who run the place, basically, on its the daily routine.

'I was in somewhere called the Exercise Wireless Office which was a communication centre set up for training. During that time I worked in a delightful little room called the Tape Farm. We used to prepare and transmit Morse code tape for people to read for their training. That was about as interesting as watching paint dry. The Morse tape machines are even less interesting than watching a telex machine all day. They had eight or ten machines, each wired into a different classroom and I just had to sit there and run the paper tapes, repair them occasionally, retype them. Dear, oh dear.

'I spent some time in the Special Communications Unit and then joined HMS *Herald* as a radio operator.' The *Herald* was a survey ship carrying a lot of sophisticated equipment. 'I got a bit more experience running a watch, because being a small ship there was one person in the watch. It meant you had to do everything.

'We were out in the Middle East for seven months at the end of 1981, beginning of 1982, doing a Gulf survey. I was on watch in the middle of the night – a quiet watch – when it all went mad. I was sitting there reading a book, teleprinters chattering away, everything normal. All the alarms started going, the flash message alarms. It went bonkers! We had four teleprinters in a bank. One was always fixed on, the others at standby, and these three others flashed themselves up. All their lights started flashing, all the frequencies came alive and in the first day we received over a thousand messages. We'd be lucky if we had twenty or thirty a day usually.

'We didn't have a clue where the Falklands were. We thought it was Scotland. The first we'd heard about it before that was South Georgia. In the NAAFI canteen someone had put up a map of South Georgia – a newspaper cutting – and we were taking bets over whether it was the one in America or the one in Russia and who was going to fire the first nuclear missile. Even when we got back to the UK, which was just before the Task Force sailed, we didn't have a *Scooby Doo* [Cockney rhyming slang for clue]. We had come back to Portsmouth at the end of deployment and see the Task Force go out. I was given a fortnight's leave having been away for seven months and I had barely got my feet warm at home when I was called back. They phoned because we had to leave the number where we were staying.

'*Herald* was converted to an ambulance ship. As a result they took out the naval communications gear under the Geneva Convention rules so they didn't need all the radio operators. I was due to be drafted off first anyway in the normal scheme of things – I got what was called a *pierhead jump*, an unexpected draft. I was sitting in the office and the boss came in.'

SCENE 1
'Pack your kit, you're going on draft.'
'When?'
'WHY ARE YOU STILL HERE?!' – meaning *now* …

Some thirty minutes later Bilverstone found himself 'standing on the dockside with a kitbag and suitcase thinking *what the bloody hell's going to happen now?* I had to go up to HMS *Nelson* and the regulator at the manpower control centre.'

SCENE 2
'Who are you?' the regulator asked.
Bilverstone introduced himself and gave the regulator his draft chit.
'I don't know anything about you. Go and sit over there.'
Bilverstone sat for a long time ('about six hours!' he swears) in a chair in the corner.

'Are you a radio operator?'

Bilverstone pointedly looked at the badge on his arm and said he was.

'What's your name?'

Bilverstone pointedly looked at his bloody great big name tag.

'As you're a radio operator you'd better go up to HMS *Mercury*. There's a minibus leaving.'

Bilverstone reached HMS *Mercury* and made his way to the regulator.

SCENE 3

'Who are you? What branch are you?'

Bilverstone pointedly looked at the badge on his arm.

'Don't take the mickey out of me, or else …'

Bilverstone was sent to a transit mess. 'I knew that something was going to happen, so I didn't completely unpack my kit, but I got my sleeping bag out, got my bed sorted out, hopped on it and someone came in.'

SCENE 4

'R.O. Silverstone?' the someone asked.

Bilverstone had always been called Silverstone.

'Yes.'

'You've got a draft.'

Bilverstone packed everything up and returned to the MACC – the Manpower Allocation & Control Centre – just in time for …

SCENE 5

'Who are you?' the regulator asked.

Bilverstone pointedly looked at the badge on his arm and his name tag.

'Oh yeah, I remember. There's a minibus leaving in two hours for HMS *Nelson*. Be outside the drill shed.'

This was nearby and he stood outside, but a fast black taxi turned up and Bilverstone thought, '*I'm not going to wait here, I'll jump in that* and I went down to Portsmouth in it. Cost me an arm and a leg, but it was better than standing around at HMS *Mercury*.'

SCENE 6

Bilverstone went to the regulator at *Nelson* and got to sit on the same chair again. Eventually he 'went over to the desk – this is absolutely true – and the regulator said, "There's three drafts here. Pick one." I just had to point at a bit of paper. I got it and it had MV *Saxonia* written on it.'

Bilverstone asked, 'What's "MV"?'

'It stands for *motor vessel*.'

'Well, what's that?'

'I don't know. It's a big yacht or something.'

Bilverstone set off, but not everything was open and he remembers 'I had to walk out of the dockyard, down Queen Street, into the main gate, all the way through the dockyard up to Fountain Lake Jetty, which was fun with a kitbag and a suitcase. There was no ship there so I waited for it. Two or three other blokes turned up. They were the other radio operators, who I didn't know from Adam. They'd had a similar runaround to me.

'Eventually this dirty great big merchant ship came round the corner and we stood there looking at it because it's unusual to see a cargo ship in Portsmouth, or was in those days, anyway. It had SAXONIA painted on the bow so we thought it must be ours, that must be our ride. She was a 510-feet long, 15,000-ton refrigerated cargo boat and she'd just come in from East Africa because she'd been on the banana run. She was full of bananas so she had to be unloaded.'

The *Saxonia*, a refrigerated cargo ship, had been requisitioned from the Cunard Line on 28 April. She'd sail on 8 May.

'We were taking dry naval stores. It means a lot of the stuff was classified but also anything that wasn't perishable, so we were carrying body bags. I think we had some collapsable coffins. We had general stores, tents, that sort of thing. We also had three Harrier engines strapped to the back of the ship, which was interesting. The ship had a very small swimming pool at the back, unlike the Royal Navy! We didn't get to use it anyway because they plated it and turned it into what they laughingly called a flight deck. It wasn't actually big enough for anything to land on it apart form the occasional Wasp. You couldn't get a Sea King on there or even a Wessex. They craned in three Pegasus engines[1] in big yellow cradles.

'The Pegasus engines spent their time sitting up there all the way to the South Atlantic, but the plating really wasn't all that strong. During one particularly nasty storm it broke and two of the engines went sliding through into the pool and there was still water in it. Two engines for Harriers stuck out of the pool and there they stayed. We couldn't move them. It wasn't until we were down there that Sea Kings came over and lifted them out. There was some screeching and grating and rending – *God, dear, oh dear.*

'The ship needed to be converted and they had to build accommodation for us. The ship's company was, I think, about thirty and then four of us Royal Navy and another thirty from the RFA, the supply and transport office, so they had to sort out the accommodation. They built wooden bunks in a stateroom and one of the ship's officers took us up there. One of our number was a petty officer and he had his own cabin. The three of us were in this stateroom. We thought this was the lap of luxury.

'The day after we left Portsmouth we were told that we had to darken ship, which meant putting up black-outs. We were called up to the wardroom. Our radio superviser, Bill, was there with a great big box full of Portsmouth Corporation dustbin liners and as much tape as I've ever seen in my life. We had to go round every window because that ship didn't have portholes, it had windows. Every window on the ship that wasn't in use, we had to black it out. It took about five days in the end. The thing is, you know how thin bin-liners are: they didn't black anything out. It *greyed* it out a bit, but you could still see lights. I always thought that was fairly amusing, but there we are.

'We had no duties other than our watch-keeping duties, so when we were off-watch we were getting bored. We'd go down to the crew mess and sit down there or wander around the ship or whatever.

'We were introduced to Board of Trade sports – that's basically lifeboat drills. It was a bit scary because the crew didn't know what we were doing and we certainly didn't know what we were doing. It took them several days to free the lifeboats because they'd never been used and were rusted in.

'When the *Sheffield* was hit, I think people realised on that day it was going to get nasty. We heard about that on the BBC World Service. The thing is, we didn't hear about it through the official system. Being radio operators you're normally the first to hear about anything: we'd have been the ones telling everyone else. We were well on the way down there by that point. Something started twitching and it was inside my trousers.'

This was just before they left Portsmouth.

'We didn't know what was going to happen. We didn't know if we were going into the war zone or stopping at Ascension or what. We did stop at Ascension and there's a silly story behind that. They welded machine-gun posts onto the ship, eleven of them. They were basically scaffold poles that they'd cut down. They welded them two on the bridge, two on the sides, a couple up for'ard. We had a chief gunnery instructor, a guy who came on board and showed us how to load and fire the machine guns, which we played with down the Channel. They took the guns away because they were practice guns and that was it. We got down to Ascension and we were told we were picking up the proper weapons there. When we got down there it was like being in the MACC again because they said, "Who are you? We haven't got any guns for you, pal." So that was that. We went with no weapons at all. Well, the captain had a pistol, but I think that was more for pointing at the crew than anything else!

'Much later on we got a bit *antsi* a couple of times because the crew did boast about the amount of money they were getting for working on Sundays and working in a war zone and all the rest of it. We were paid a war allowance – would you believe? – and it was 75 pence a day, taxable, but I suppose if you are in the armed services you don't really expect any extra, do you? Mind you, a little bit wouldn't have hurt if we'd found some beer to buy with it.

'We were in South Georgia for most of the time. What was that like? Bloody cold. I didn't go ashore. We didn't stay anywhere for any length of time. Basically we'd get into somewhere like Cumberland Bay and we'd meet up with another ship, transfer some stores, and then we'd be moved because at that time there was considered to be a submarine threat. We thought the Argies still had their submarines out. This was after the *Belgrano* had been sunk and we didn't know they'd all cleared off back to BA [Buenos Aires]. Even the Admiralty still thought they were out.'

The South Atlantic was itself a hostile environment. In a storm off South Georgia the *Saxonia* reportedly lost an anchor and four shackles of chain.

'We spent a lot of time hiding amongst icebergs and that can be quite scary when you think about how big they are. There were four floating around in a rough rectangle and we were literally in the middle of them. When you're in a ship with only one screw, that's fairly deep in the water because she's laden, and not very manoeuvrable, it's a bit of a worry. With icebergs it's one-ninth on top, eight-ninths underneath.

'That was nerve-wracking because we didn't know whether we were going to hit an iceberg or take a torpedo or what. The satellite equipment kept breaking down. They had very hastily installed military radio gear, which was why we were on there, and a Marisat terminal. Marisat was still in its infancy then.'

The Marisat system had been developed by the Hughes Aircraft Corporation from 1973 to provide communications with ships across the Atlantic, Pacific and Indian Oceans by satellite for the first time. The satellites were launched in conjunction with NASA from Cape Canaveral in 1976.

'They put the dome on what we call the bridge roof and the merchant seamen call the monkey island. They put it very close to the mast and unfortunately whenever the disc tried to lock on to the satellite it couldn't. It kept falling over and we couldn't use it. Very often in the middle of the night you'd find yourself climbing the ladder up the side of the bridge to the monkey island with a red torch in one hand and a spanner or a hammer in the other. Then you had to get up into the dome. You could only get your head and shoulders into it, and you'd hit something until it moved. This was maintenance! I did that countless times. You'd think, *here we go again* and, in the middle of the South Atlantic where it's pretty rough, you're trying to climb all over a darkened ship – with no safety net – to knock the crap out of a satellite dish. I don't know if the dish eventually survived, although I do know it was still working the second time we went down there.

'I don't think that the services were at all prepared for the real thing. We practised for the Cold War, didn't we? We never expected a hiccough from the Second World War to happen, which is basically what it was. It was all a little bit Heath Robinson,[2] to be honest with you.

'I've spoken to a couple of my counterparts on some of the other merchant ships and they tell similar stories of the equipment just falling over: one minute it's working and the next it isn't. We found ourselves on several occasions trying to read fast Morse being transmitted by the merchant fleet because it was the only communication we had. Of course, merchant radio officers are trained to a much higher standard than we ever were – and we were trying to read 25 words a minute whereas we were trained to 16 or 18. We'd be taking that and writing it down – and that's encrypted messages – and then we would be trying to make that into a tape to decrypt on the equipment. The equipment would get so far and just wouldn't decrypt it any more because we'd written a letter down wrong or something, so it was taking hours and hours to receive fairly urgent messages. When I look back on it now, it was farcical, really.'

The *Saxonia* entered the war zone on 20 May.

'What really upset us, I think, was that we were getting more information via the civilian radio services than we were via our own system. I have to say that none of us were at all impressed when they broadcast on the radio an item about the Argentine bombs not fusing properly, which implied some of them weren't going off. It was after that that the *Coventry* got it, and the *Ardent*. Someone forgot that the Argentines were listening to the same British radio service, too. It was just such a breach of security it was unbelievable. I don't really understand journalism now and I didn't understand it then. I thought, *why don't they just keep their bloody mouthes shut?* That's the first time I remember feeling seriously frightened about the situation.'

The *Ardent* was in San Carlos Bay on the day after the *Saxonia* entered the war zone. She was protecting the transport ships taking the marines and paras ashore. The Argentinian Air Force attacked her with nine 500lb bombs, causing extensive damage and fires. They attacked again, although the ship was able to limp to Grantham Sound, where she sank the following day. Twenty-two men died.

On 25 May the *Coventry*, accompanied by *Broadsword*, was attacked by A-4 Skyhawks and shot two down. The Argentinians attacked again and the *Coventry* was struck by three bombs. Two exploded and the ship listed. She was abandoned in twenty minutes and sank the following day. Nineteen men died.

'To be honest, if you'd sat and thought about it you'd have gone out of your mind, so you just didn't think about it. We were only 20. It was a big adventure.'

Between the sinkings of the *Ardent* and *Coventry*, Bilverstone had had personal experience of tragedy.

'We went over to the Falklands a couple of times and you knew what you were being scared of. Things happened. When the *Antelope* went up I realised *that could happen to any of us*. That has stayed with me. The thing is – and not just with us – when everybody heard about the *Antelope* we thought that she still had the ship's company on board. We didn't know the full story, we didn't know that they had been evacuated and we thought there were 300 blokes getting blown up. A couple of soldiers were blown up: one was killed, the other lost his arm.'

The *Antelope*, a Type 21 frigate commissioned in 1976, had not been fitted with Exocets. She reached the war zone a day after *Saxonia*. On 23 May she was guarding the entrance to San Carlos Water and protecting the beachhead. Four Skyhawks attacked her: *Ardent* drove the first off with a Sea Cat (a surface-to-air missile) but the second dropped a 1,000lb bomb. It killed a steward but did not explode. The third was hit by cannon fire and crashed into the main mast. The bomb penetrated the ship but did not explode.

'People had been killed on the *Antelope* during the afternoon when she was being bombed. That was out in Falkland Sound and her captain brought her into San Carlos, I think because it was shallower water and it would perhaps be a bit safer. Night was coming down and the Argentines didn't attack from the air at night. You could set your clocks by them. In fairness to them they had a long way to fly and they only had a few minutes over the targets. If they didn't set off back they didn't make it so it had to be timed pretty tightly.'

The *Antelope* limped to a point where bomb defusal experts could come aboard to tackle the two unexploded bombs. One could not be reached and three attempts on the other failed. They tried with a small defusing charge, but this made the bomb explode, tearing the ship open and lighting fires. The ship was becoming white hot and the commanding officer ordered the 175 crew to abdandon ship immediately. Some few minutes later the missile magazines exploded. One of the explosions, framed by the darkness, was said to be an image from hell; the ship smouldering then suddenly flinging an immense arch of fire into the sky.

'As I understand it, Warrant Officer John Phillips – who I've come to know quite well – and his sergeant tried to defuse the bomb and it went off. There was this almighty bang which of course was caught on camera [the immense arch of fire]. If you look at a map you'll see what sort of shape San Carlos Bay is. It was big enough to get several large ships into and I think the *Canberra* was in there at one time. Certainly the *Norland* was. I went back in 2007 and I was standing on Blue Beach, near Port San Carlos, looking up San Carlos Water. I was surprised at how narrow it *actually* is.'

The fires continued through the night and at dawn another major explosion broke the *Antelope*'s back.

Bilverstone returned to South Georgia on the *Saxonia* and 'we heard that there was a *de facto* cessation of hostilities, as we called it at the time. We were anchored. I'd been on nights – night watch'. It meant he was in no mood for flippancy.

Jacko, one of Bilverstone's oppos [friends], arrived.

Jacko: 'They've packed it in.'
Bilverstone: 'Who's packed it in?'
Jacko: 'The Argies – they've surrendered. We've won.'
Bilverstone: 'Clear off. I'm going to go back to sleep.'

Next ...

Ginge, not one of Bilverstone's oppos, arrived.

    Ginge: 'Get out of bed, they've packed it in.'

Bilverstone went down to the crew mess and 'they were all down there. The British radio service was on and they were announcing it every few minutes. It came on again. "The Union Flag flies over Government House. God Save the Queen." We had a very quiet drink. There wasn't any shouting or whooping or anything like that – a quiet drink, and, although I didn't used to drink at sea, I made an exception on that occasion. I remember I had a Scotch. Being a merchant seamen's crew mess they have booze, which in the Royal Navy you don't. I had just one drink and thought that's enough of that. Then we felt the engines starting up. The ship left.

    'We came back to Portsmouth, which took a couple of weeks. We anchored in St Helen's Road [at the Isle of Wight] the night before. We couldn't get into Portsmouth because there had been a NATO exercise, would you believe, and one of the German warships had run aground on the sand bar. Clearing that delayed entry and exit into Portsmouth, creating a bottleneck which left only one way in and out.

    'We went in the next day. My parents were there and we had a good welcome because we were the first of the big merchant ships back. We had the tugs and all the water fountains and the rest of it. There were people on the side cheering. I remember the *Foudrayant*[3] was still tied up in the middle of Portsmouth harbour and all the cadets were on there cheering us in. I've still got the ensign we were flying when we came in, our rather tattered and damaged ensign. I took that down and put up a new one and tucked it away.

    'Then I got my leave, went on leave – we weren't told anything, just to go – and when I returned I didn't know whether I was going to be joining *Saxonia* or what. I went down to the MACC at *Nelson* and he said:

    '"Do I know you?"

    'I had a bit of a giggle about it. He recognised me ...

'He said, "You are rejoining *Saxonia* because you are going south again." I felt joy unbounded, as you can imagine, because I really did not want to rejoin that ship. I absolutely hated it. It wasn't the ship's fault, it was that it just didn't sit with me. I wanted to go back into the Royal Navy.

'We went straight back down to Port William, which was just out-side Stanley. We couldn't get into Stanley because we were too deep draught to get across the bar into the harbour. There were a lot of ships all anchored in Port William and we were discharging stores to Royal Corps of Transport Mexi Floats.[4]

'We had a little routine set up because we were in competition with the other ships to give the best service. All the soldiers living ashore were on chicken supreme and stuff like that so we'd get them on board. They weren't allowed to load the Mexi Floats themselves because of union rules. The merchant seamen would do the loading. Once the soldiers were on board we'd take them down to the mess deck, get them pissed, show them porn movies and give them steak and chips. They loved us, funnily enough! They used to come back time and time again!

'Strangely, I think more of us were more apprehensive going down the second time because we thought that it wasn't over and the Argentinians were going to come in with their air force again. Again, we didn't have any weapons and we were very vulnerable. You could see the batteries around Stanley. That's all very well, but the jets are just going to fly past them, aren't they? Then nothing happened. It was as if we'd prepared, as if we'd practised and – just nothing. When I was there in 2007 I went out in a small boat in the middle of Stanley harbour and out in Port William and it is very, very open – very, very vulnerable. And by now everybody knew about Exocets, and that they were everything they were cracked up to be. An Exocet would have done us straight away, and no doubt.

'In actual fact we were anchored where you go through from Port William into Stanley and I don't suppose they'd have bothered with us much, they'd have gone for the ships on the outer end to try and block-ade the port completely. That's my guess. They were mad enough to try and do it and I think they are mad enough to try and do it again now.

'We kept on unloading and I got a draft chit because by that time the military operation was winding down. I was due to leave the navy in October 1982, but obviously that had been put off. They said to me, "Do you want to go home?" and I said, "Yes, please." Apart from my fortnight's leave I hadn't been home since the middle of 1981, because I'd been out in the Middle East, so I thought it would be quite nice.

'I had been ashore in Stanley. At that time, through no fault of the population, it was a mess, quite frankly. Filthy. The Argentines had left it in a right old state and although the army had got them to clean it up it was in a mess, nothing like the picture-postcard image. Now it appears as a prosperous town but back then it was just sad. A lot of equipment had been moved to the side, out of the way, but there was still mine clearance going on. The people weren't overly happy at us being there. They were relieved to have been liberated but they were pretty sick of seeing uniforms. It was understandable. Also, servicemen being servicemen there'd been a little bit of trouble and things had happened.

'I got into a row with an officer and I was thrown out of the Upland Goose Hotel because he was a pompous idiot. He was what the Americans call a REMF [use your own imagination] – a second-waver. He hadn't been down there during the fighting. I was ashore and my little bit of increased status that had gone on during the actual scrapping was gone. I was back to being a bog-standard radio operator. I had a message to take him from the sargeant-major who was controlling the public jetty. He said, "You'll do, you're navy – take this message to Captain Whatever-his-name-was." So I took this message into the Upland Goose Hotel, which was being used as an officers' mess by then and Captain Whatever-his-name-was proved to be a pompous twat. I'd had enough. I gave him a mouthful and then went back in and gave him the message. It was a verbal message.'

Officer: 'Well, why didn't you do that in the first place?'
Bilverstone: 'Oh, **** ***.'
Officer: 'Stand still, you are under arrest.'
Bilverstone: 'Bollocks.'

It was not dialogue by William Shakespeare, but it was conclusive, or, as Bilverstone puts it, 'that was that. That was also the sort of level of tension there was, and there was a lot of Them and Us at that time as well. You'd either been there or you hadn't. The army didn't think much of the navy and they didn't think much of the army and you didn't take much notice of the RAF anyway – the usual old rubbish. It was all a bit like that.

'Once, I was walking outside Stanley. The farmers had been told that they would be paid for every sheep killed by mines. They were driving sheep across the fields and every so often there'd be a loud bang and a flash … it's terrible, really, but that's the sort of gallows humour you get.

'When we were in Stanley we only got a short time and we had the choice of either mooching off on our own or jumping in a Land Rover and being taken somewhere and dropped for a couple of hours. Whatever we wanted, really. There wasn't that much to do, anyway. I got dropped off at some beach or other fairly close to Stanley. It was a beautiful afternoon – howling half a gale and pissing down with rain! A few of us were there wearing our camouflage stuff because that was what we were issued with. We said, "Let's eat our compo rat packs [ration packs]."

'We sat there eating sandwiches and the bloody penguins were bold as brass, had no fear at all, and I turned round and there's this dirty great big penguin looking over my shoulder. I had a sandwich and he took it out of my hand, very calmly reached over and I saw this bloody great big beak coming over. I thought, *well, you have what you want, mate.* He took it, and walked away with it. I thought, *you cheeky git.* And he came back for more. They just stood and looked at you. Did he like the lunch? He ate it, so he liked it more than I did …

'I had to do a leaving routine, so I spent a lot of time flying round different placements around the islands. I had to get a chit signed by various people. While I was doing that we were made duty postmen so we had a sack of post.

'We had a change of the sea auxiliary personnel, and one of the chaps who came on board was called Bo'sun Bill. I don't know what his surname was, but even now I know people who, if you say "Bo'sun Bill", they know who you mean. I don't know what he was like professionally, but I do know he knew everything about everything, but didn't know anything about anything, really.

'They'd repaired the flight deck and we were carrying baulks of timber. We used to get helicopters fly by and, as they flew by the bridge, the captain would say to us, "Tell them it's OK to land". We'd go out and wave to them. That was the routine: just wave to them. They didn't actually land, they'd come over and hover, winch up the cargo and go away.

'One day Bo'sun Bill came flying out of the crew mess: "I'll deal with this, I'll deal with this." He picked up a pair of table-tennis bats and he ran up onto the flight deck. He started trying to bat this helicopter in like he'd seen in the films. The pilot was leaning out giving him the finger: "★★★★ ★★★, get out of the way." Bo'sun Bill stood there in the downdraught, nearly getting blown away giving it plenty with these bats. The flight-deck crew hooked on the baulk of timber, the helicopter flew away and nearly took his head off.

'He got up their noses because after that he *kept* going out with these bats.

'One of the days I had to go to the *Rangatira* [a general cargo ship] with a postbag and they sent a Sea King over. When they hovered over the deck to pick up people they'd drop a weighted line which had a magnet on the end. That would be put on the deck and ground the helicopter. Then you'd be allowed to get in the strop and go up. I went up first because I had the post. As I got in the crewman patted me on the shoulder and said, "Watch this." As they were putting Bo'sun Bill in the strop he lifted it so Bill's feet flew up in the air and he was dangling like a lump of pork. He got into the helicopter and all his hair was standing up. The crewman said, "Sorry, mate! I didn't have a clue!" We could hear it on the intercom – the pilot was laughing his socks off.

'We had to jump out and it was quite scary. The pilot just put one wheel on the back of the *Rangatira* and we had to jump. I'd never done that from a helicopter. The bloke said, "This is how you do it," and pushed me. He threw the sack of post after me.

'I came back to the UK and I spent the last few months at HMS *Drake*. I was working in the communications centre in Plymouth. I went on Christmas leave in December and terminal leave in January.

'While I was in Stanley I looked around [at the debris of war and the cost] I thought, *well, what was all that about?* I think quite differently now. I think it was absolutely the right thing to do. Whatever the politics around something, you don't allow one bully to walk in and take over the territory of another country, especially when the people who live there so desperately do not want to be part of the country that's taking them over, and have no history of being part of it.

'Had they been Spanish people down there – or let's say Hispanic people – I might have thought, *well, OK*, but it wasn't even as if the Falklands were a colony: *the place is a British enclave.* I feel the same about Gibraltar. I think the Spanish imagine they'd get a duty-free trading port, but of course they wouldn't. What they *would* get is a lot of Brits who don't want to know anything about them.'

Bilverstone, reflecting, distills the war into one sentence: 'The whole thing was a monumental cock-up followed by blundering about in the dark with a bit of luck.'

It worked.

Notes

1. Rolls-Royce-built engines used in all Harriers, notable for being able to give downward thrust for vertical take-off and forward thrust for conventional flight.
2. Heath Robinson: once upon a time a fabled figure specialising in fiendishly complicated and amateurish contraptions to make things work.
3. A training ship.
4. Flat pontoons with outboard motors which can be hooked together to form huge rafts.

4

THE MARINE ENGINEER

'It's all right, boys, emergency over, you can get up now' – he said as calm as you like. Apparently, a steward came down with a brandy glass and a decanter on a silver tray and said, 'Would you like a drink, sir?' He said, 'Yes, please,' and his hand was shaking to hell, but he didn't betray that.

Steve Wilkinson was born in Chesterfield in Derbyshire in 1960. 'A couple of years before I left school I played in my town's colts Rugby Union side as well as for the school. I was a three-quarter. You wouldn't imagine that now if you saw me! I used to enjoy reading. I was a bit of a loner although, I had a couple of friends. I was into aeroplane modelling. Academically, I was Mr Average; never to the fore, never at the back.

'The area around where I was born was coal mines. There was a little bit of heavy industry as well because I lived in Derbyshire: the tube works and a company making pumps, there was a chemical firm just up the road and quite a few coal mines in the surrounding area. To be quite honest none of it actually appealed to me, although I didn't know what I was going to do when I left school.

'My father died in 1975 and my brother-in-law took the reins after that. He and my sister helped mum, what she was entitled to and everything else. I'd been in the Sea Cadets for three or four years beforehand and my brother-in-law obviously thought it was going to be a good idea to keep me in that kind of environment. I thought maybe the armed services were the way to get a good, steady job. I joined up in 1976.'

Some people join up to find a surrogate family?

'I didn't do that, no, not really, because I'd had some good times and prior to father dying I'd been – almost unknowingly – looking after him. He'd had a stroke and I'd go swimming with him. If he had a problem I'd help him out. He used to work for the local transport company, so if there was a problem on our way back from the baths or whatever I'd just put my hand up. Because we were known, the driver would stop exactly where we were and help me and dad onto the bus to get him home.

'Joining up was a job outside the norm for me and I think my brother-in-law thought it would give me a change and get me away from the heavy industry and the coalmines.

'Initially I applied for an apprenticeship as a marine engineer. You go into a lot more detail – on the theoretical side, if you like – of it. Once you've done a lot of the theory you'll pick up the practical side. I failed on my maths. It let me down a little. I was then offered a place as a marine engineer and I took that. When I joined, my title was Junior Marine Engineer (Mechanical). I liked the services. I enjoyed the usual things, the alcohol and the camaraderie. I got a sense of purpose, that I was doing something with my life.

'Within heavy industry it was a case of you being part of a company. You work with your mates, you go out to the pub and everything else with your mates, but in the forces you were never in the same place twice, really. We went to some nice places and some of the other places would have been [pause] … not what you'd have expected. How can I put it? I went to Karachi. You'd love to see Karachi? No, you wouldn't. It just wasn't nice.

'I was on board HMS *Exeter*, a Type 42 destroyer, and we were in the West Indies doing a three-month stint as guard ship out there.'

The *Exeter*, built by Swan Hunter on the Tyne, started service in 1980 and would be based at Portsmouth. She was the seventh Type 42 built and was designed to give air defence to other ships as well as naval gunfire support and undertake anti-submarine operations. The crew was 260.[1]

On 4 May the *Sheffield* was attacked and crippled.

The West Indies stint was 'very nice and pleasant,' Wilkinson says. 'The locals were very friendly and there were were quite a few barbequeues and parties to be had. I think we were just about coming to the end of our time there when the Falklands developed and in no uncertain terms we were told, "You're not coming home, you can turn right and go south about 6,000 miles. Away you go.'"

They were ordered to go south on 5 May to replace the *Sheffield* and set sail on 7 May.

The captain, Hugh Balfour,[2] would remember: 'Our anticipation of Antigua's delights received the original cold douche as we spent 12 frantic hours offloading all of our surplus kit into a convenient container … Like moving house it's always amazing to see the huge mound of baggage and wonder wherever you kept it all. Golf clubs, bicycles and huge cuddly toys appeared from the most mysterious of stowages. There was time enough, though, for many of us to get ashore for a last look at the Caribbean before slipping out to sea to the encouraging cheers and waving Union Jacks of our disappointed hosts.'[3]

Wilkinson says, 'No, I didn't know where the Falklands were – I was sketchy because it was like the Shetlands and the Orkneys, just another bunch of islands. Because the UK had sovereignty on all sorts of bits and pieces, unless you were a geographical whizz you didn't necessarily know. I didn't even know about South Georgia. I'd followed some of the news and I'd been looking at South America as part and parcel of looking into life. I'd come across Tierra del Fuego – the Land of Fire – which was right on the bottom of Chile. You look at that but you don't look just slightly out to sea, where you've got the Falklands.

'Before we left the West Indies I read the paper and by all accounts we'd been sunk – and we'd not even left the West Indies! It cost me an arm and a leg to phone my mother up and say, "No, I'm fine. We've not even left yet. Let everybody know." I can't remember which newspaper and it might have been a propoganda stunt [by the Argentinians].

'On the way down it was a strange situation because most of the guys had been to Newcastle to fetch the ship. We picked it up from the Neptune yard in Wallsend. We brought it down to Portsmouth and we took it through all the work-up phases: we were the brand new crew of the *Exeter*. We'd been through all the different scenarios but, to put it bluntly, we were now going into the sharp end because people would be using real bullets and bombs at you – not an exercise in the West Indies at all.'

Balfour remembered the 'high-speed dash' and how the mood began to change at Ascension Island. They were only there for eight hours and during it were 'piled high with huge mounds of stores by a very insistent Chinook helicopter who kindly took away the remainder of our peacetime chattels'. *Exeter* left 'under the watchful eye of a Russian spy ship'.[4]

Wilkinson remembers 'we'd been practicing all the way down after we'd found out what we were actually doing'.

The *Exeter* arrived at the Total Exclusion Zone on 21 May, the day the troops went ashore. She went on patrol about 20 miles in front of the Task Force because, as a guided-missile destroyer, she ought to have been able to deal with enemy air attacks. The fates of the *Sheffield* and the *Glasgow*, however, induced a certain nervousness.

Then on 25 May the *Coventry* was hit.

'We thought, *oh hell, what's going on?'* Wilkinson says. 'We were told over the tannoy, "If you want to go onto the upper desk you can see one of the ships burning on the horizon." Did I go up and have a look? I can't remember. My memories are sketchy.'

This, Wilkinson feels, is perhaps because subconsciously that's the way his mind has decided to deal with it.

The burning ship must have been the *Atlantic Conveyor*. Balfour remembered the 'red glow on the near horizon' as darkness fell. This was only hours after the *Coventry* sank.

'We were gunnery support. We spent a lot of time in San Carlos Bay,' Wilkinson says. 'The Falklands looked rugged. We went into this piece of water and it resembled Scotland. Rugged countryside. Of course we didn't see any people whilst the conflict was on – they were all in Stanley. In San Carlos Bay we'd anchor for the night facing west so that we could provide an anti-aircraft barrage if required until the guys on shore had set up the Rapiers and got them ready. This happened on quite a few occasions. Then first thing in the morning we'd pull the anchor up and away we went out of San Carlos Bay again.

'My action station was down the after engine room. The British Type 42 destroyers had a black line down the centre to distinguish them from the two Argentinian 42s. My action station was right behind the black line so if they'd have used that as a bomb mark or aiming mark ...'

Wilkinson might face a delicate task in an emergency. The mechanism for making the ship go forward or back was electronic – Controllable Pitch Propellor Controls, to give it a proper title – but if power was lost he and one other would have to do it manually, using mini-steering wheels. They only had to do it 'in anger' a couple of times, and 'you had to be very gentle otherwise you'd lose it'.

He'd have other concerns. They all would.

'In San Carlos we were attacked a few times. In my life before I had never been under attack and most people in the services hadn't, either. We have been credited with [bringing down] four or five aircraft.'

One source says:

30 May. Two Argentine Étendards, one equipped with an Exocet mis-sile, attack the British Task Force containing the two British aircraft carriers. According to the Argentine account the HMS *Invincible* was struck. The British account states the missile passed between HMS *Exter* and HMS *Avenger*. HMS *Invincible* returned to England showing no damage to the carrier.

As a planned follow-up attack to the Exocet attack, four Argentine Air Force Escuadron I Grupo 4 Skyhawks with 500lb. bombs attack what they believe was the target of the Exocet, the *Invincible*. However what they find is the HMS *Avenger* and the nearby HMS *Exeter*. *Exeter* shoots down two Grupo 4 Skyhawks using Sea Dart Missiles. First Lieutenant Vazquez in C-301 and First Lieutenant Castillo in C-310 ware killed in this action. First Lieutenant E. Ureta, First Lieutenant Alférez G. Isaac were able to return to their base convinced the attack was against the *Invincible*.[5]

There is a measure of controversy, however, over whether the *Exeter* brought down an Exocet with a Sea Dart.

'When we were attacked by the Exocet from an Étendard the skipper came on, a very relaxed, pleasant guy. His words were, "AIR RAID WARNING RED, hit the deck." I mean, you *hit the deck*. You become part of that steel. You make love to that piece of steel because you don't know what's going to happen. You heard the chaff go because they were 3-inch rockets, then you could *feel* the Sea Dart ignite, you could *feel* the front of the ship drop as it was pushed into the water and this 2-ton missile left, you could *feel* it through the ship.

'It could have been seconds not minutes, but it felt like an age and the captain came on. "It's all right, boys, emergency over, you can get up now." He said it as calm as you like so it was a case of thinking *what the hell was that about?* But apparently a steward came down with a brandy glass and a decanter on a silver tray and said, "Would you like a drink, sir" and he said, "Yes please." And his hand was shaking to hell as he had this brandy – but he didn't betray that.

'People still question the fact that an Exocet was hit. We put our chaff rockets up for protection and this missile went into the chaff. Our Sea Dart missile went into the chaff, too, and then all of a sudden the "picture" [of an Exocet on the radar screens] disappeared. Friends of mine who were in the ops room have said, "Yes, this is what happened." The ship was not actually hit. We were credited with the four or five aircraft but you can't credit a missile because it's always questionable. And how the hell can something supposedly *that* good built by the French be hit by something *that* old – the Sea Dart – by us? They've still got the Sea Dart now …

'Normal action stations – or the normal course of events – they would call, "Hands to action stations, close all doors and hatches." You'd get yourself up, get your mates up wherever you were on the ship. We were doing half-and-half: 7 hours on and 5 hours off, 5 hours on and 7 hours off, 5 hours off … so there was always half of you awake at any given time. But when they called the "hands to action stations" everybody was up. You'd leave the mess or wherever you were and you'd close up in your action stations, which could be a damage-control post, could have been down one of the machinery spaces. You'd close all the doors and hatches behind you.

'However on the one occasion I was down the mess and we were just chilling out, having a break when it was piped up "AIR RAID WARNING RED incoming". That could have been bombs, rockets, missiles. We got "hit the deck" and that was the time when somebody slammed the door and everybody went down flat. You put one arm under the side of your head and then you fold the other arm over the rop of the head: you were cushioned against the deck. When they said, "The threat has passed, you can get up now" – because everybody had done the same thing, hit the deck no matter who they were and where they were – you could get up.

'After the attack you get back to normal.'

Most British people have never been under fire. Is it real when it's real?

'We, being at sea, were in a different position to the soldiers, the army guys. They were being fired at by another human. When we were attacked it was by somebody flying at 600, 700, 800 miles an hour trying to lob something at you or aim it at you and we were trying to shoot them down. It's a strange feeling: you knew somebody was trying to get you but you were also trying to get them. Luckily we didn't get hit.

'One of my early ships was armed with Exocets. That was the *Ardent*. You'd seen the films about how it goes in and then explodes inside the ship and what damage is causes – and, of course, *Sheffield* had gone, *Coventry* had been hit, the *Atlantic Conveyor* had been hit. The *Ardent* had been hit by bombs, her back had been broken and she'd gone. You think *what's going on? A modern navy, they send these planes over and suddenly they are beating the living crap out of you.*

'It was very strange. You do all your training – thunderflashes and the lights go out, there's water coming in and this and that and everything else – but you can't mimick what could really happen, like the guys on *Sir Galahad*. You can't say, "Right, in you go, you go in there" and then all of a sudden you put a roll of fire towards them and it's real fire. So there are some things that you cannot train for. We trained to firefight but it was still controlled. You can't simulate an explosion to train people because you'd kill them. And you can't simulate a ship having its back broken and sinking.

'The Marine Engineering Officer and the Weapons Engineering Officer in one of the section bases kept up a commentary. If you walked past while you were doing your patrols they'd get you up to speed on what was happening. They were running a map of the Falklands. You'd obviously pop round into the ops room and you'd get information from there: as you were passing and you'd ask, "What's happening, sir?" and they'd say, "Oh, so and so". "Oh, right, OK." It meant you could keep in touch with it all in some sort of way, piece things together – because mail wasn't over-frequent and news wasn't, either. We were a long way away and this was a little while before satellite television was around.'

On 7 June the *Exeter* shot down an Argentine Lear Jet on a photo-reconnaisance mission using a Sea Dart.

'There was a strange thing. They always seemed to attack at the same hour every day so you could time your showers and so on around it: never have a shower before, never have a shower after, but you had ten safe minutes to wash your smalls, have a quick shower, get dressed again and back to wherever. This was during the evening, when we'd done shore bombardments – we'd go to wherever we were needed – or supported the troops and come back in, dropped the anchor.'

'They were for ever coming around San Carlos Bay doing the bombing, trying to get the civilian ships. When we could we took them out. The Rapiers on the land needed quite a while to become operational.'

On 14 June a Sea Dart from *Exeter* brought down a Canberra B62 bomber, and one of the two crew survived. It was the last Argentinian aircraft to be brought down.[6]

'The planes were definitely confirmed,' Wilkinson says, 'although of course when you're at action stations down below you don't see anything outside. You're just in contact with other engineers in the machinery space and you're looking after different things but you don't know what's happening up there. You just talk among yourselves, although you are thinking *what the hell's going on?*

'After a while, and when we weren't tasked too much, we went ashore at San Carlos Bay. There was about half a dozen of us. A boat took us ashore. We were told, "Don't go too far, don't do this and don't do that and we'll come and pick you up in an hour." We walked around. You'd see the ejector seat out of a plane just lying there, a small wheel off a plane

– I don't know which plane it was. We went walking across a couple of fields and *there's supposed to be a freezer station or something over there, let's go and have a "nose"*. We were ambling and looking and a helicopter – I think it was a Wessex – buzzed us. We wondered what was going on. Over the loudspeaker the message was, "Don't go any further, guys, just over there down at the freezer station is the Argentinian prison camp and we don't want you getting too close. Turn round and sod off." We thought *all right, OK*. When you see a guy with a machine gun up there you think *I think I'll take that advice*. You turned round quick and legged it. We had about an hour ashore before we had to go back to the pick-up point and return to the ship.

'We were down there well after the surrender. We came round in to Stanley harbour because the previous *Exeter* – after the River Plate – had quite a few of her dead buried in Stanley cemetery. There was the *Exeter*, the *Ajax* and the *Achillies* that held the *Graf Spree* in and after *Exeter* had had a mauling she went to the Falklands to bury her dead, get patched up and go home to Devonport.[7]

'We went so close to Stanley that standing on the ship you could see the jetty and the scrapped armoured cars that the Argentinians had left. We stayed on board because there wasn't anything on land at the time.

'How do you describe to people what the conditions in the Falklands were like? I always say, "I've got slides, I've got a picture from the ship of lovely countryside" and in the space of winding on *one* frame the next picture's white, totally white. The snow dropped so fast and so suddenly it closed off the whole picture. People wouldn't believe it.

'After everything had been settled we started to make our way towards Ascension. I was lucky enough to get off there and fly home. We'd got the duty frees before we boarded it and we were *blathered*. We had to land in Dakar to refuel and the RAF changed the crew.

'I do remember we were asked to leave the plane at Dakar because personnel were not allowed to remain on during refuelling. Where do you go? You sit down on the apron away from the aircraft. You had all these matelots – everybody who was coming back – laying on the apron fast asleep for an hour. Then we were told, "Right, you can get back on now." The plane goes off and you're *still* blathered and then it's coming in to Brize Norton. It was an unreal experience.

'As the ship made her way from Ascension I had about ten days' to a fortnight's leave. After that I came back to Portsmouth, picked up a boat and sailed out to the *Exeter*. I was one of those who took over from the crew that had brought her up so they could get changed and meet their families. And we brought her in. It was weird.'

Before Wilkinson left the services he 'did all my mechanical and welding and pipe-bending and ship-wright stuff and then as I left I cross-trained and became an electrician. They said, "Would you be interested in this course or that?" and I thought *hang on a minute, I've got fifteen years left of my working life. Yep, I can do that: another bit of paper and it will give me more outlets.* I am now an electrician.'

He remembers working with a colleague 'for a couple of days outside on street lights. We'd come back in and he'd had problems with his heart. I said, "Are you OK?" and he said, "No, I don't feel quite right." He went into a fit, I shouted for help and next thing two paramedics were there.'

He was taken to hospital and Wilkinson went there to 'try and find out what was happening. They said, "Are you family?" I said, "No, but I was there at the time." The nursing sister said, "I'm sorry to say there was nothing we could do. He's died." He was just a work colleague but the point is I'd been bombed, shot at and everything else and it seems as if I've come through unscathed but a work colleague died next to me. It threw me, it really did. It took me days to get over it.'

Notes

1. The *Exeter* retired from service on 27 May 2009 after twenty-nine years. She was the final surviving operational Royal Navy warship involved in the Falklands. A ceremony to mark this took place at Portsmouth Naval Base. Falklands veterans were there, and ten of the ship's twenty-one commanding officers. The *Exeter* had also seen service in the 1991 Gulf War escorting a United States battleship and in 2005 took part in celebrations to mark the 200th anniversary of the Battle of Trafalgar. In the

twenty-nine years she covered 892,811 nautical miles, which is 1,027,428 miles (1,653,439 kilometres), or forty-one times round the world.

2. Rear Admiral Hugh Balfour commanded *Exeter* in May 1982. His father was serving in the Mediterranean when Balfour was born in Malta in 1933. He joined the service in 1951 and died in 1999. Wilkinson says: 'He was proper. He took command of the ship and I think it was going to be his last trip before he retired when we went to the West Indies but after the Falklands I believe he became a commodore. I met his wife and his daughter last year [2009] when the ship was paid off and it now sits at the top of Portsmouth harbour. She was the last veteran of the Falklands, if you like.'

3. www.hms-exeter.co.uk/Falk_82_1.html

4. Ibid.

5. a4skyhawk.org/2e/argentina/falklands.../argentina-malvinas.htm

6. Ibid.

7. The *Admiral Graf Spee*: a heavily armed German warship which sank nine Allied merchants ships before three British and one New Zealand cruisers cornered her in Montevideo where the captain scuttled the ship. It brings this memory from more modern times: 'Before we left the islands we had a last duty to perform in meeting the friends of the "Old Exeter" who still live in Stanley. Our famous predecessor anchored there in 1939 to lick her fearful wounds after the Battle of the River Plate. A few of the crew are buried there and many of Stanley's older generation remember her men with affection. We sailed proudly into the inner harbour of Stanley (the first warship to have been allowed to do so) and landed some 40 of our men dressed in their best uniforms for a thanksgiving service in the cathedral. The warm welcome and smiling hospitality of those who remembered our old comrades of another war left us in no doubt that our struggle for the Falklands' freedom had been a worthwhile task.' (www. hms-exeter.co.uk/Falk_82_1.html)

5

THE HELICOPTER EXPERT

Some of the gravy from my roast dinner had gone into the white sauce in my pudding. I thought, *that's not on, I'm not going to be able to eat that now.* I hadn't grasped the enormity of the situation.

David Buey was born in Hitchin, Hertfordshire, in 1962, 'so I was 20 when the conflict happened. As a child I had always had an interest in aircraft and I wanted to work with them.' He'd been to an RAF careers evening with his dad and when they emerged ...

> Dad: 'What do you think?'
> Buey: 'No, I'm not interested in that.'
> Dad: 'What about the navy?'
> Buey: 'Dad, I want to work on aeroplanes, not ships.'
> Dad: 'Well, there's the Fleet Air Arm.'
> Buey: 'OK.'

They looked into it and went to the careers office in Luton. They talked to the recruiting officer who, at the end, asked them to have a think about it and come back. They emerged and his father started walking towards the car ...

> Buey: 'Where are you going?'
> Dad: 'We're going home.'
> Buey: 'No, he said to have a think about it and come back.'
> Dad: 'Yes, he means go home and have a think about it.'

Buey: 'No, no, I've *had* a think about it and I want to do it.'

David Buey was clearly single-minded and knew what he wanted, but his training would be extensive. He joined up on 8 May 1979.

'My mother told me that she'd lost a brother in the War and the worst thing was when the policeman came up the path with the telegram.'

He 'originally joined for nine years. I went to HMS *Raleigh* in Torpoint, Devon, and I did my basic training there.'

Raleigh is, according to the official *Navy News*, 'the Royal Navy's initial training establishment for ratings, providing a wide-ranging and intensive course in general training.' Final military exercises included a:

weapon-handling test, a simulated smoke walk, an endurance course and teamwork exercises. Once finished at *Raleigh* the rookie recruits go on to further training in their chosen professions – some, such as logistics specialists and submariners, will attend the relevant schools at HMS *Raleigh*, while others go to training establishments in other parts of the country.[1]

Buey 'then went across to HMS *Daedalus* which was based at Lee on Solent. I did my Part 1 and Part 2 training there which was the theory of flight and basic aviation.'

Daedalus was a leading Fleet Air Arm airfield, set up in 1917 for seaplanes. Subsequently it became the Fleet Air Arm's main training and administrative centre.

'Then I was drafted to HMS *Heron* at Yeovilton in Somerset, where I joined 707 Squadron working on Wessex 5 helicopters' – the Wessex HU (Helicopter Utility) Mk 5 has been described as a Royal Navy commando assault helicopter capable of carrying sixteen commandos and their equipment into battle.

Heron, according to the Royal Navy description, consisted of:

around 1,400 acres of airfield sites at Yeovilton and the satellite at Ilton (Merryfield). Royal Naval Air Station (RNAS) Yeovilton is a large multi-role air station and one of the busiest military airfields in the

UK with an annual budget of some £17 million. It is home to Royal Navy (RN) Lynx helicopters and RN Commando Helicopter Force. RNAS Yeovilton operates over 100 aircraft in four different categories and is manned by around 4,300 personnel, service and civilian, including MoD employees and permanent contractors. Training of aircrew and engineers of resident aircraft types is carried out at Yeovilton, and it is also the location for the RN Fighter Controller School and RN School of Aircraft Control, training fighter and helicopter controllers.[2]

'The 707,' Buey says, 'was a second-line squadron, so it was essentially for people who were training and who had been training. They'd done their front-line service and come back to offer the benefit of their experience. Then I got drafted to 845 Squadron, which was the front-line squadron from 707 – the active squadron, if you like, doing tours of duty in Ireland and places like that. I was an AEM M(1), an Aircraft Engineer Mechanical Branch.'

The Royal Navy says:

845 Naval Air Squadron primarily provides 3 Commando Brigade of the Royal Marines with tactical troop transport and load-lifting helicopters. 845 NAS operates the Sea King Mk 4 which has a clear cabin space to minimise weight and to maximise the size of cargo carried. It is capable of carrying underslung loads of up to 6,000 pounds such as 105mm guns, Land Rovers and air defence missile systems. 26 troops can be accommodated in the cabin.

On 19 March the Argentine civilians occupied South Georgia. The *Endurance* – whose withdrawal as a patrol ship in March had arguably provoked Argentina to invade the Falklands – was despatched with marines to reclaim South Georgia. She got there on 25 March and would return to the Falklands.

On 29 March the supplies and support ship *Fort Austin* was ordered to leave Operation SPRING TRAIN in Gibraltar and go south to replenish the *Endurance*.

Buey 'didn't go to Ireland and that was a reason we were one of the first ones to leave the UK – because our flight was the active flight. We were *prepped* and ready to go to Ireland and of course when the Falklands conflict came up it took precedence. We were called to the briefing room at work one afternoon and, when we arrived, there was a lot of secrecy going on, although we were given a brief about what was happening. At the time they didn't say "down there", it was the Falkland Islands and of course – as many, many people did – we thought it was something off of Scotland. We thought, "Well, the Argentinians are a long way from home. What's this about?" Very few people did know where the Falklands were, I think.

'We were told that, in the event things kicked off in the way they might, we needed to be in a state of readiness to go, which of course we were because we'd been due to go to Ireland. The timescale went *48 hours* [readiness] then *24 hours* down to *12 hours*, and then we were told, "If you can get home and back in eight hours we suggest you do it." We knew it was getting serious.

'Essentially we were sworn to secrecy. We were told that we couldn't say anything to anybody and I remember – I believe it was a Tuesday that I went home – I had only just gone back to camp on the Monday. I went to see my brother in the pub and he said, "What are you doing home?" and I said, "Just got some bits and pieces that I need." I went home and mum and dad said, "What are you doing?" I said again, "I've got some bits and pieces that I need." My dad is not a tactile person but when I left that night he followed me out to my car.'

Dad: 'What's going on, son?'

Buey: 'Dad, I can't tell you, but something may come up in the news in the next few days and when it does you'll know where I am. Tell mum not to worry.'

Dad (putting his hand on Buey's shoulder): 'Good luck, son.'

And that, Buey says, 'was it, really. We went back to camp and were on our way. We left Yeovilton in a Hercules flown in from RAF Lyneham. We'd

stripped two helicopters down and put them in the back of a Belfast –
a big, big cargo plane – which had been chartered from HeavyLift at
Stansted.' (HeavyLift specialised in what they described as carrying 'all
manner of dangerous goods'.)

On 7 April, a group of ships – the *Antrim, Plymouth* and RFA *Tidespring*
– were ordered to go to Ascension as fast as they could to accompany the
Fort Austin on her way to replenishing the *Endurance*.

The *Fort Austin*, commissioned in 1979, had two flight decks and could
store six Sea Kings in the big hangar. Buey would be joining it.

'We flew via RAF Gibraltar,' Buey says, 'a four-hour flight, and had
something to eat. We flew off early the next morning but it was sev-
enteen hours in a Hercules to Ascension. We were the first to arrive
on Ascension so there was no-one there. Ascension is a volcanic island,
almost like a moonscape, although there is a place there called Green
Mountain when they imported things that would thrive in that climate.
I'm sure it's quite different now. It's always been UK owned but was on a
lease to the Americans. There was a garrison of US people there manning
the radio stations and Wideawake Airfield.

'They didn't have any accommodation for us or anything. I remember
sleeping on a pool table and lads were sleeping underneath it and around it.
It was a very tiring time for us because we'd left the UK in April in English
weather and Ascension was very, very hot. And of course we needed to get
these aircraft together so that when the ships came in they were ready.

'We were using them to fly stores to and from, so it meant some very,
very long days and people falling asleep. I remember I was wiring the
No 1 driveshaft on one, I looked down and my colleague, Jimmy Stuart,
who was putting the troop seats in the other helicopter, had fallen asleep
on them. We put the helicopters together and we stayed there for a little
while helping. Other aircraft were flying in and we were assisting them.
Then we embarked with our aircraft on to *Fort Austin*, a Royal Fleet
Auxiliary with a twin hangar.'

On 8 April, *Fort Austin* left Ascension after taking on three Lynx and
two Wessex helicopters as well as 120 men of the SAS and SBS[3] and a
Royal Naval surgical team. She headed south to meet the *Endurance*.[4]

Buey describes the *Fort Austin* as 'essentially a Royal Navy support vehicle which carries stores but is manned by a Merchant Navy crew. It's what's affectionately known as the grey funnel line – it's the same colour grey as a warship. Their purpose is to replenish the ships while they are at sea so that they don't need to come back into port and lose their operational viability.

'Nobody really thought there was going to be a war, absolutely not. While we were on the *Austin* we were of course going through all the drills that you would expect in terms of packing and re-packing your kit, and doing training with SLR, self-loading rifles. Whoever thought of giving sailors guns was a bit loose in the brain, I think. Would you trust a sailor with a gun? Sailors with guns are generally called marines! Through basic training you are obviously taught to handle weapons, submachine guns and general purpose machine guns – but clearly you never expect to have to fire those in anger.

'The ship was blacked out at night-time with black curtains on the inside of all the doors so that even when you opened them the light didn't extrude. You've got to think that at sea the smallest light is visible for miles and miles around, and you want to make it as difficult as possible for your enemy to know where you are and pinpoint your position. Curtains mean people can move about inside and outside, and you do need to get outside at night-time to work. It always used to amuse me that when we were at Yeovilton we'd had the Dutch navy come in and they'd finish at 5 o'clock. You'd think *hang on, a war doesn't finish at 5 o'clock.*'

On 12 April, *Fort Austin* 'sighted *Endurance*, and over the next day the SBS and SAS men heading for South Georgia were cross-decked to *Endurance* along with their stores, equipment, boats, and supplies for the *Endurance*. Two Wessex helicopters helped with the shipping. HMS *Endurance* and *Fort Austin* were joined by HMS *Antrim*, HMS *Plymouth* and RFA tanker *Tidespring*. The reoccupation of South Georgia was planned aboard HMS *Antrim*.'[5]

On 25 April, South Georgia was recaptured.

'The moment I thought it was going to get serious was when we heard that we'd hit the *Belgrano* via a British radio service. It was at that point you suddenly thought *well, we've fired a shot in anger now and there is going to be some retribution for that.*

'You'd always had the thought of the possibility the longer you were down there the more likely it was going to become, but at that point none of us had seen anything actually fired. We'd see the Harriers take off in the morning and come back in the evening or later that morning. You'd count them back in as well. It was true what Brian Hanrahan said.[6] There were times when six went out and six came back and you stood on the flight deck and cheered them. By this time there was a massive, massive, almost overwhelming sense of camaraderie. It was very, very strong.

'You ended up communicating with people you would have given a wide berth to in peacetime and finding out a bit more about those people. You were now ultimately reliant upon them for their piece of the jigsaw, the bit that they could bring to the table, and you were going to need every piece of the jigsaw.

'Before we knew it we were subjected to an AIR RAID WARNING RED, the highest, once we got into the Exclusion Zone. We had not seen the Falklands at this stage. The Argentinians were encamped on them and if you could have seen them you were far too close, certainly as a Royal Fleet Auxiliary, because it's not a warship and it doesn't have the firepower or the arsenal of a warship. On top of that, you don't want to lose a support vessel because whatever it was supporting you with you now have to manage without. You sail with the fleet because, obviously, when the fleet needs you, it's important to be right on the doorstep. It means you can sail alongside them and, although you are military personnel, you are still in a Merchant Navy vessel which is part of the grey funnel line.

'So we had WARNING RED and everybody went to the stations that they should go to. I have a very, very vivid memory that I just desperately wanted to urinate so regularly at that time. Fear and trepidation, I suppose. Then somebody said – I can't remember who – "How do we know if it's one of ours or one of theirs?" It was a very valid point and there was a pregnant pause. Then somebody else piped up, "If you see something glowing under its belly let's just shoot it and we'll ask questions later." Everybody laughed – a kind of nervous laugh, like *we might have to do this,* but somehow that settled everybody down again. It seemed like ages but it was probably over within five minutes. Your brain can cover a lot of territory in five minutes when it's working fast.

'So we are now in the Exclusion Zone and we are doing what we can to keep our aircraft airworthy. Our aircraft were flying off and other aircraft were flying on to our ship – these are the helicopters. If something needed a bit more maintenance on it and a warship needed its aircraft to be active then we would send our aircraft across to them and they would send theirs across to us. We'd service them and send them back. It was a heavy workload and it's the one and only time in my life when I've worked twenty-hour days. Strangely enough, you do. Your body adapts even though in the twenty-hour day it sometimes won't sleep in a four-hour batch. It was a catnap here or a catnap there. You'd just get your head down and then the air-raid warning would go off and you'd be back up to your action stations wide awake again.

'We had some SAS guys parachute out of the back of a Hercules and our aircraft was tasked to go and pick them up out of the water. I believe there were six of them. They came on board which caused a bit of a stir because we knew they were coming and we knew we were responsible for picking them and their equipment out of the water. They are macho people, absolutely, and they are also very private people.

'A colleague and I were having some lunch one day and an SAS guy came in and sat down at our table. We introduced ourselves and he looked like a South American, dark hair, dark moustache, nice suntan. We asked him what his name was and he pondered for a moment, looked up at the ceiling and looked back at us and said, "You can call me George. If you call me George I will respond to you" – so he obviously wasn't called George, he just didn't want to disclose his correct name or anything like that.

'One of the lads on our flight recognised one of these SAS lads. He said, "I know him; he used to be an aircrewman with the navy." He went across:

'Hi.'

SAS man: 'Do I know you?'

'Yes.'

SAS man: 'No, no, I don't.'
'You used to be a crewman.'
SAS man: 'You've got the wrong bloke, mate.'

Buey says that 'when we went away our lad said "I'm telling you now he was such-and-such." We were three or four weeks into the conflict and these guys were sent down there with a job to do. That wasn't making friends.

'In some respects you become in awe of them. There is a persona that they have. You've been brought up to believe they are gods and here they are demonstrating to you at first hand that they are really like that. They don't let on to anybody, even wives who don't know their husbands are in it.'

The sinking of the *Belgrano* was one decisive psychological moment because everyone knew this was now serious. The sinking of the *Sheffield* was a second psychological moment because everyone in the Task Force knew this was now serious for them.

'When the *Sheffield* got hit we took on board some of the survivors. I remember distinctly having a dialogue with a guy – because obviously they repatriate you after something like that – and saying to him, "When you get back to the UK you are going to be such a hero" not knowing myself that exactly three weeks later the same thing would happen to me. We weren't expecting it to happen at all.

'We transferred from the *Fort Austin* to HMS *Hermes* on about the 15 May and spent five days on there. During it we were responsible for stripping an aircraft down to its flying controls only – it was to fly a group of SAS people a very long distance. We were literally asking, "What about this chief, can we take this out?" He'd ask, "Does it need it to fly? No? Then get it out."

'If you remember seeing the development of the Harrier – when it looked like a flying bedstead, no wings on it, just a frame with an engine – that's essentially what this was like. It wasn't coming back. As I understand it, subsequently the aircraft did its dirty work and then flew to Chile and was burnt out by the crew. The Chileans registered a protest that their airspace had been violated because they didn't want to be dragged into the conflict and that was word to the [UK] government that the mission had been a success.

'We spent four or five days on the *Hermes* and the *Atlantic Conveyor* joined us in the Exclusion Zone. It had come down with a payload of Harriers. They flew the Harriers off the *Conveyor* onto the *Hermes* and the *Invincible*, and our helicopter was flown off the *Hermes* with us to the *Conveyor* on 20 May.

'The *Atlantic Conveyor* was a container ship, quite big and essentially a third aircraft carrier, because although it didn't have any fixed-wing aircraft it had Chinooks and Wessex 5s. As you'd imagine with a container ship, it's got no watertight integrity whatsoever, because you could drive articulated trucks on to there, unlike a warship, where, if a compartment gets hit, you can seal that and it still keeps its buoyancy. On the *Conveyor* there was all sorts of stores, tented villages, lorries full of frozen meat, oxygen bottles – the whole lot, everything geared up for when we landed on the Falklands to kit the forward operation bases out so that we could advance on Stanley.'

The *Conveyor* was a 14,950-ton roll-on, roll-off Cunard. Because of the urgency of the whole Falklands operation, a decision was taken not to make it 'a high-value unit' and there was a measure of controversy over whether it was legal to arm auxiliaries. The consequence was that *Atlantic Conveyor* didn't get a defence system!

Buey says that 'the *Conveyor* had come from Liverpool. My parents didn't even know I was on it. As far as my parents were concerned I was still on the *Fort Austin*.'

At 7.30 on 25 May a possible target was picked up by Argentinian radar and passed to Rio Grande. The target was placed at 110 miles northeast of Puerto Argentino [Stanley] and a mission to attack it was programmed for 9.00. The target (or targets) is not clear, but may have been HMS *Ardent*. The attack had to be delayed until evening because of the lack of a refuelling plane.

Two Super Étendards took off that afternoon[7] and set a course for the refuelling plane 160 miles away. The rendezvous was successfully completed and the Étendards now set a course for the target, still some 300 miles away. At 150 miles they dived to get beneath the radar and one source says they flew at no more than 8 or 10 metres above the sea.[8]

'At about 6.00,' Buey says, 'there was a pipe over the ship's tannoy that our squadron and one or two others would be going ashore next morning. We'd go in under the cover of darkness and disembark at dawn. We should prepare ourselves for that.

'We still had some work to do. Because we were a commando squadron we were supporting the Royal Marines. What we'd have been doing was set up forward operating bases so every time there was an advance helicopters would have flown the troops in. The troops would have secured the area. We'd have been picked up and flown there, and that would have been our most advanced operating base where we could carry out routine maintenance to keep the aircraft flying. It would have been like a piggyback. Once we were there they would push for the next base.

'We'd been at sea for six weeks and we really wanted to get some land and *somebody bring me a pint of fresh milk, please. I'm sick of having my breakfast with powdered milk.* I remember what it was called, Millac. It was disgusting – you can't call it food. It was white and liquid but it tasted nothing like milk.

'That night was spent tidying up the aircraft and doing the after-flight inspection which we did on a routine basis. It got to towards 7.30, I'd finished my jobs for the evening and I decided to go for some dinner. We had aircraft tool kits with shadow boards [containing outlines of tools showing where they should be stored] in them. You'd take them back to the tool control; the controller would check them in and make sure that all the tools were in the box. It meant nothing was left on the aircraft which could get into the flight controls and render them unserviceable. The lad's name who was doing tool control was Adrian Anslow. I said to Adrian, "Are you going to dinner?" He was just wrapping up. "No," he said, "you know what I'm like, Dave. My gear's all over the place. I need to go and get it all ready for the morning." We walked together down the side of the ship and then towards the galley. I took my anti-flash gear off and I left my gas mask outside the galley because by this time complacency had set in. We'd had so many AIR RAID WARNING REDS and nothing had happened. I had my anti-flash gear with me but my life-jacket and my gas mask were strapped together and I left them on the floor outside alongside everybody else's.

'Adrian went past the freezer units to go down to A deck to pack his stuff up. I went into the galley and got my dinner. I had a roast dinner and I remember thinking *I'm going to make the most of this because it could be the last I get for a while*. On the menu was chocolate sponge with white custard so I thought *I'll have some of that as well, thank you*. I sat down and I remember my anti-flash gear being alongside me.'

The Super Étendards launched their Exocets at 7.31.

The *Alacrity*'s radar picked up the Exocets travelling at 300 metres a second. She fired chaff to distract the Exocets and so did other warships. The Exocets flew through the chaff and now their radar picked up the *Atlantic Conveyor*. She had no chaff and, as someone said cryptically – and tragically – 'was not built for agility'.[9]

Buey remembers 'the air-raid warning came and I thought *oh, here we go again*. I carried on eating my dinner. Then there was a big thud, not a bang but a thud, a very loud thud that shook the ship enormously. Everybody stopped eating and was looking up and looking around at each other. They knew it was going to take something to *shake* the ship.'

That was the first Exocet.

'There was an urn full of boiling water and, given the impact, it dropped off its shelf and fell to the floor. There is now boiling water pouring all over the place. I looked down at my dinner and the fluo-rescent light tube cover – the plastic, opaque cover that goes over the fluorescent bulbs – had fallen onto the table in front of me. Some of the gravy from my roast dinner had gone into the white sauce in my pud-ding. I thought *that's not on, I won't be able to eat that now*. I hadn't grasped the enormity of the situation. Then a pipe came over the tannoy that we had been hit by an as-yet unidentified object, that we should close up at the emergency stations.

'I don't really remember it word for word but while it was going on I do remember it being interrupted. "HIT THE DECK, HIT THE

DECK, HIT THE DECK." You knew something else was coming and so everyone threw themselves to the floor, under tables. We were laying there and we were hit by something else. This time there was a bang.'

That was the second Exocet.

'Now the ship was alight. You could hear the heat affecting all the oxygen containers and everything that was down below. The containers were going off like balloons popping and every time one went off you could feel it through the metal of the ship. You couldn't feel the engines any more because they weren't working. The ship was dead in the water. The propellers had stopped, the power had gone and it was dark.

'I remember laying there and looking at a chap called Jimmy Stuart and he was *white*. Honestly I have never, ever seen anybody as pale as I saw Jimmy. He was whiter than the custard which now had the gravy in it. I looked at him and I thought *God, am I that scared?* and of course I was. Looking through Jim's eyes I was looking back to me and *seeing* the same complexion.

'Then some power was restored to the ship – auxiliary power. The telephone rang and there were five Royal Naval ratings. I believe one of them, Charlie Bishop, was the leading hand and he picked the phone up and gave a briefing to the bridge. We were tasked to go along past the freezer unit to try and make our way down to A deck to see who we could save, what we could salvage and also see what firefighting capabilities we had.

'That was the start of the most frightening part of it, really, because it was a smoky environment out there and we had learnt from the experiences of the *Sheffield*. Some of the lads on the *Sheffield* had reported that you could get up to a minute's more time in a smoke-filled environment if you put your gas mask on, even though they weren't designed for that. We had them, we put them on and we started crawling along the floor because the smoke was now billowing to the ceiling. We got quite a way along and we could hear people screaming and shouting "help" but we couldn't go any further. You couldn't see and the deck was so hot – we were kneeling down. You couldn't put your hands on the deck anymore. The paint was starting to blister because it was getting so hot.

'We returned to the galley.

'I took up some firefighting with the fire hydrants which were there and working. Shortly after that the order came to abandon ship.'

This was twenty minutes after the Exocets struck.

'Our life-raft station was at the point of the ship where an Exocet had come in and, in that situation, what you do is go to the other side of the ship, to the place which is the mirror image of it. So we went over to that side, which meant going through the kitchen area itself. There was a civilian steward in there – or chef, I can't remember – and he had gone into shock. He was sitting huddled in a ball in complete shock. We tried to get him to come with us, but he was just staring into oblivion, shaking, and the medics said to us, "The only way you're going to move him is to break his arms. You have got to preserve yourself."

'After what seemed like ages of trying, myself and Don Pryce – who was a Leading Aircraft Engineering Mechanic, Electrical Branch – went through to the life-raft station where there was a few people, very, very calm, very, very cool and collected. Very polite. No panic. That's shock as well, perhaps, because I still don't think the enormity had struck home at that stage.

'We did know we were in serious danger, but I think that the camaraderie which had shown itself earlier in the trip – and sustained itself throughout – was at the fore now. It was about *listen, we're in this together, let's get out of it together* to the point where I remember Don and I standing at the top of the ladder, one either side, saying, "You go," "No, you go." I remember Don saying he was senior and that I should go. I said something along the lines that, "If you're senior to me, you go down and if I fall I'll fall on you."

'Don went over and then I went over onto the ladder with wooden slats on it. Unbeknown to us, one of the vertical ropes had severed so half-way down it flicked over. I came over the top and then people were coming over the top onto me and they were standing on my hands as they were coming down. I'd only got down about half a dozen rungs and I was shouting, "You're standing on my hands." They lifted their feet but I hadn't got a grip and I fell what has been estimated as about 60 feet into the ice-cold water. I had a marginally inflated lifejacket. I remember going into the water and it was black, so black. I was under the water for a second or two and it was so dark, it was just so dark. I was thinking *I'm not coming up, I'm not coming up.* All of a sudden I popped out.

'As I did, there were life-rafts everywhere and it was light. Helicopters flying overhead had their searchlights on the surface of the sea. HMS *Alacrity* was en route to us. The swell between the two ships was forcing me towards the bow of the *Conveyor* and the bow of the HMS *Alacrity*. I managed to swim and, strangely enough, Jimmy Stuart was sitting in the doorway of one of the life-rafts. I managed to swim close to him, he leant over and he assisted me getting into the life-raft. Then Jim and I sat in the doorway pulling in everybody that we could once they got close enough to us.

'We were still tied to the *Conveyor* – lashed to the side – and the *Conveyor* was completely unstable in the water. She was well alight, although, because we were so low down and on the opposite side of the ship, we couldn't see all that. You could see the smoke which was filling the air because the hull was hot. Every time it touched the water you got steam off it and because we were lashed to the deck every time the stern came out of the water it dragged us under – then as it came down again it washed us out. At that point the propellers were clearing the water and you could see that they'd stopped.

'We managed to cut ourselves free. I believe the knife in the life-raft had been lost and one of the last people we pulled in was an aircrewman who had one in his flying suit. We used that to cut it. If he hadn't had the knife we would probably have chewed through the rope with our teeth.

'We were freezing cold. I didn't have a life-suit on, I'd just gone in my combat inside the lifejacket and now it's probably 8.15, 8.30 at night, dark and cold. I'm frightened, but not panicking – never panicked, never panicked. The fact that you can look around at others who aren't panicking, and know that you are all there for the same reason, again gives you the feeling *we're in this together, let's get through this together.* People were not panicking. People were bewildered, people were staring and wondering what had gone on, but essentially it was those people who hadn't got anything to do. It wasn't any fault of those lads staring into space: they were sitting there in a safer environment taking it all in. Jim and I were still engaged in trying to pull people in, and it gives you a purpose. You don't think about anything else. We couldn't stop and realise the enormity of it because our minds were still focused.'

One report suggests that seventy-four men and three bodies were pulled from the sea against a backdrop of constant explosions from the *Conveyor*.

'When you're at sea and they do what's called an RAS – a replenishment at sea – there's a gun with a projectile on it, which I think is made of cork, and attached to that is a bit of string. It is fired across from one ship to another and you pull the string which becomes rope which becomes a steel cable. It's how they manage to hang fuel lines and things like that across.

'*Alacrity* had come alongside but because of the unstable nature of the *Conveyor* it had to withdraw. It wouldn't be leaving us behind. It fired out these ropes and I managed to pick one up and wrap it around my hand. The consequence was that, as the *Alacrity* withdrew, it towed us via my hand. When we were at a safe distance the *Alacrity* started to get the people out of the life-rafts. A scramble-net was thrown down the side, people were disembarking from the life-rafts onto the scramble-net and some of the *Alacrity* crew were hanging over the side, literally pulling you on board.

'There was a chap, a chief petty officer who was a member of our flight. His first name was Eddie, but I can't remember what his surname was. He was a fairly – dare I say? – unpopular person, a bit aloof, but one of our lads nonetheless. He mis-timed his approach to the scramble-net and fell into the water. He got washed along the side of the ship and was going to be washed away. The spotlights were on the water and I could see a rope was hanging off the side of the *Alacrity* and I followed it across the top of the water, straight to my hand. I started thrashing my hand around and Eddie managed to grab the rope. He pulled himself along it to my hand and Jim and I pulled him in the life-raft.

'It came to my turn and I came up the side. Because we knew some of the lads on HMS *Alacrity*'s flight – they had a Lynx helicopter on there

– and because the Lynx was based at Yeovilton as well, we went up and gathered with them on the flight deck. We saw we were making headway away from the *Conveyor*. Perhaps we were a mile away by this time. It was so bright – burning away there – it was like the sun on the water. It was almost like looking at a phosphorous glow.

'I remember it was great to see the lads of *Alacrity*. I asked one of them how Tottenham had got on in the Cup Final against QPR and he said, "If I'd known you were a Tottenham fan I'd have thrown you back in!" – he followed Arsenal – so there was a good bit of banter. By the time we got onto *Alacrity* at 10.00 and they told us that we'd been in the life-raft for up to two hours I was bewildered. I said, "You've got to be kidding me, we've only been in there for five minutes." And it *was* two hours.

'We went below decks and managed to get dried off. We were issued with survival packs – clothing that didn't fit – and then it was a case of going up to the galley to look at the names that were appearing on the list as either having been brought onto *Alacrity* or onto *Broadsword* or *Hermes* or *Invincible*. They asked you your name when they got you on board and that was relayed to the other ships. You might read that so-and-so was "alive and aboard HMS *Alacrity*". It was at that point I saw on there that Don Pryce who had gone down the ladder before me. His body had been recovered by, I believe, one of the petty officers of our flight. He was found floating face-down in the water and they managed to get him into a life-raft to try and resuscitate him, but it couldn't be done.

'You were looking at the list and the list grows and the one list you don't want to grow is the list of fatalities. I couldn't see Adrian's name. A day or two later, when all the final lists were in, Adrian's name was listed as "missing, presumed dead". Bear in mind we were a flight of a dozen people, and for two of those people to be missing is quite a large proportion of the flight. It was my one and only experience of a burial at sea as well. We buried three people.'

That was the day after the attack.

'Eddie very kindly came down and said, "Thanks for saving my life" and gave me a can of beer. Quite funny really because it was a warm can of beer and the junior ratings on the *Alacrity* said, "Give us that." They put it in the front of the air-conditioning unit and gave me one of the cold ones that they'd stored in there earlier.'

Twelve men died on the *Conveyor* and the loss of munitions was significant: ten helicopters, ammunition (including cluster bombs), tents for 5,000 men, spare engines and pieces for the Harriers, a plant to make sea-water drinkable and materials for a mobile runway for the Sea Harriers. The *Conveyor* was the first British merchant vessel to be sunk by hostile fire since the Second World War.

'We spent a couple of days on there. The *Alacrity* still had its job to do and the crew were fantastic. They would sleep on the floor and let us sleep in their "pits" and I am forever indebted to those lads. We had an opportunity to send a telex home, with no more than twenty words on it. I sent mine to my sister and it read:

'"SIS, SENT TO YOU SO AS NOT TO ALARM MUM. AM OK. WILL SEE YOU ALL SOON."

'My sister has passed away now but she did say to me in a quiet moment that that was the most compassionate thing she'd ever known me do!'

After the two days on the *Alacrity*, Buey and the others were airlifted onto the *British Tay*, a fuel tanker, 'then we sailed back to Ascension Island. We were repatriated from there to Brize Norton. It was an incredible feeling, really, an incredible feeling. We flew on a VC10 and we saw the first women for nine weeks with the aircrew on the plane.

'The pilot seemed to be taking ages from when we landed to when we were tied up on the hard stand. The passengers started singing *why are we waiting?* because it was the RAF, you see, and the other forces call the RAF civilians in uniform. We got off the aircraft and in those days I smoked so I'd taken advantage of the duty free. I had a bottle of whisky in one hand and 200 Rothmans in the other. We were walking across the hard standing and my mum and my sister came running towards me. I think I swept them both off their feet. There were big cheers. They'd been through an awful lot.

'I had been on an emotional roller-coaster. There was so much going on around you it was a bit like being a kid at a funfair. And I was only 20.

'At Brize Norton there was a party atmosphere tinged with a bit of sadness in moments when you had a chance to reflect by yourself about those who weren't coming back – Don and Adrian, for example – so you were experiencing quite mixed emotions, really, but in essence it was a kind of a funfair atmosphere.

'The first thing was a large consumption of alcohol. My brother had told the pub I used to frequent that I was coming home on leave. There was a lot of national fervour at that time and they arranged a bit of a party. The local newspaper was there. You're on a high.

'It was 7 June when we got back and the country's following what's going on in the Falklands, the World Cup was to start in three day's time in Spain, the weather was fantastic so it was *surreal*: I'd been in one situation two weeks beforehand and now here I was back at home in the sunshine looking forward to the World Cup, watching the news, understanding that we're now on top in the Falklands and it won't be long now before it all draws to a close and hopefully the killing stops.' (Incidentally, Buey says that the *Conveyor* was 'a major loss because I've heard it stated that, had the *Conveyor* got through, the conflict would have finished two weeks before'.)

'The first morning, I'd said to my mum to wake me up early because I wanted to get out and get some bits and pieces. I had taken most of my stuff with me when we originally sailed because we didn't know how long we were going to be away. As a 20-year-old I didn't really have that much, anyway. My living quarters were at my air station so the morning after I got back was about hiring a car and buying some clothes. She came into my bedroom and pulled the curtains open. Of course I'd been in with lads for nine and a half, ten weeks and swearing is rife. The curtains opened and I said, "What the ****'s going on?" then I looked up and it was my mum ...

'I said, "I'm sorry, mum." She patted the bedclothes and said with a smile, "That's all right son."

'We'd been issued with temporary ID cards which had "Falklands Survivor" written on them and all your mates wanted to see that. You're going around places and your mates are telling everybody you've just come back from the Falklands. Everybody's proud and they want to shake your hand. People *were* proud.

'I remember going into Dixon's in Stevenage with a friend who was in the navy but hadn't gone to the Falklands. The *QE2* had come home and all the TVs in the shop were showing the news. I stood there and cried my eyes out. My friend gave me a wide berth and let me get on with it. It was the first time since I'd been back that I'd come off the high. It was the reality of it all that suddenly struck home.

'I left the services in 1985, three years on, because unemployment outside was pretty dire and that meant people just weren't leaving so promotion had become dead man's shoes. I didn't want to be doing the same thing at the same rate six years down the line as I'd been doing the previous six years. I'd also met a girl and it just seemed the right thing to do. I put in for what's called Premature Voluntary Release. I was on eighteen-month's notice and I ended up serving twelve months of that.

'I always knew before I went in that when I left I wanted to be a salesman, a rep out on the road. I didn't know what I wanted to sell. Because I'd been in over five years I was entitled to a resettlement course, which I did. I spent a month in professional selling and after I'd done that I managed to get myself a job.

'I was 23 years of age and everybody was telling me that as a 23-year-old I had experienced much more than some 53-year-olds. I was very proud to have joined the navy and pleased to have been involved in what I had been involved in. I was very proud to have been involved with the people that I had been involved with. It all seemed to go so quickly, there one minute, then it wasn't.'

Notes

1. www.navynews.co.uk/articles/2004/0406/0004062801.asp
2. www.royalnavy.mod.uk for Naval Bases & Air Stations.
3. SBS (Special Boat Service): a unit for special operations at sea which also operates on land and has a maritime counter-terrorism capability.
4. www.royalnavy.mod.uk/operations-and-support/.../print

5. www.britains-smallwars.com/Falklands/sbs.htm

6. Brian Hanrahan, BBC reporter on HMS *Hermes*, found a way to circumvent reporting restrictions when he said, famously, after a Harrier raid on the Falklands, 'I counted them all out and I counted them all back'.

7. There was a one-hour time difference between the Task Force and Argentina.

8. www.britains-smallwars.com/Falklands/Exocet.html

9. www.hmsalacrity.co.uk

6

THE HEAVY MOVER

All their rights were observed. I wouldn't say they were happy, but I wouldn't say they were unhappy. They were alive, they were safe, they were getting fed and they knew they were going home.

Mark 'Mario' Reid was born in Huntingdon in 1962. 'I joined up in 1981. I worked in a factory with my father, who sadly passed away when I was 18. The only way for promotion was normally following in dead men's shoes. I thought I'd try a different career. The services appealed to me because they were something different and it probably had something to do with getting away. Huntingdon's not that bad at all. I haven't been back for a few years but when I did go back the same old faces were still there.

'I joined the Royal Engineers as a sapper and after training I volunteered for paratroop training – or I was volunteered by my training officer: 9 Para.'

9 Parachute Squadron, RE is an Airborne detachment of the Royal Engineers. In the Royal Engineers, the soldiers are called sappers. A sapper – or combat engineer – multi-tasks, including building bridges, laying or clearing minefields, demolition and a variety of construction roles.

'In the Corps you are a soldier first, sapper second and a tradesman third.

'I got a few injuries and was unable to complete para training.

'We were in barracks at Aldershot when we got the word that we were going to the Falklands. Word of command, they call it – it comes down!

'Did I know where the Falklands were? No, of course not. Most people thought they were near Scotland. That's an ignorance about our history, isn't it? To be fair, though, it was an extremely obscure place before the conflict.

'We got all the kit ready and I was on the *QE2* with 3,000 other squaddies – the Welsh Guards, the Gurkhas and attachments, which would be our squadron and a few others from logistics and so on. I didn't hear of any trouble.'

The *QE2* had been sailing from Philadelphia to Southampton when she began to 'pick up commercial radio broadcasts' that she was being requisioned for the Falklands. Mrs Thatcher, initially reluctant to risk the most famous ship in the world, accepted that her enormous capacity was needed. She'd take the 3,000 squaddies.

Some thousand officers and crew volunteered to go and of them 650, including thirty-three women, were selected. The ship was quickly refitted:

Art work, silver, furniture, and casino equipment was taken ashore for storage. Wooden panels were laid down to protect the carpets from the soldiers' boots. Hundreds of cots [beds] were brought aboard … In addition, military communications equipment was brought onboard and a secure communications centre was constructed. Tons of military stores and cargo were brought on including vehicles, jet fuel and ammunition. Since there was more than would fit in the hold, some supplies, including ammunition, were stored on the open deck near the funnel.[1]

'It wasn't too good for me,' Reid says, 'because I wasn't a para I was given a lot of the crap from my own squadron, who were Airborne. I didn't get to see any of the farewells. I had to look after the weapons for the troop. They were all outside waving goodbye.

'The food at first was too posh. They were giving us caviar and all we wanted was bloody baked beans. You don't believe they were giving us caviar? They were, first of all. Caviar: you had to try it – and it was horrible. We were getting through the stocks they had on the ship, you see. We'd eat our way through that first but it soon changed because there were enough complaints.

'I was in the stewards' accommodation right down at the bottom so I was on this luxury liner, but not in luxury. Four of us managed to squeeze into one of their rooms, maybe 4 metres by 3 metres. In fact, I don't think it was that big. This was crew quarters, not for passengers. We used to run around the deck and I did loads of getting fit. It was brilliant. Super-fit we were. It didn't seem strange running round a cruise ship because you were army-barmy, weren't you? You did as you were told.

'I managed to see one film, *Escape from Victory*; I remember the abuse Ossie Ardiles got when he came on screen! I didn't venture out much, just kept my head down writing letters.

'In fact I got the name Mario when I was on the *QE2*. Because I'd done Spanish at school, they nicknamed me Mario. I turned black at Ascension – suntanned – and they said, "You're all right, you can swap sides" as a joke. They called me "Mario the Argie", although I think Mario is more Italian. Never mind. My real name is Mark so it's not that far away and it's just followed me throughout my army career, In fact, I use it today here in Spain.

'We went to Ascension although but we didn't land. We changed over to the *Canberra*. Near the icebergs!'

The Ministry of Defence had requisitioned the *Canberra*, the first large cruise liner built in the United Kingdom – by Harland & Wolff, Belfast – after the Second World War. The *Canberra*'s career mirrored the changes in travel. She'd been built to transport migrants from Britain to Australia, but numbers decreased and she switched to cruising the West Indies from New York. She was moved to Southampton and became famous for world cruises.

Now she was a troopship.

More than that, the *QE2* was regarded as too vulnerable to be sent fully into a war zone.

Reid explains that 'a boat pulled up alongside the *QE2* and you had to jump on it and hope you didn't fall in the gap. I heard one or two did. On the *Canberra* we might have known it was getting serious because it came over the World Service that we had landed [in the Falklands] or were getting ready to land! We were annoyed about that. They had told the world and we might have got a hot reception. In the end we were quite lucky.

'On the *Canberra*, once again, I was down in the crew's quarters and it was the first time I'd seen an Asian toilet, where you squat. There is no toilet, just a hole in the floor.

'Again I couldn't see anything at all, I saw icebergs but all we were doing was training, just training – weapon training. I don't think we ran round the *Canberra's* deck.'

On 21 May, the *Canberra* was in San Carlos Water for troops to disembark. Interestingly, because of her size, even if she'd been badly hit she wouldn't have vanished under the waves – San Carlos Water was too shallow. Reportedly the Argentinian pilots were ordered not to attack the *Canberra* because she was thought to be a hospital ship.

'We landed at San Carlos on the jetty. It wasn't like the D-Day landings; it was follow-the-man-in-front. We got off the *Canberra* by jumping on to little boats – landing craft – and they pulled up alongside the jetty. Then we dug in. 3 Brigade had already landed and secured the area some weeks earlier. We were 5 Brigade. As a four-man team we dug in, which meant foxholes, small at first so your body could lie in it.

'The Falklands struck me as pretty amazing having come from Huntingdon, which is flat and green. The Falklands were like Wales and, because I'd been there to do a bit of training, that had prepared me for it. When you saw all the peat it was nice and green but very bleak when you got to the rocky patches of the island.

'You didn't see the fighters – well, you did but they were so fast. It was just a flash. They were *that* fast. You only heard the roar, really. We all shot at them. I only had an SMG, a submachine gun; a little 9mm weapon the same as the ones in the Second World War. Pointless! They went over Carlos Bay to get the ships. I didn't see any of the ships hit but I did see the flash of one of the planes being hit. We all did. I think one of the Rapiers got it, not us.'

Reid had some truly amazing encounters.

'I did bump into quite a few school mates. Jumping into a trench I met someone I'd joined up with and someone else who was my next door neighbour's best mate! I didn't even know they were there. This was at San Carlos during an air raid when I went into the nearest trench. There were two other Royal Engineers there from 11 Squadron.

'My next door neighbour was called Michael Gray. Michael had joined the Corps and at that time I didn't know anything about it. I believe he'd left by the time I was in. So when I jumped in to the trench there were two sappers in there, one I'd joined up with – which means I was in the same training party – and his corporal, who was called Dixie Dean. We got chatting. "Where you from?" Dean said: "Oh, I've got a friend called Michael Gray [who lives there]." I said, "That's my next door neighbour!"

'When I was in a shed I mentioned stupidly to the commandos, "Do you know so-and-so?" and they said, "Yeah, he's in a trench out there!" I met three school mates, all commandos: one was in hospital with trench foot, one was a signaller and the other was in that trench outside. It's called a small world ...

'My daily routine was moving stores forward, then I went up to Fitzroy once all the stores were there. We were in sheep sheds, kipping on the wood, with the smell of sheep not very far away – the smell of humans was better! Well, not really ...

'Helicopters were doing all the moving. I was the net man, shall we say, attaching the stores to the helicopters. I was REMF – Rear Echelon M★★★★★ F★★★★★. The helicopters could lift quite a few tons. All the stores would be prepared and a pallet loaded in a net. We'd do that all day long, although I didn't know where they were going. They'd vanish over the horizon.

'We finished up at Stanley on the day after the surrender. I got there on the only Chinook that they had on the island. They shifted the whole squadron on a one-er. Because we were the engineers, we had to get straight in there, didn't we? There were about eighty of us and I think a Chinook can only take eighty, anyway – eighty bods, fully kitted. We all stood up: you just walk on, stand there with all your kit on and then walk off. The trip wasn't that long.

'Stanley was different, weird because there was not a traffic light in sight. That was funny. *Way back in time*, you'd think, *like when you grew up in the '60s*. I'd never known a little village but I imagine it to be like that. I think the conflict brought them into the twentieth century.

'I never got to a bar or anything. I wouldn't have been allowed in and in fact I didn't even get to the church service in Stanley[2] because once again I was looking after the weapons.

'I tried to find accommodation and I ended up in an attic by the jetty. I moved from the attic to someone else's house and that was nice. We'd put on a Neil Diamond record and it was played every day. It was his greatest hits – *Sweet Caroline, Song Sung Blue* and so on. I still play it because I play guitar. I give guitar lessons.

'I was driving a Merc Land Rover – pretty posh, they were, and doing PoW work because of my Spanish and in fact the Argentinians gave me some souvenirs, chevrons and stuff. Because I "did" some Spanish they'd always come and see me. I ended up with lieutenant's pips and sergeant's chevrons which they gave me when they left.

'I was guarding them and taking them when they went up to clear the mines – they would show us where the mines were. I also went to the hospital when one of them lost his foot. He'd stepped on a mine. I tried to do the translation and that was a bit upsetting because then you realise that they are just like you. You're face to face and you're thinking *it could have been one of us.*

'In my Spanish I was trying to say, "Thanks for your help, really" because they were doing the mine clearance. They didn't have to do it – well, I don't know the ins and outs of that, but I presume they didn't have to. They wouldn't have had to.

'The Argentinians were demoralised. A right mess. I came to understand they were just human beings like me. At the time they were the enemy and then afterwards you looked at them and thought *they're conscripts and we're professionals.* I think they were treated scrupulously fairly. I didn't see anything go wrong, put it that way. All their rights were observed. I wouldn't say they were happy but I wouldn't say they were unhappy. They knew they were going home, they were alive, and they were safe and getting fed. They lined up like we all do at the cookhouse. They had lots of their own food, too.

'We went home on a ferry which had been called *St Edmunds* and was renamed the MV *Keren*.'

Thereby hangs a tale. The *Keren*, in the Tyne, was an ex-Sealink ferry bought by the Ministry of Defence just after the conflict ended and urgently needed down south. The National Union of Seamen and the MoD fell into dispute over whether they'd be paid 'ferry' or 'deep sea' rates and they struck.

The MoD 'hatched a plot to take the ship over with a Royal Navy crew' who would sail it to the Falklands. Thirty-five of them boarded it at night and a 'Commissioning Warrant was read and the ship became "HMS" *Keren*, thereby making it an offence for any member of the public including NUS to step on board'.

The navy personnel spent three days learning how to sail the ship and did sail it to anchor off South Shields. The NUS now asked for their jobs back, she sailed back up the Tyne and was decommissioned, becoming MV *Keren* again.[3]

Now Reid was on it.

'We got to Ascension and waited for a plane. Then there was a toss of a coin for who got on it between my people, the engineers, and 10 Squadron, which was REME paras. We got on. It was my 20th birthday, 29 July.

'I watched 10 Squadron open up all their duty free. It was normal duty free. We were flying back from Ascension Island and I think I bought a bottle of whisky for my brother and perfume for my girlfriend. We flew back to Brize Norton and there was no family to meet me. I was obviously a bit upset, as you would be when you see everybody else getting met. I thought *what's going on?* One of the officers said, "Don't worry, son, your family is waiting for you in the squadron bar [at the base]." I said, "I'm not allowed in the squadron bar" – it was normally for personnel who had passed Airborne, or P Company. Every squadron has a squadron bar, but I hadn't passed Airborne then. He said, "You are allowed ."

'So the perfume went to my girlfriend – who I eventually married and am now divorced from – the whisky went to my brother and there was nothing for my mum. At the time I didn't realise. My mum thought

I should have cuddled her first and not my girlfriend, but you don't think like that.

'I ran away from home. I was living back there and had a hard time, really. My brother thought I was a big hero but you're not a hero if you upset your mum or anything like that. At 20, you don't know that, do you? You're still growing up and going through your own faults. When I left home I went and lived with my girlfriend's dad. Then I went back, made up with my mum and got engaged to my girlfriend.'

By contrast …

'I remember going to a fairground, I was getting on a ride and Diane, an old school friend I hadn't seen for years – and who's a mate of mine now on Facebook – came over to me, gave me a hug and a kiss and said, "Well done. Welcome back." That was nice. I went to the welcome home party of one of the marines who'd had trench foot at San Carlos. That was quite good because he had all of us there.

'I left the services in 2003 so I did twenty-two years. I got my pension and came out here – Spain – to live.

'Looking back, the Falklands helped me grow up.

'In November 2010 I was fortunate enough to be selected to go on the Pilgrimage. It was a true honour to go back and pay my respects to all those we had lost. It was great to see Stanley thriving; the people there are so helpful, considerate and appreciative of what you have done. Was it worth it? You bet it was!'

A postscript: the *Canberra* was used to repatriate Argentinian prisoners and then returned to cruising. Her reputation made her very popular. She ended her career in 1997. She was a stubborn old girl to the end and took a year to break up instead of the anticipated three months.

Notes

1. www.beyondships.com/QE2-Falklands-1.html
2. The service, in Christ Church Cathedral, was taken by Chaplain David Cooper, who'd been with 2 Para. In his own words: 'I asked our soldiers always to remember how they felt at this time, remembering themselves

without any sort of veneer as they were facing death, remembering what they were really like and what really mattered to them. I read out the complete list of killed, wounded and who had been evacuated. Many learnt for the first time of the deaths of friends and even family. This was followed by a normal church service, during which our emotions caught up with us.' (www.timesonline.co.uk/tol/news/uk/article1595742.ece)

3. 'The Story of HMS *Keren*' by Tony Dyer: www.btinternet.com/~warship/Feature/keren.htm

7

THE LUCKY PARATROOPER

We weren't going to give in, we were Airborne, we'd have rather died. Honestly. Everyone was saying we are not going to fail and let the regiment down. So that was in everyone's minds.

Dave (Charlie) Brown lives in a 'lovely little Yorkshire village, but I was born in Glasgow, believe it or not. My dad was from Belfast and my mum was from Scotland. My dad was in REME. I was born on 21 May 1961 which is an ironic date – 21 May was the day we set foot on the Falkland Islands. I got a mention in *Pegasus* magazine[1] that I had a 21-gun salute by the Royal Navy and a fly-past by the Argentinian Air Force. They started flying over and having a bloody go at us from the day of the landings, didn't they? The regiment said it was a fly-past in my honour. That is my claim to fame.

'I joined in 1979 – the Parachute Regiment. I always wanted to be in the Parachute Regiment. I spent the first day in the guardroom at the depot in Aldershot! I was on my way down, like a whole bunch of others – it was a bank holiday Monday and it turned out to be the same day as Warren Point and Mountbatten getting killed.[2] When we got to the depot they didn't have any time to mess about dealing with young recruits so, what they did, that night they accommodated us in the guardroom. Then two days later they gave us rail warrants and said, "Come back next week."

'I'd been a brass bandsman, and in a classical orchestra and I originally joined to go into the band. However, what I wasn't told by the band recruiting officer was that you don't go for your wings and you aren't even supposed to wear the red beret if you're in the band unless you have got them. I wanted to get my wings, my parachute wings.'

In simple terms, this would qualify him as a paratrooper who also happened to be in the band, rather than just being a musician.

'I felt it was not right being in the Parachute Regiment without the wings. I was told that I would be allowed to do them later. I joined the band in Northern Ireland. When I arrived at 2 Para that's where they were, and I felt like a fraud because the bandsmen were the lowest of the low, even underneath the chefs. Chefs were useful, after all: they cooked the battalion meals. I felt *this is not right*.

'I kept asking to go for "P Company," because that's the important thing: pre-para selection. Every single Airborne soldier has to do it before they go for their wings.'

P Company is an abbreviation of Pegasus Company, run by the company of that name and involves long-distance running against the clock, an assault course, a 2-mile march, a steeplechase, an endurance test and so on.[3]

For those who are not military experts, here is the Parachute Regiment breakdown – three regular battalions and one reserve: 1st Battalion, the Parachute Regiment (1 Para), which is now part of the Special Forces Support Group providing specialised support to SAS and SBS operations; 2nd Battalion, the Parachute Regiment (2 Para); 3rd Battalion, the Parachute Regiment (3 Para); and 4th Battalion, the Parachute Regiment (4 Para), a territorial unit which supplies reserves for 2 Para and 3 Para.

'The bandmaster kept refusing me and I ended up having a fall-out with him. In his office I called him a craphat, which meant I was marched up to the jail thinking *I am going to be in some serious trouble here. I have just called a warrant officer class 1 a craphat.* I went in front of the RSM [Regimental Sergeant-Major] and he said, "Sit down." When the RSM said sit down, you sat down.'

RSM: 'Well, what's the problem?'
Brown: 'Sir, I know I'm in the band, but I want to go for my wings. That's what I joined the regiment for. It's an insult to the lads who have got their wings that I am allowed to walk round with a red beret on without them. I feel it's wrong I should be in the band of the Parachute Regiment and not have them.'

RSM: 'Right, no problem.'

The RSM rang the bandmaster.

Bandmaster: 'How many days have you jailed him for?'

RSM: 'I haven't, and by the way he's not in the band any more.'

The RSM said to Brown, 'Right, when we get you back to England you'll go on fitness training' – and that's how Brown began the process of becoming a paratrooper as he thought paratroopers ought to be.

Brown earned his wings in 1982, 'the proudest day of my life'. 'It was a turning point, but to be honest I would have been quite happy to go back to the band after I managed to get my wings because I love my music. I played trumpet in orchestras and soprano cornet in brass bands. Anyway, I got back to the battalion just in time for the big showdown in the south.

'Normally when you've got your wings you spend two weeks marching up and down the square learning how to do drill. I didn't really want that. I was told to pack my kit because "you're going back up to 2 Para". That was the start of the great adventure. Of course, I didn't realise it was going to be such a great adventure.

'I was up at home in Leeds for the weekend, Easter leave. My plan of action was watching Leeds vs Liverpool at Elland Road and then travelling over to see my sister in Holland, who was just about to have her first baby. Unfortunately we got called back. I managed to stay over for the Leeds game – which I think we lost, by the way – and then I phoned my mate up, who was on guard duty, because obviously nobody had mobiles in those days.

'All the married people in Aldershot were easy to get hold of, but the others were harder. Notice boards were being put up in railway stations and they were sending military policemen round to people's houses to get hold of them, not to arrest them but get hold of them. Everybody wasn't on the phone and, more than that, some lads had gone home on leave and had a home address – like I had my mum and dad's (they were out in Malaysia) – but might be elsewhere. I might have been over at my friend's house or in Holland seeing my sister. It was absolute bedlam.

'I warn you there were two Dave Browns in the battalion. I was Dave Brown, C Company, which was Charlie Company, so I ended up being called Charlie. If you hear people saying "Charlie Brown", that's me.

'When I phoned up my mate he said, "Charlie, do yourself a favour. Don't come back for at least three days because everyone is packing kit and so on. Just make sure you come back within the three-day limit, otherwise you'll be classed as AWOL." Aldershot was chaos because they were unpacking kit, weapons, ammo to move. There was no way they had ever moved the whole battalion for war before and it was basically all hands to the pump.

'I reported back to Aldershot. When I got there we spent a week getting briefed about the Falklands, the Argentinians and everything that was going on. Nope, I did not know where the Falklands were. I don't think 80%, 90% of the lads did. Probably a couple, one of them because he'd served down there in the Royal Marines at some point. The lads were saying, "What the **** have the Argies invaded Scotland for? They must be after the oil wells."

'People had been thinking *great, the battalion's going to war, we're going to parachute in like Arnhem* and the next thing we realised was that the Falklands were little islands 8,000 miles away. We eventually got hold of a North Sea ferry called the *Norland* – God bless the little boat.'

The *Norland*, a P&O roll-on, roll-off ferry built in 1974, had been plying her trade between Rotterdam and Hull and was now requisitioned as a troop ship.

'We sailed from Portsmouth and the first two weeks it was a bit of a relaxed atmosphere. We were doing fitness training and weapons training, we were having medical briefings. We thought when we got to Ascension Island the Argies would say *OK, we're going to pull back out* but, now as we know, all the Argies were doing was delaying and delaying and delaying until they could get more men on the islands and build their defenses up. They were not going to pull back out. They kept blaming [General Alexander] Haig and Britain for being stubborn, but they had no intention of withdrawing. People forget this. The negotiators could have talked about it forever and it would have made no difference.

'The next stage was getting to Ascension Island. Because we left a couple of days later than everyone else, most of the Task Force were there and they had already practised beach assaults, landing craft drills and so on – you name it. They'd even been ashore for a couple of days sunbathing and swimming. All we'd got was the *Norland*, a roll-on, roll-off ferry – drive on at the back, drive off at the front, which you can't exactly do in the middle of a South Atlantic conflict zone, can you? So they had this brilliant idea: we'd all step out of one of the cargo holds in the side onto the landing crafts.

'At Ascension Island it worked brilliantly. We had a lovely, tropical, sunny day and a calm sea. It was like getting on a pleasure-boat trip round Scarborough. That was our first ever, ever trip in a landing craft. The Royal Marines do it all the time but we jump out of planes. That wasn't the problem. When we did these landing craft drills we only had an hour in the landing craft and none of us had Bergens on or were carrying heavy kit, all we had was personal weapons and a lifejacket.

'Eventually we moved forward with the Task Force and got down there on 19 May, ready for the 20th.'

The *Norland* moved towards San Carlos Water with her cargo of Royal Artillery and paratroopers ready for the landings. The British had realised with their possible supply-line problems they needed a beach for the landings where they would be unopposed and which they could defend. Many places were considered. The Argentinians had some forty men in Port San Carlos and twenty men manning a radio observation post at Fanning Head to the north. The SAS and SBS cleared the area.

'We sat there waiting for briefings and signals for when we were going to go in. We got the all-clear. We'd lost all track of time. We were just told we were going to go ashore at some point. That's when I'm sat there all kitted up and loaded up and I realised *hang on, it's my birthday*. It was the most unbelievably scene: 600 paratroopers all sat in this lounge, weapons and everything going to war on a cross-Channel ferry, and I'm thinking *I'm 21!*

'Then the real chaos began. We were going from the top deck of a North Sea ferry right down the hold, which is about G Deck, all kitted up with Bergens and everything, in total darkness apart from some red lights marking your route down. Every deck you went down you were given something: radio batteries – stuff them in your smock. Next deck – 200 belt rounds for the machine guns, sling them over your shoulders. Don't forget we'd already packed our own kit. Then we got to the final deck – right, each man is carrying two mortar bombs each. The average Bergen was already 150lbs with the weapons and everything else.

'They brought the landing craft forward but this was in total, pitch darkness *and* in South Atlantic waters: a bit stormy. We had to wait for the landing craft to rise to get across into it, and this was like one at a time every time the tide rose. They hadn't realised the difference between when we got on the landing craft at Ascension Island and now with these massive rucksacks and mortar bombs. One of the lads slipped. He got trapped between the boat and the landing craft and he broke his back.

'The nights down there are very long in the winter. The *Norland* was at sea off Fanning Head. They couldn't bring the ships in so we had to do a run-in to the shore – like they did in Normandy on D-Day in the Second World War – to secure the beachhead. We're not Royal Marines *but* who was first ashore? 2 Para. The marines sent *us* in to secure the beach.

'As we got down to the last deck, Royal Navy lads issued us with lifejackets. The marines and navy have their own green ones. All we had on the *Norland* were those bright day-glo orange ones so if you go overboard on a pleasure cruise they see you, but we were doing a night beach assault here.'

The navy: 'You've got to have your lifejackets on or you might drown.'

2 Para: 'Yeah, we might drown, but we'd rather drown than have every Argie on the islands seeing us.'

So 2 Para were taking them off.

The navy: 'You've got to have them on.'

2 Para (chorus): 'Bollocks!'

One historical source sets out the context of the operation:

At 0440 hours local time, sixteen landing craft carrying troops from 2 Para and 40 Commando from the *Norland* and HMS *Fearless* passed by Fanning Head, where the SBS force were still in action against the Argentine outpost. 2 Para landed first on Blue Beach just south of San Carlos on the eastern side of San Carlos Water. The paratroops immediately set off for their objective, to dig in and prepare defensive positions overlooking the landings.[4]

They waded in. Brown says that 'we got ashore in the end and we were told there were three code signals from the special forces on the beach. I can't remember the three colours but one was BEACH UNSECURED, one was BEACH SECURED and the other was ENEMY FORCES IN THE AREA. We never got a signal so we were sitting around in these landing crafts trying to run in and we're thinking *well, are we going to get shot to ★★★★? Are we going to step off and no Argies around? Or are we going to step off and get further inland then start fighting?* No-one had a clue what was going on. Suddenly, out of the darkness, two SBS lads flashed us.'

SBS: 'Who are you?'
2 Para: '2 Para.'
SBS: 'You're not due in until tomorrow.'
2 Para: 'Someone might have told us that.'

This happened shortly after they got ashore.

'We had to go a place called Sussex Mountains to prevent the Argies attacking the beachhead. Not a problem: we always run with weights long distance *but* the ground in the Falklands is slightly different, and don't forget the lads were carrying all sorts of extra kit that had been dumped on them. We did 10 miles, which normally we would have completed in under 2 hours. It ended up total chaos. Daylight broke and half the battalion were still scattered all round the bottom of the valley. Everyone was all over the place.'

One historical source describes how this came about:

The British 3 Commando Brigade waded ashore at San Carlos a few minutes before 4 a.m. on Friday 21 May [Brown's 21st birthday]. 2 Para waded ashore an hour later and took their positions on the summit of Sussex Mountain to protect the approaches of Goose Green soon after first light. A few minutes after 2 Para's landing, 40 Commando came ashore a few hundred yards further north behind the Scorpion and Scimitar armoured vehicles of the Blues & Royals to be met by the filthy SBS reception party who had been on the hill for days.[5]

Brown says 'we dug in. We were there to stop any Argentinian forces coming over the top and attacking the Task Force or the beachhead. The next few days we sat and watched the navy get pounded in bomb alley, and it was bomb alley. We were thinking *we've got to do something here – it's going to be like Anzio.*[6] Eventually we got the order – "You are moving forward. We are going to do a raid" – a raid on Goose Green, like the SAS: we'd hit them hard and clear off. C Company, on patrol, had gone forward and checked the whole area out and sent D Company forward to join them and it was 8 km each way – which again in daylight and in normal conditions is not a problem, but in full tactical conditions at night was something else. It wasn't like along roads, it was over hills, through rivers, everything. D Company managed to get there. C Company were waiting for them and then we got told a day later: "Operation's cancelled." D and C Companies came all the way back, we'd just got in – and an hour later it's on again.'

The battalion was at a place called Camilla Creek House, 10 miles from the Sussex Mountains and midway between them and Goose Green, and prepared to move into action with artillery support plus support from HMS *Arrow*.

'We sat there overnight. We hadn't been compromised, as far as we knew: the Argies didn't have a clue where we were. This one house had a few outsheds and we had the whole battalion crammed into every nook and cranny in the house. There were people sleeping in cupboards, there were people sleeping in the coalshed to get out of the wind and the rain. Suddenly one of the signals lads is screaming at everyone, "Get out." "Why?" The BBC World Service had said paratroopers from the 2nd Batallion, the Parachute Regiment had attacked and taken Goose Green. It supposedly said "had taken Goose Green". This was a signal which was due to be released after we'd done it.

'You've never seen so many lads coming out of one house and thinking *trenches very quick*. H. Jones was fuming. He said, "I am going to sue the BBC, I'm going to sue the lot of them if any of my men die." That's when it got serious because obviously the Argies knew that we were on the way to Goose Green and they also knew there was only one way we could come in. The single good thing in our favour was the Argie in charge [Lieutenant-Colonel Italo Piaggi] thought it was a bluff. He said *no, the British wouldn't be so stupid*. He didn't react to it and move his defences round to block us off. He expected us to come in from the sea side, which was where his main defences were.'

So 2 Para prepared for a night attack against an enemy whose number was not known, and prepared to do it across open ground 1 mile wide and 5 miles long.[7]

'We moved forward about 4 o'clock on 28 May. A Company started taking out the first positions. It was a hell of a hard fight. We had been misled about the number of Argies that were there, and their positions. Not only that, we didn't have enough artillery support and we only had half a battalion's mortars. We had naval gunfire from HMS *Arrow* but after firing three rounds the gun jammed.

'The first few phases went well. Companies were taking objectives. They were fighting through and the Argies were well dug in, but we do a lot of our attacks at night so we were able to over-run most of the early positions without a problem. The problem was that daylight broke. All the companies were caught out in open ground – exposed – and we hadn't actually got to the main Argentinian defence line. As soon as it got daylight we were in trouble, and I mean totally in *it*. We were spread out and we still had to get across Darwin Ridge, which was their main defence position, before you got into Goose Green.'

One historical source says:

At 3.30 am, A Company moved off on the left and attacked Burntside House, believed to be occupied by an Argentine platoon, but found no-one there other than four unhurt civilians. At 4.10 am, B Company started forward from the other side of Burntside Pond down the right flank with D Company following them along the middle. With artillery support on both sides, B and D Companies were soon in confused action against a series of enemy trenches, and as they slowly made progress, A Company moved past unoccupied positions at Coronation Point. Leaving one platoon of A Company to provide covering fire from the north side of Darwin, the remainder started to circle round the inlet to take the settlement. As dawn broke, the attacks on both flanks bogged down as B Company came up against the strongpoint of Boca House and A Company found that a small rise, later known as Darwin Hill, was the key to the Argentine defences.[8]

Brown says: 'That's basically when we, A Company, took every casualty going. I came close to being hit. This is where H. Jones realised the battalion was in trouble and the plan wasn't working. He went forward to try and find a way to clear some trenches and he got killed. That was how it happened. He realised he had to do something.'

As the same historical source details:

Not until midday did 2 Para break through. As A Company was hit and went to ground, Lt-Col. Jones and his Tac HQ came up, and another attempt to push forward was made which led to two officers and an NCO being killed. Col. Jones moved off virtually on his own, and was soon shot and dying in an action which led to the award of a Victoria Cross. Maj. Keeble was called up from the rear, and leaving A Company to slowly wrest Darwin Hill and pulling B Company slightly back from Boca House, ordered D Company to move round them on the far right along the edge of the sea. Now in daylight, the battle continued with the Argentines helicoptering in their first reinforcements and flying more support missions.[9]

Brown says that 'everyone goes on about the fact that when H. Jones was killed that was it, the Battle of Goose Green was over and the Argies surrendered, but it wasn't. My company, C Company, which was patrols and recce, had to sit back for A Company to clear Darwin so we could follow forward to go for the airfield. We were getting all the overshoots from the Argie positions onto A Company, so every time we moved out of the way to find somewhere safe we were getting mortared. The Argies had some spotters in the mountains.

'We kept moving round trying to find somewhere safe. This was C Company, which had not been committed to battle yet. A Company did clear Darwin Ridge at a heavy cost and we were sent over this gorse line – something like 3km from that gorse line to Goose Green itself, broad daylight, down an open slope. The last famous words we heard from the company commander were, "Fix bayonets". I thought *Battle of Waterloo job here*. Three km over this undulating open moorland in daylight and the Argies in Goose Green had obviously got a main artillery position, they'd got the mortar defences and they also had the anti-aircraft guns in two versions, 20mm and 40mm. Because we were going down an open slope they were firing head-high at us with these 40mms and 20mms; in the first fifteen minutes C Company took eleven casualties. A ******* nightmare, put it that way.' As the book *Razor's Edge* details: 'Private Holman-Smith was killed, Jenner and ten others wounded – many horribly – in a few minutes.'

'Mark Holman-Smith, along with Charlie Holbrook, was one of two signallers attached to C Company HQ. When Steve Russell was caught in the neck by AA fire coming from both sides, Mark, with no thought for his own safety, ran down the slope to help Steve. Mark was then hit. I sprinted down towards them with OC Major Roger Jenner and we started to treat them both. Whilst doing so, a mortar shell landed behind and wounded Jenner. Around the same time, as Charlie Holbrook was sending a casualty report, he was also hit. Sadly we could not save Mark, despite all our efforts. Mark Holman-Smith should have received a medal for what he tried to do, giving his own life in the process. Out of the four-man company HQ, I was the only man not wounded that day.

'They hit us with everything on that hill because they knew we were going for the airfield. The only thing that helped us a bit was the soft ground. The artillery and mortar shells were exploding in the ground. Had it been chalk and hard we'd have been ripped to pieces. B Company tried to come round on the airfield end and help us out – come across – but they had to do the same: face this totally open ground and minefields.

'Then B Company came up with a secret weapon, called the Milan anti-tank, and they started bunker-busting [Argentinians in bunkers] – first time they had ever been used in action and they were using them to take these bunkers out. We had had the ★★★★ shot out of us all day and suddenly we were actually hitting the Argies back.'

The Milan, made in France, was intended as a portable medium-range weapon to be used against tanks.

'The rest of the day was individual battles, trench-clearing all round these positions and just before last light a Harrier cluster-bomb attack on their main gun-line. That was brilliant to watch. What I didn't know was that, while two Harriers came over, another Harrier from another direction acted as a decoy. The anti-aircraft guns went for him and the other two Harriers came screaming over and cannoned their whole gun-line, silenced all their artillery and mortars. That gave us a chance. We were literally patching wounded up and leaving them because that was all we could do.'

A historical source explains:

> With evening approaching and the Argentines squeezed in towards Goose Green, more reinforcements arrived to the south by helicopter … Two Argentine PoWs were sent in to start negotiations which lasted most of the night, and next morning, Group Capt. Pedroza surrendered all his forces to Maj. Keeble. British losses were fifteen men from 2 Para, a Royal Engineer and the marine pilot, and 30 to 40 Paras wounded.[10]

Brown says that 'one of the saddest incidents, and it did affect the whole battalion, involved a Scout helicopter – the small, teeny-weeny ones – from the Royal Marines. They were on casualty evacuation duty: casevacing, taking casualties out. They were flying Argie wounded back as well, there was no differentiation. This Argie Pucara shot them down. He knew it was a Red Cross helicopter and he shot it down. It meant we couldn't risk any more casevac helicopters.

'It started getting dark and we were in the middle of this bloody open battlefield. We were told to go back up to the gorse line and reorganise, which we did. We got to that gorse line and we were sat there thinking *we're ******, we're just wiped out.* Of our company of fifty-five, at one point there were nine of us up there. The next thing was *they are either going to blow us off this gorse line the next day with artillery, they are going to send troops up under cover of darkness and over-run us, or* – and the worst scenario – *we will go back down the hill again tomorrow in broad daylight.*

'We weren't going to give in, we were Airborne, we'd have rather died. Honestly. Everyone was saying *we are not going to fail and let the regiment down.* So that was in everyone's minds. We all had the same spirit.

'Eventually elements of C Company managed to start extracting themselves and I think by morning about thirty had managed to get back up that slope through the night. The next thing we knew, Chris Keeble sent a surrender bluff down. He was very clever. He said, "You have fought bravely and honourably. We will be coming in, we are the Airborne soldiers and we will finish the job. You are trapped. You have only got the sea behind you." An Argentinian sergeant came back up and agreed to surrender. The biggest military bluff ever in history, that was, but it saved a lot of lives on both sides. We were sat on that slope cleaning weapons, loading ammo and getting ready for the bell to start round 2, if I can put it like a boxing match.

'An average battalion strength is about 650 and obviously not all of the 650 were committed at Goose Green. There were echelons and signals and various other things. We went into Goose Green with under 400 anyway, and that morning we had 190 men left to fight. We were told to advance with caution, in other words guns still loaded. We got on the outskirts of Goose Green and the Argies were all stood around. We looked at the airfield and there were hundreds and hundreds of them coming out and laying their weapons down. Thirteen hundred actually surrendered. We were stood there and this Argie officer came up.'

Officer: 'Hello. Good battle, good fight? Yes. Where are your men?'
The British: 'We're here.'
Officer: 'Yes, but where are your men?'

'We thought *get the rest of the lads down here quick, they might realise.* We still had a wary couple of days and then they brought the Gurkhas in to reinforce us and take over Goose Green.

'We pulled another bluff. There was a famous phone call made by B Company to Fitzroy. They send a patrol out and it came to a local landline telephone box, one of those wind-up dial and press-button jobs. They got hold of Fitzroy settlement and said, "Are there any Argies there?" The voice said, "No." Next minute a Chinook which was being used to take Argie prisoners was comandeered. *Get everybody off there, get us on and take us to Fitzroy.* Which we did.' One historical source explains:

> The Guards were sent to support a dashing advance along the southern approach to Stanley. On 2 June a small advance party of 2 Para moved to Swan Inlet house in a number of army Westland Scout helicopters. Telephoning ahead to Fitzroy, they discovered the area clear of Argentines and (exceeding their authority) commandeered the one remaining RAF Chinook helicopter to frantically ferry another contingent of 2 Para ahead to Fitzroy (a settlement on Port Pleasant) and Bluff Cove.[11]

'Sadly,' Brown says, 'a couple of days later while we were sat in Fitzroy, the *Galahad* came in and we know the story of that. We were pulling the wounded off the *Galahad*.' A historical source explains what happened:

> On 3 June Fitzroy on the south side of East Falkland was occupied. The campaign on land had been going reasonably well with troops crossing the main part of the island from San Carlos but it was decided to open up a further line of advance from Fitzroy. In doing this two of the landing ships *Sir Galahad* and *Sir Tristram* were sent carrying equipment, ammunition and several military units including part of

the Welsh Guards. On 8 June they were at anchor there in daylight. Before unloading could be completed the ships were attacked by five Argentine Air Force A-4 Skyhawks. Bomb and cannon hits were taken on both causing fires, worst in *Sir Galahad*, leading to her being abandoned. Unfortunately there was heavy loss of life, especially on board *Sir Galahad*, a total of 50 men killed or missing with more wounded. It might have been worse without timely rescue efforts by helicopter and boat and rapid medical assistance.[12]

The fate of the *Sir Galahad* and her crew provided some of the most graphic images of the whole war.

'The next move forward from 2 Para,' Brown says, 'was Sea King helicopters up to Mount Kent. We were sat on there for two days freezing our nuts off – we had just light fighting order on – and then on 11 June we started off on a really, really long, horrendous night march across a valley.

'While this was going on 3 Para were taking Longdon on the 12th, so we were watching all the firefights going on in the mountains thinking *that's our sister battalion up there, that's our mates.* We wanted to break off and go up the side of Longdon to help them, because with the Airborne brotherhoods you are very close to any Airborne warrior. We were saying *look, we really need to get up there and help them out.* We could hear it on the radio but we were told to keep on and we moved through this valley at night. The next day we went into Wireless Ridge, which was one of the last Argie defensive positions before Stanley. This time we'd got every bit of fire support we wanted: we had the machine guns and mortars from 2 and 3 Para, the anti-tanks, Blues & Royals[13] with the Scorpions [armoured reconnaissance vehicles], everything. And we just plastered them. We only lost three and one of them was by a British shell dropping short. We cleared Wireless Ridge on the night of the 13th.

'When 3 Para took Longdon they were reinforced so 3 Para could get the hell off it. The Royal Marines were so far behind and if 3 Para had had to sit a night on Longdon they'd have got shelled and anyway they lost nearly as many killed and injured after taking Longdon as they had during the battle.

'On Wireless Ridge we thought *to hell with this* and we moved back about 600 metres into the open ground. We sat there freezing all night long, and it was snowing. Sure enough the Argies did start shelling Wireless Ridge. If you've taken an enemy position they know exactly where you are and can call in defensive fire, so we spent that night watching them waste their artillery on Wireless Ridge.

'Next morning we were told "cease fire, unload weapons" and that was it: the great Stanley race was on. Berets on, straight into Stanley. We just wanted to get in there and it was a great feeling at first but we suddenly realised that a lot of the lads were down to the last few rounds of ammo *and* we were thinking *hang on a minute, there's up to 9,000 Argies in Stanley*. There's us lot racing down this bloody road, with a couple of Blues & Royals as our fire support, we were actually going past Argie gun-lines and the Argies were sat there just looking at us. They'd *gone* [given up].

'When we got into Stanley, Julian Thompson realised how few of us there were, how far the rest of the units were behind us and his reaction was "hold fast", which is what we did. Today it's called Holdfast Road. That's where 2 Para got in first and 3 Para followed down from Longdon.'

The 'holdfast order' was given because at that point the Argentinians had not officially surrendered. Today the Falkland Islands Museum is on the road. It shows many aspects of island life, including artefacts from the war.

'Afterwards we were held back for about another month so we weren't in the big homecoming. We didn't get any of it, and that's the Parachute Regiment for you. We had to wait because the *Norland* was transferring prisoners over to Argentina. We just wanted to go home and there was absolutely nothing there [in the Falklands]. We stayed in Stanley, based in houses for three weeks and eventually we got back on board the *Norland*. They put 2 and 3 Para together, which was a very wise move, because there were a lot of angry people about various things that happened down there. If they'd have put marines on board with us they'd have been swimming. Any paratrooper is not a good person to pick a fight with.

'The biggest battle of the whole Falklands campaign was the Airborne forces on the *Norland* on the way back between 2 and 3 Para. There were more casualties on board the *Norland* and that is even in Julian Thompson's book *No Picnic*. It's not like if you have a big punch-up and the MPs can come in. We were on a North Sea ferry in the middle of nowhere and a battle went on all night long. The next morning over the tannoy system came an announcement that anyone with a self-inflicted wound would be charged – there were lads who'd got broken collar bones. They classed it as self-inflicted if you were fighting. It's self-inflicted because you have gone in with the intention of fighting knowing that you could get hurt. Some lads were done for self-inflicted wounds because they went sun-bathing and got burnt. Basically they were saying *you put yourself in the situation where you received that injury*. So the lads were running round finding the medics to *stitch me up, please*.

'*Norland* went back up to Ascension Island, we were taken off by helicopter and about eight hours later flown home in a VC10 to Brize Norton. We went straight in the back door.'

Notes

1. *Pegasus*, the regimental journal of the Parachute Regiment, published three times a year.
2. On 27 August 1979, eighteen soldiers were blown up by IRA booby-trap bombs at Warren Point, near the border with the Irish Republic. Two hours later the IRA killed Lord Louis Mountbatten using a bomb on his yacht, which happened to be in Irish waters.
3. www.eliteukforces.info/parachute-regiment/
4. www.raf.mod.uk/falklands/dday1.html
5. www.britains-smallwars.com/Falklands/land-war.htm
6. Anzio: the landing of Allied forces in Italy in January 1944 with the strategic goal of outflanking the German forces and moving on Rome. It resulted in a costly stalemate until May, and the plan remains controversial.
7. www.naval-history.net/F48goosegreen.htm
8. Ibid.
9. Ibid.
10. Ibid.
11. en.wikipedia.org/wiki/Falklands_War
12. www.royalnavy.mod.uk and search for Battles/Falklands Conflict
13. The Blues & Royals were an amalgamation, in 1969, of the Royal Horse Guards (Blues) and The Royal Dragoons (Royals).

8

THE UNLUCKY PARATROOPER

It sounds ridiculous but I put my arm around my head thinking *I'll save my head. When the lads are walking round in the morning they'll be able to find my head and go, 'Oh, there's Scouse's head.'* It seemed logical at the time because I assumed I was going to get blown to pieces in a minute.

Jimmy O'Connell was 'born in Bootle in Liverpool in 1960 and I joined the army in 1979, so I was 19. I had been in 4 Para – the Territorial Army – and I enjoyed 4 Para. I thought *I might as well go full time* so I joined the Parachute Regiment. And was sent to 3 Para. At the time we were based in Osnabrück in Germany. We came back to England, did a tour in Northern Ireland and I went on Easter leave. I didn't know where the Falklands were. I don't think anyone knew. We thought they were in Scotland – I had never heard of them.

'We sailed down on the *Canberra*, a lovely ship, lovely food and very good staff. We enjoyed it, as you'd imagine a gang of lads would on a liner. We went to Ascension and we test-fired our guns there before we sailed on to the Falklands. We changed ship and were put onto the HMS *Intrepid*.'

By a great irony, HMS *Intrepid* was in the process of being sold to Argentina. She had been built in 1967 as a Landing Platform Dock (LPD), based in Devonport and Portsmouth.

'We came off the *Canberra* and got onto the HMS *Intrepid*, because that had landing craft, which we sailed out the back of. We came ashore in darkness. At San Carlos one of our rifle companies (A Company) had an encounter: two helicopters had both been shot down by the Argentinians and both crews died.'

This was now 21 May.

'As it got light, for some reason the SS *Canberra* – I have no idea why – had sailed right into the middle of the Sound. It was acting as a hospital ship – that was its role after we got off it. I was watching bombs drop around it and everyone said, "What's that doing there?" It stuck out like a sore thumb. When the Argentine planes came in and they were dropping bombs all over the place they were missing the SS *Canberra* by feet. It turned round and it sailed out – too big a target. It was ridiculous: she should never have came in so close and they were very, very lucky it wasn't sunk.

'We stayed at San Carlos for about a week and then it was decided to make the break-out and start walking across – we did the long march right across the Falklands. The battalion strength at that time was about 550 men, and most of them walked the 35 miles to Teal Inlet, all spaced out, right through the night, in what we call the Battalion Snake; we carried what we thought was essential, which was different from the marines, they took big heavy bergens full of kit, we stripped out all non-essential kit. We went with what we call fighting order, which is nothing but ammunition: in fact, just what you need for fighting – no sleeping bags, no spare kit, no nothing except ammo, and then it's *let's go*. I had a machine gun – a GPMG – which has a very high rate of fire, something like 200 rounds a minute, so you have to carry lots of ammunition. Every member of the section will carry 200, 300 rounds. The whole section carried what we call *food* for the guns – it is essential, you can never carry enough ammunition. You always need more. That's the way we worked it.

'We stayed at Teal Inlet for about fourteen hours, slept in a sheep barn and the next day we walked another 30 miles to Estancia House. It wasn't just walking; it was very hard physically. The weather was terrible – the snow, the rain – and you're physically and mentally exhausted, but we did it. There were a couple of Argentines taken prisoner, stragglers basically. No fighting, just men who'd come in and surrendered. Then we waited for the marines and everyone else to catch up with us. The *Atlantic Conveyor* had gone down with the helicopters on board, so they were very limited in the number of helicopters to bring ammunition forward for the battles ahead. We waited at Estancia for about a week and it was freezing. I have never been so cold in my life. We didn't have tents or anything like that. You just dug a hole, a shallow hole that you can take a bit of cover in.

'Estancia House was an ordinary Falklands house. They were not like houses in Britain. It was a big farm at the bottom of Mount Estancia and 3 Para were on top of it. The farm was like a base and the companies were out in the hills, which were very, very rocky.

'While we were at Estancia the Argentine Pucaras were flying over at night randomly dropping 500lb bombs and you didn't want to get caught by one of them. You'd hear a boom. The only one that got hit by one of them was a lad from 2 Para. Well, he wasn't hit by the bomb. He was in his sleeping bag, it went off quite a bit away from him and a piece of shrapnel hit him.

'We waited for all the ammunition to come forward and be stockpiled for the coming night battles. 3 Para's D Company Patrol Platoon carried out reconnaissance patrols of the forthcoming objectives and they led the battalion, they carried out numerous reconnaissance missions on Mount Longdon for us. In 3 Para we had A, B, C, D and Support Companies and HQ Company. HQ and Support Company were integrated between A, B and C. We all got our orders to advance on 11 June to Mount Longdon and attack it.'

One historical source gives the overview:

With minefields to the south, the Argentines on Wireless Ridge to the east, and given the long and narrow summit ridge of Mount Longon, Lt-Col. Pike decided to launch a silent attack from the west. With C Company in reserve and fire support teams staying on the start line, the plan was for B Company to take the length of the summit ('Fly Half' and 'Full Back') while A Company occupied the northern spur ('Wing Forward') as a fire support base for the B Coy attack. Once Mount Longdon was secured, A and C Coys would, if possible, move on to Wireless Ridge. After a short delay, A and B Coys started off from 'Freekick' at 00.20 (ZT).[1]

That was Friday 11 June.

'On the move from Estancia to Longdon the terrain was just open and boggy and horrible. The main thing was the cold: it was really, really cold. It was also the stopping and starting because you are bringing up the entire battalion with all the attachments and ammunition and everything. The stopping and starting was to make sure everyone gets there together, and when you stop you get cold. The ground was very boggy underfoot and your feet were soaking. There wasn't really a way to get out of the wind. Eventually we were at the Murrell Bridge where the engineers had arranged a ladder for the entire battalion to cross the river, which proved to be a task in itself! We all moved into our various company positions and waited to be called forward to do whatever we were supposed to do. I was in Support Company, attached to C Company; B Company would be assaulting, A Company would do fire support for them, and we (C Company) were held back in reserve. While we were waiting we started taking small arms fire – light fire, not nice, and then we started taking some heavy artillery fire which was exploding all around us. Just to the front of us A Company had taken their first casualties: one dead, Tim Jenkins, and one wounded, Stevie Hope, who would die of his wounds later, was passed through to C Company with another wounded man, Jock Brebner. I was then wounded by a piece of shrapnel from one of the many rounds landing around us, it passed through my nose removing the bridge of my nose and took out my right eye and cheekbone as well as my front teeth. My mate Geordie Nicholson said, "Have you been hit?" and I said, "Yes, I've been hit." He said, "Where have you been hit?" I said, "My head." He crawled over – as we were still being shelled – he reached me and again asked where I'd been hit. I think he thought, because I was talking, that I couldn't be that bad, but when he shone his little torch he went, "******* hell." I said, "Right, get some shell dressings on my face now!" Just after I was wounded another bloke, Paddy Rehill, was shot in the side of his face, and pretty soon we had a small group of wounded. We stayed in this location for hours constantly being shelled.

'I assumed I would eventually be killed as the shells were landing extremely close and our group had now grown to six. It sounds absolutely ridiculous now, but I wasn't that upset about it. You know when you have reconciled yourself to your fate? I thought *it's just going to be a matter of time now; I'm going to go any minute.* I decided to put my arm around my head thinking *I'll save my head. When the lads are walking round in the morning they'll be able to find my head and go, "Oh, there's Scouse's head."* It seemed logical at the time because I was sure I was going to be blown to pieces.

'My condition gradually worsened and Paddy was having difficulty breathing as a bullet had passed through his face and lodged in the back of his throat. Stevie Hope who was with us had been shot through the head and was in a bad way, too, so it was decided at 0903 hours, about four hours after being wounded, that we needed to see the doctor on Longdon. This would entail the lads in C Company carrying our group through a minefield under heavy shellfire to reach the doctors and medics at the base of Mount Longdon. A number of times we would have to stop as rounds landed around us; Paul Wray was one I remember laying across me to try and cover me.

'We eventually arrived at the regimental aid post at 0950 hours. The doctors (Captains John Burgess and Mike Von Bertele) were rushed off their feet with the flood of wounded: 3 Para would suffer twenty-three dead and forty-eight wounded on Mount Longdon. The aid post was constantly shelled. At one stage I was confused with having died as I had gone into hypothermic shock – which is a sort of suspended animation due to extreme cold (-10°). As I was being taken away by the stretcher-bearers, however, one of them spotted me move and said "this one is alive" and carried me back to the triage area.

'I was loaded onto the next Snowcat vehicle available with a number of other wounded and we were then taken to a helicopter landing site 4km away. This took another 1½ hours, and by this stage we were all in an extremely poor state. Eventually we were picked up by Gazelle helicopter at approximately 1200 hours and arrived at Teal Inlet at around 1230 hours. From being wounded to evacuation to a field hospital had taken around eight hours, we had been promised forty minutes. The first helicopters to arrive at Mount Longdon would arrive twenty-four hours after the battle, around 1300 hours. A lot of 3 Para's wounded would have to wait up to thirteen hours in extreme, freezing conditions.

'When I arrived at Teal Inlet I was carried in and they cut all my clothes off, looking for secondary injuries, as sometimes you don't know you've been hit somewhere else. I didn't have any, just my face. I was classed as non-urgent as there was nothing *they* could do with my injuries; they would be dealt with by a facial surgeon when he was free. I was given blood and put into a warm area with other wounded blokes. I mistakenly assumed I was being put to one side, but it was just that my injuries required a facial surgeon. Even though I was bad there were people a lot worse; I now understand how triage works, and the difficult decisions that doctors and surgeons have to make.

'There was one lad, who'd also been shot in the head. He was classed as unsavable and put outside. They didn't have the time to work on people who may not live, and those are terrible decisions to make, but those surgeons did down there. You've got to work on the people who you can save; you can't afford to spend half an hour on someone who is not going to make it. So the lad was put outside. When the rush hour finally finished – well, it was more than rush hour – he was checked, brought back in and saved.

'From Teal Inlet I was flown by helicopter to the SS *Uganda*, a hospital ship. I was booked in for 0215 hours but a nurse asked, "When did you last eat?" I said, "Two days ago." She said, "Get him in theatre now" – they could do that because I had nothing in my stomach – and they began the process of putting me back together again. We sailed to Montevideo, because Uruguay was a neutral country, and from there flew back to RAF Brize Norton then onto RAF Wroughton and then a series of hospitals. Putting me back together this would take five years and eighteen operations. They took bone from my hip and rebuilt the cheekbone. They gave me a glass eye, a new plastic centre of my nose and new front teeth, but I still suffer today with my breathing due to nasal damage.

'I left 3 Para in 1985. I was an anti-tank gunner and there's not much call for that when you get out. I couldn't get a job. There was no call for one-eyed anti-tank gunners. I applied to the Post Office and – you wouldn't believe this – you have got to have two eyes to be a postman. I applied to be a traffic warden and you have got to have two eyes to be a traffic warden. You're putting tickets on parked cars! You're putting letters through letterboxes! I applied for everywhere and I just couldn't get in anywhere. Eventually a friend said to me, "Why don't you try the taxis?" I said, "I've only got one eye." He said he had a mate who'd got one eye and he was on the taxis, so I applied. You would think the minimum requirement to drive a taxi would be two eyes, not for a postman or a traffic warden but for a driver. Anyway, I got a job on the taxis and I have been a taxi driver ever since.

'I applied to the Post Office again just recently and got knocked back again because of the two eyes. I applied to the MoD as a doorman in a building checking door passes – never got it – and you would think *here's an ex-army veteran who lost an eye in the Falklands?* If you're going to give the job to anyone give it to him. I applied to the Prison Service. I declared I had one eye and they never said anything. I had to do the maths test; I had to do the English test. I passed the maths, I passed the English, and they said, "Right, come up to Wakefield for the interview." I got on the phone and said, "You've sent me a letter to come to Wakefield for the interview. Before I take a day off work to do that I am telling you I have only got one eye. I don't want to travel to Wakefield and be told, 'You've only got one eye'." The man said, "I'll just check it out and we'll get back to you." They got back to me and said, "No."'

Note

1. www.naval-history.net/F54longdon.htm

9

THE PRISONER

I carried this one into the showers and he didn't even know what day it was – you were talking to him and he was very incoherent. I was in there for about twenty minutes with him, constantly talking. You got a bit wet yourself: I still had my clothes on.

William (Billy) Field was 'born in Cardiff on 28 April 1961. I have always been a very keen fisherman from when I was a kid. I used to sneak out of the house and go fishing. I loved the sea and I always needed to be by water. As it happens, my father was ex-military, even though he was a National Service conscript in the Welsh Guards. My grampie was Royal Navy, Merchant Navy and army. He served in Burma. My uncle was in the army as well, three tours of Northern Ireland. He was there during the Troubles.

'I applied to go on the fishing vessels, but having not done any school at all – I'd finished by the time I was 12 – the fishing industry wouldn't take me because I didn't have any certificates. I was going to be a diesel engineer and fitter but they wouldn't take me because I didn't have any paperwork, either. I went and sat the exam at the navy instead. I passed maths and English and they took me. That was it, off I went. I ended up in the navy and I was in by the time I was 16½. Loved it. It was a big adventure and I never realised what I was letting myself in for. I joined up at Christmas.

'I saw the world, absolutely. I was very, very lucky to have three ships one after another: Bermuda, Barbados, Grand Caymen, Dominica, Antigua, Stavanger. I think I've seen about seventy different countries altogether, which is not bad for a lad from Cardiff with no qualifications. I had the fortunate pleasure of coming to Cardiff on one of my warships when I was 18 and I was photographed with two other boys on the dock-yard in uniform – you know, *local boy comes home*. We berthed into Cardiff when I was on a ship called HMS *Fife*. It's gone now because it was a rust bucket then, but what a pleasure it was to come to my home town!

'I was a steward, catering. A steward basically serves officers: you cook food, you serve food, you look after officers and dignitaries coming to the ship, you take care of cocktail parties. I was a captain's steward on HMS *Newcastle* for some eighteen months and that was a fantastic job, that was. Really fantastic. When he finished he was going to Washington as a naval attaché and he could take a steward, but basically one of the higher-ranking stewards, like a petty officer. They had to have a driving licence and I hadn't. He said, "Right then, where would you like to go?" I said, "I'd like another ship straight back to America" – I was fortunate because I'd been to the States and the West Indies on a few occasions. I did manage to get another ship straight away which took me off again.

'It was great when you came home because you had a pocketful of money. You really looked smart, you were young and fit and you'd learned how to drink: not like your friends! Two, three pints and a smell of the barmaid's apron was enough for them; I wanted to fight the world! You are already drinking many more beers than them and you're the one still on your feet at the end of the night taking the barmaid home. That was a fact. All the women used to love a uniform and it was a pleasure.

'I was on HMS *Brilliant*, a frigate. We'd been doing Exercise SPRING TRAIN out in Gibraltar, which normally was round about the January/February time, when all the navies meet. After SPRING TRAIN there were quite a few arrests due to men being drunk in Gibraltar. We got kicked out of Gibraltar and we took stores off the *Glamorgan* and other ships. We are now told we are going to the Falklands, leading a group of ships and heading south at high speed. We were the first Royal Navy ship to put to sea. We just thought it was one big adventure and nobody realised that anything was going to happen, certainly not fight a war or anything. After we'd taken a lot of stores off two of the ships – extra armaments and food – we were on our way. Nobody had gone into combat since Aden,[1] really, and there wasn't even a big skirmish there with the military at the time. So we set sail for the Falklands as the first ship there – and the last to bloody leave. Yes, I knew where the Falklands were. Top of Scotland! We thought *what do the Argies want to go up there for?'*

Brilliant was a Type 22 frigate.

'She was accepted into service in 1981, so she was a new ship, very new,' Field says. 'We had 25 officers, 75 senior rates and a 150 junior rates. Then you'd got a detachment of Royal Marines as well, about twelve.'

Field was already involved in his own mini-war, because he had been stopped by the police at 5.30 one morning for riding a bike without lights. As he says, 'I was on my way to the ship. This happened at Crown Hill, Plymouth – from the married quarters, which is just by the police station. I was going to do my duty and I couldn't believe it.'

He was on the ship and 'we then had the orders to divert to the Falklands. The captain got a signal as a warrant for my arrest for non-appearance in court. I was tried and I was fined £50 without being there. They took it straight off me. The captain sent a signal back to the courts saying, "Which police station would you like me to hand him over to: the one in Buenos Aires or the one on Ascension?"'

Brilliant left Gibraltar on 28 March and reached Ascension on 10 April. Reflecting, Field says it would all prove 'a very interesting deployment. We didn't get off at Ascension going. It was just black volcanic ash.

'There wasn't a moment when we realised it was getting serious, well, not for myself, no. I was still a young boy thinking it was a great big adventure. I did notice a change in everything that was going on within the ship; for example, like certain things had to be stowed away, certain things had to be jettisoned, certain things tied down. You were doing more exercise and getting ready, but it was one of those things where it was just a laugh, it just seemed a joke.

'As we were sailing down Admiral Sandy Woodward came over to visit us and he spoke to us all in the lower mess, the junior rates and the senior rates and the officers. Basically all he said was, "It's all right, boys, we're going to go down there, we'll be there about two or three weeks.

They've only got Second World War material so we should have it over quite early and then we can all get back." Lo and behold, it wasn't that easy, was it, Sandy?

'I mean, they had some sophisticated aircraft with which they did a fantastic job. We came close a couple of times to actually having nothing [in the way of material and stores] because they sank the *Atlantic Conveyor*' – of which more in a moment.

Brilliant carried two nuclear depth charges, but on 16 April these were transferred to the *Fort Austin* to prevent complications under the Treaty of Tlatelolco. This had been signed in Mexico City in 1967 and essentially kept Latin America and the Caribbean nuclear-free. The British Caribbean islands were British territories before their independence so Britain signed the treaty on their behalf, as it were. Interestingly, only Argentina and Cuba did not sign, meaning that at the time of the Falklands War the treaty did not protect Argentina.

On 22 April, *Brilliant* was diverted to South Georgia, where 'we took part in the crippling of the Argentina submarine *Santa Fé* and the landing of troops to recapture the islands. We also took with us about ninety SAS and SBS on our ship. We had to double up bunks and take all their equipment with us. The men were all right, very fit, obviously, glorified Royal Marines I'd call them. I'm not afraid of these people, see! My claim to fame was – later – sticking a thermometer up their asses! *You're not that hard, mate, not that hard!*

'So we cleaned up South Georgia. You'd manage to get out now and again onto the upper deck and you could see it. It looked like just a little piece of land, cold. We flew one helicopter mission over there of which one of the boys was Mentioned in Despatches. I don't know what for – I think because he went for a ride in the helicopter! That's what it was like. We didn't have Argentinian prisoners.

'We then turned for the Falklands and a week later we were on the edge of the Total Exclusion Zone, ahead of the main carrier group which arrived on 1 May. Then we all went together into our war. You still weren't quite sure what was going to happen. You were put into a combat mode: on for twelve hours, off for twelve hours. I was unfortunate and copped the night shift, so I'd be awake all the evening and the Argentines were bombing us in the daytime. I was getting very little sleep.'

On 12 May, *Brilliant* in company with HMS *Glasgow* was off Port Stanley conducting naval gunfire and they were attacked by twelve Skyhawk fighter-bombers. *Brilliant* was responsible for repulsing the first wave with Sea Wolf missiles – she was the first Royal Navy warship to fire one – and also became the first ship in the Task Force to engage and destroy enemy jets. She shot down three A-4 Skyhawks that day. The second wave of attackers were unsuccessful and the third remained in the distance.

'Because you are shut down and you're inside, you can't see it. You can only hear it. You hear the chaff going up, then you hear bang-bang – the guns going – so you know something's happening, but because you can't see anything it's like being cocooned in a submarine. You had to listen to the reports they managed to put over the tannoy system.

'From 12 May up until the invasion, *Brilliant* was involved in special operations. We were making sweeps of the Falklands coast and goal-keeping for HMS *Invincible* to make sure she was safe from missile attack. Myself personally, I *still* thought it was an adventure. It was not like one of your typical war films. You carry on as normal.'

One historical source comments:

On 19 May, the [SAS] regiment suffered a tragic loss when a Sea King crashed while cross-decking troops from HMS *Hermes* to HMS *Intrepid* and killed 22 men. The Sea King had taken off from HMS *Hermes* at dusk. The aircraft was slightly over-loaded but because it was a short flight the pilot reduced his fuel load to lighten the helicopter. At 300ft the Sea King started its decent towards HMS *Intrepid*. Those on board heard a thump, then another from the engine above them. The Sea King dipped once then dived. Within 4 seconds it hit the water. Some men were killed instantly and others knocked unconscious in the initial impact. Amazingly nine men managed to scramble out of the open side door before the helicopter slipped below the waves. They were the only survivors. Rescuers found bird feathers floating on the surface where the helicopter had impacted the water. It is thought that the Sea

King was the victim of a bird strike. One theory is at the Sea King was
hit by a Black Browed Albatross which has an 8ft wing span. The SAS
lost eighteen men on this night. The regiment had not lost so many
men at one tine since the end of the Second World War.[2]

Field says: 'there were some thirty men on board the helicopter. The first
lifeboat that we had sank. It was an inflatable and it got bust. We went
out to the quarter-deck to where we picked up the lifeboat, launched
it at about 20.20. They were in severe shock and stages of hypothermia
because they were so laden down with ammunition – they had more
ammunition than a gun shop. They carried everything themselves. So
with that amount of weight, as soon as they helicopter came down and
they were in the water, you can understand what happened.

'We weren't quite sure how far away the helicopter had crashed. All we
knew was that a helicopter *had* crashed and we were on the scene to pick
them up. In the lifeboat was myself, Leading Seaman Robson, another
good friend, Taff Rossi. Robson dragged them out of the water and we
put them into the boat. It's pitch black, you can't see anything. Well, you
could see the liferafts in the water. We were on the upper deck with the
duty diver – he was ready in his diving suit – and this bright orange flo-
tation suit came down the side of the ship very slowly. I asked, "Should
we retrieve it" and was told, "No, let it go." Even being under the water,
about 3 or 4 feet, the water was so clear you could still see him. At that
moment you let it go, but on reflection I keep thinking *that is somebody's
son*. That's what bothers me: that somebody's son is still floating about.

'The lifeboats are like rubber dinghies – a fibreglass hull with a rubber
band all the way round. They are like the little inshore ones. They've got
an engine. My mate went off on the other boat towards the helicopter. As
it happened, that sank and they were picked up by another boat.'

Field went in another lifeboat. 'It was only forty minutes from the
time the boat was launched to the time we were back on. It went very
quickly, actually. We brought them back to our ship and brought them
in through the quarter-deck. We took them straight to the senior rates'
showers and started putting them through cold water because you can't

put them directly into hot water or you'll kill them. They were very incoherent. They had been in the water for some time and they were so cold they were unaware of what was going on.

'After a good half an hour or forty-five minutes we put them into one of the petty officers' messes. There were blankets ready, soup, baths and whatever treatment they might need. They were in such severe shock some of them couldn't stand properly and we had to hold them up. I carried this one into the showers and he didn't even know what day it was – you were talking to him and he was very incoherent. You got in the shower with them, stripped them off, get their clothes off, keep talking to them to try and bring them around.

'You got a bit wet yourself. I was in there for about twenty minutes with the one fellow, constantly talking. I still had my clothes on. I was still warm. After, you strip it all off, put it in a bag and get some more clean clothes on. Sharing a shower with the SAS! *Do us a favour, mate, scrub my back!*

'I was given the task of overseeing the observations for the night. That was because of my first-aid training. One or two of them had intravenous drips to give them some fluids. Some had already started coming around and you were having to get temperature readings to keep your charts up to date. I was keeping observations every half hour. We had the nine of them there at close quarters so it was easy to look after them. I smoked sixty fags and drank about thirty cups of tea or coffee in the space of six hours.

'As the night went on they had come around. They started talking with each other and so on. Breakfast was soon upon us so I got eight meals. They were asking about their mates and I couldn't tell them anything. They kept asking but I didn't have any answers. We kept them all night and then we had to fly them off the next morning to the *Canberra*. I did notice one thing when they left: they all shook my hand and said, "Thank you."

'Through the night there was nobody about. Everybody had gone and got their heads down but in the morning it was surprising how many wanted to come and say goodbye to them. People want a little bit of a claim to fame, I suppose, especially with them being SAS. Everybody wanted to say, "I did this" and "I did that."

1 The *Atlantic Conveyor*.

2 Another view of the *Atlantic Conveyor*.

3 Mark
Hiscutt with
Kirsty on their
wedding day,
shortly after
his return
home from
the Falklands.

4 Mark Hiscutt
today.

5 Steve Wilkinson at San Carlos Bay in 1982.

6 Steve Wilkinson at Veterans' Day in 2010.

7 David Buey at his homecoming at RAF Brize Norton.

8 David Buey today.

9 Mark 'Mario' Reid.

10 The Royal Navy's route to the Falklands in 1982.

11 Dave Brown on his 21st birthday on 21 May 1982, the day of the landings.

12 Dave Brown returning to Mark's grave on Valentine's Day 2009. A lady from the island presented him with a rose to put on the grave.

13 Jimmy O'Connell on
Ascension Island in 1982.

G. COLVIN 1980
S. HOPE 1982
I. HOLT 1991
M. J. BESWICK

14 Jimmy O'Connell
at Cpl Stevie Hope's
memorial in 2009.

15 Graeme Golightly, back row furthest right, in 1982.

16 Graeme Golightly today.

'I said to these people, "Enjoyed your sleep, did you? Have a good night's sleep, did you?" *Steward Field is the one who's sat up and looked after them all night!*'

On 21 May *Brilliant* was near San Carlos Water and the Argentine air force attacked her, inflicting light damage with cannon fire.

Field noted in his diary: 'The *Brilliant* got hit. Late last night – about 2 in the morning – we moved up the Sound escorting the rest of the fleet. The Sound is as wide as 10 miles in places and down to 3 miles in others. We moved in very silent motions and then anchored in the coves to give air cover. The SAS were ashore knocking off fuel dumps and radar and ammo dumps and the sky was lighting up with the explosions of these attacks. The codes that they used – I was listening to these boys talking – was chocolate bars. Aero, Mars, Topic, Marathon. It came over that an aircraft had been blown up and they knew exactly which boys were doing it.

'We'd had air attacks, air threats. I was below deck all the time. They took us into the Sound and we'd been caught by cannon fire from aircraft, the Skyhawks or Étendards. We got hit on the starboard side from the fo'castle down to about midships – twenty-one holes in the side, I think, but it was only cannon fire so they weren't large holes. A bomb went right between the main mast and the funnel and we had three bombs bounce over us. One bounced over the flight deck, one between the main mast and the funnel, one over the fo'castle. The most damage that we received was cannon fire.

'We'd gone to action stations and we were under our first wave of attack. As it happens, my first-aid post – in a weapons systems control room with two men in there, a chief petty officer and a good friend of mine, Scouse Markham – was at the back end of the ship.

'I ran the full length of the ship with another first-aider. This cannon fire came through the side of the ship and had gone straight through Scouse's survival suit and into his leg. Reflecting now, I think you just go into overdrive, you seem to know what you are doing *automatically*. This petty officer, who'd been in the service some twenty years, was in shock because he didn't know what to do.

'Then there was a leading stores accountant – basically, everything that comes to a ship has to be booked in and booked out – but I don't talk too much about him, I smacked him once. He was with me as well and he didn't know what to do. They had much more service than I had.

'I took control of the situation straight away. On the right-hand side there's a bit of a fire and smoke and a bit of water. It wasn't so serious although the officers' toilets got a bit shot up and their bathrooms got shot up a fair bit, too. The chief petty officer and Scouse Markham were on the floor. The first thing I did was to put a packing on to Scouse's leg, then I fireman-lifted him over my shoulder and ran back through the ship through about three or four doors. I suppose it's just technique being able to do that.

'At the same time the guns were going off again and you could hear that because they were right above you. It came over the tannoy to take cover, and every time we had to take cover you lay down flat. Now I can't lie down flat while I've got a bloke hanging over my shoulder. By the time I'd got to the wardroom – which, because it was the largest space, was used as a first-aid theatre and operations centre – there was a bloke lying on the floor with his hands on his head. I said, "Get up, what are you doing?" He said, "There's an air attack." I said, "I know, get the ******* door open." It was a door on hinges – rollers – and I kicked it straight off the rollers. I went in, put Scouse on the floor and laid next to him until the air attack had subsided. Then I took closer account of his injuries.

'He had a large hole in his left leg, the top of his thigh. He also had the shrapnel that took the packing of his survival suit into the hole with it. I had to get hold of the proper medical fellow and take advice from him. Scouse didn't require morphine because he wasn't in pain – as a first-aider, you carry 5 ampoules of morphine, whereas everybody else just carries 1. My task was to look after him until he was flown off to the *Canberra* where they'd got proper operating facilities.

'By contrast, there was a leading seaman who had a bit of a graze on his head – just clipped the top, bit of blood. I've had worse on a Saturday night in the street. When I did manage to get up to him on the upper deck I gave him a plaster. You know, kiss it better, and say *there, there, there* ...

'We spent forty-eight hours under mass Argentine air attacks, suffering slight damage. I was below decks and you can't see outside. All you hear is BOOM-BOOM-BOOM – bangs going off all the time. All the hatches are shut down. You're turning this way, that way, they are launching things up in the air. At the time I can honestly say I thought it was a big adventure. It's hard to explain. It didn't frighten me – because you couldn't see what was coming it didn't really worry me. I know it might frighten some people more that they couldn't see to get out of the way but ... I don't know, it just didn't seem real.'

Two days after the attack, *Brilliant* joined *Yarmouth* in chasing a coaster called ARA *Monsunen*, actually a British vessel which the Argentinians had captured. A Harrier spotted it moving towards Port Stanley with fuel and flour on board. *Yarmouth* opened fire and the captain beached the vessel at Seal Cove.

Brilliant rescued twenty-four survivors from the *Atlantic Conveyor* on 25 May.

'The *Atlantic Conveyor* was hit by, I think, an Exocet. The rumour was that the Argentines thought because it was flat it was an aircraft carrier – whether that is true or not, I'm not quite sure. The *Atlantic Conveyor* was the one that had the Chinook helicopters on and the supplies – everything. Next thing we heard it had been hit – we didn't see that – and, "Stand by to receive survivors".

'The boats and survival rafts had come alongside. We had scramble ladders over the side and they came up there themselves. None of them were injured in any way. Physically they were OK, but they just looked a bit worse for wear at being dumped in the water. One of the boys, I think it was a petty officer, used to be a leading hand at Yeovilton air base and my instructor. His name was Pete Cherry and the first thing he said was, "Hello, Bill!" I said, "Hello, Rocks!" I'd never thought after Yeovilton I'd be seeing him again.

'The survivors from the *Atlantic Conveyor* were in a better condition than the boys from the helicopter. They weren't in the water that long. Three minutes and that's your arse, really, you're already feeling the effects by then. We checked them over and made sure they were all right. Then it was a question of blankets, new clothes, food and making sure their registration was taken: who they are, date of birth, so they could be accounted for.

'I think it was one of those situations for them where you just do what you have to do, you don't think about it.'

Field had 'my 21st birthday while I was down there. The usual procedure: everybody will sign your cap and you keep that as a memento. The SAS boys that we had down in our mess – all signed my cap for me, but I can't find it now …

'I have another souvenir. It's the declaration from the queen herself: *I wish you to pass on to all officers and subordinates, your country is proud for the liberation of the Falkland Islands.* I've got the main signal in my wallet. I saw it and I wanted it. It was just left hanging about on a table.'

Field also held a wonderful memory. Every ship had its own Chinese laundrymen and, evidently, the Chinese kept themselves to themselves. The Chinese 'we had on our ship never went to action stations'. Instead, one of them 'used to hide in the tumble dryer. They gave him the BEM – British Empire Medal. I said, "What for?" "Because he's a foreign national." The BEM!

'We returned home on 13 July after 107 days at sea. We came back through Ascension. We had to fly home on a Hercules, which was a very, very long trip, refuelling in Dakar and then into Brize Norton. My first day home I was arrested for drunk and disorderly fighting with my brother, who was in the Royal Artillery – me against him. We smashed the toilets up in a local pub. Then the police came and we turned on them. They went to arrest me, he didn't like it, they went to arrest him, I didn't like it so they threw the two of us in the cells. We both went to court on the Monday. We were both in uniform. The judge took one look and said, "Go and have a pint. Case dismissed." This was Cardiff!

'I left the services in 1984; pretty much within eighteen months of the Falklands I decided *I'm gone.* I was unhappy, I had come across so much hypocrisy and I just thought *naah.* Don't get me wrong: I came home and things were seen differently outside. You always think the grass is greener on the other side. I never realised I was giving up what I had enjoyed. It was the biggest mistake of my life ever, coming out of the navy, but then again I was also too young when I entered. You've gone from cub scouts, it's not all glamour and there are people that will dislike you.

'I was 23/24 when I came out. It's still very young. The navy was the only family that I knew. You never wanted for anything: you had your food, you were on good money, you were travelling, all your accomodation taken care of, and you're with your mates. Your age dictates what kind of company you keep, I suppose. Those with a bit more experience look down at you.

'I just carried on drinking on a sociable level but as time went on it escalated in a very big way. You do then start to get into problems. I think it was a bit of both: the culture that I had grown up into and the Post Traumatic Stress Disorder, really, because of what you've been through and you've seen and you've accepted. You've gone through it, you've done it. When you actually do come home you're not recognised because it's an entirely different kind of life, the social system and everything. In the navy you've got people that you can rely on, but when you come outside there's nobody there that you can rely on. Trying to explain to people then is difficult.

'I applied for a job as a fireman because I was cross-trained. You have to learn all aspects of fire safety because you can't phone the fire brigade when you are at sea. So I learned a fair bit about firefighting. I was shortlisted – this was under Maggie's government – from about 4,000 down to the last 200. I went and sat the exam and passed, only to find out that they had to advertise the job, which was a local government rule I suppose. They took back eight ex-firemen, so why give people the expectation that "oh, you're going to become a fireman" when there's no job there in the first place.

'You can hurt people and that's exactly what happened to myself. I felt let down. Of course once you start with one leg down, then the next leg down, you're not getting any real social assistance. When they lose paperwork, or this goes wrong, or that goes wrong, you get infuriated.'

Brilliant starred in a BBC documentary series called *HMS Brilliant* in the early 1990s. She decommissioned in 1996 and was sold to the Brazilian navy on 31 August 1996 and renamed *Dodsworth*.

Notes

1. Aden: the Aden Emergency, 1963–67, when British forces when engaged in counter-insurgency operations in what is now Yemen, which ended with their withdrawal from the former crown colony.
2. www.britains-smallwars.com/Falklands/sas.htm

10

THE 29-YEAR-OLD TEENAGER

I went over to him and he was just a fumbling wreck. I was a professional marine but you don't want to see that in another human being. Let's be fair about this, war is not a nice place at the best of times. You either kill or be killed. Straightforward as that.

Graeme Golightly was 'born in Knowsley, Merseyside in October 1962. I didn't have an easy childhood and it's interesting because I guess most people who join the forces do it to get away. It was unfortunate for me because I had a stepfather I didn't get on with. I know that's what motivated me. Actually, from an early age – 8 – I was going to move on and join the military. As an 8-year-old I distinctly remember thinking this on a school bus: *I am going to join the marines*. I did it for another reason, too. My stepfather was ex-navy and I suppose he held the marines in esteem of some kind. I certainly know that when I publicised it he said I wouldn't be able to make it. It stems from there, really.

'What sort of a young lad was I? Easy question, difficult answer. I would say I was fairly easy going and laid back. We lived on the edge of what's known as Lord Derby's estate, which is a big park. I would think nothing of going out from 7 in the morning until 7 at night. Fundamentally, because of the difficult upbringing and my relationship with my stepfather I chose to spend a lot of the time out with friends, and if I wasn't out with friends I'd be doing my own thing in the wooded area.

'I'm jumping ahead here but after I'd left the services and was working for a brewery company up in Oxfordshire someone asked me about my career. I said I had been in the military. He said, "Don't people who join the military want to get away from their home life?" Straight back in answer I said, "Oh, no, no, no, no," but on reflection it was such a true statement that I have been truthful about it ever since. In the network of marines I still deal with, and serving guys, they have all done it for the same reason: to get away from either a disruptive homelife or they needed to have a clean break.

'You are not, however, going to go into the services for an easy option.

'Anyway, from that age of 8 on a school bus I knew what I was doing and I also knew failure was never an option for me. That is interesting because had I not made the marines I wondered what I would have done. I knew quite simply that more than failure not being an option as soon as I left home I was not coming back. Come what may, I couldn't go back to my disrupted homelife with my step-father.

'I'd been to boarding school in Angelsea, North Wales, and I was 16 when I left. I passed all my entrance details to get into the Royal Marines. I had three or four months off between school and my start date with the Corps so in fact I was 16½ when I joined. All I can remember is that when I left school I went back home, doing nothing and thinking *I don't want to be here*. Then I got a start date for the Royal Marines training, and – this *is* interesting – I know the date because it still sticks with you, as things do in life: 6 August 1979.

'The other one is your service number.

'Of course I was young because I was what's known as a Junior Marine on a thirty-week training programme to become a marine. As daunting as it was getting off at the train station at Lympstone, Exmouth, where Commando Training Centre Royal Marines is, I relished the challenges of what lay ahead because, and I keep referring to it, there was nothing for me in my home life. If I didn't make the marines I would have gone to the Canadian Rockies and built my own log cabin and led a life of isolation. I say that jokingly but I did have a get-out of doing something else.

'I passed out thirty weeks later in April 1980 and I had had my 17th birthday by then. I was with 40 Commando based in Seaton Barracks in Plymouth. We happened to be at Altcar, a weapons range in Southport, which is still there. We'd just gone up for some weapons training. When the Falklands call came in we were recalled to Seaton Barracks to get our spearhead [a unit ready to deploy quickly] kit all ready for whatever was going to be happening.

'Truthfully, no, I did not know where the Falklands were. A lot of people thought it was North Orkney. However, when it was announced that the Falklands were a problem we knew that the marines had a detachment down there. Simply put, initially no, we didn't know, but after a few questions by the senior marines we realised.

'The Argentinians had had a skirmish in South Georgia and we were put on notice to move. It all happened quite quickly. I still recall getting in the coaches in Plymouth and being driven down to Southampton to board the *Canberra*. We had three fighting companies: I was in Bravo. Alpha Company were airlifted off to HMS *Bulwark* or *Ark Royal*, doing the provisions and storage on the way down. We realised that, polticians being politicians, there was something likely to happen but not in a month of Sundays – right up to the day that we landed on San Carlos beach as the beachhead unit – did we think we would be going to war. Sorry, it's not war now, is it? It's a conflict.

'What we had was a strong-willed prime minister in Margaret Thatcher who was the right person in the right place at the right time. She was obviously motivated to stand up for British rule on the Falkland Islands

'We went from Southampton. We sailed at roughly midnight and it is poignant for me, this, because we have a Bravo-Zulu operation which happens with naval ships where you all form up round the outside in your stand-easy position. That's how you come into port and that's how you leave port. With the *Canberra* it was a totally different environment. The marines and the paras, we were all on the side looking at the quay as we left. It was total darkness, no great fanfare, but as we sailed down towards the Solent, on the Southampton side there's a stretch of road which is quite high. The local news had said we were setting sail and the traffic turned round in the road and were flashing the ship with the headlights on high beam. I always remember that send off.

'From there it was gearing ourselves up to be combat ready, doing the physical and weapons training. We built flight decks on the *Canberra* for the Sea King helicopters and the Wessexes to come on board.

'The bars? Fantastic. We were limited very much in what we could drink and do. Our morale was supported and boosted by the fact that we had Royal Marines band people with us and in war situations they act as stretcher-bearers or whatever. What goes unsaid in many a story is just what a morale boost these musicians give you either going down or coming back. Certainly in the night time when we'd gone through the various weapon stances or preparations or physical exercise – and some of it was quite hard going – we could then have a few beers. There was a guy who used to play the saxophone and we'd have a whole knees-up. They kept us and the paras apart from each other …

'I can reflect in a more mature way now. We were youngsters with coiled springs ready to rock 'n' roll, and sometimes with coiled springs you have to have releases. Our little releases was getting entertained by the Royal Marines band in the evening and having a few beers. Not once did any of us get totally blottoo – in fact you weren't allowed to – because they were restricting the beer by cans. What I remember about that set-up was the marines and the paras were fundamentally kept separate. When we had what was known as the promenade deck – it circumnavigates the ship and I think it worked out at a mile if you did so many times round the ship – and were using it for physical exercise, running round with weapons or whatever, there would be no paras in sight. In fact, we had to book the use of the promenade deck.

'You were youngsters, you all thought you were Schwarzenegger and you could take on anybody. The potential flashpoint was – and the paras must have thought the same, because I have spoken to many a para since – that any small reason would have set it off.

'I remember General Haig, the American Secretary of State, doing negotiations while we were on Ascension Island, where we stayed there for a couple of weeks, or maybe a bit less. We were kept briefed by our intelligence people and also the BBC World Service. That was fantastic, that was. There were discussions going on with General Haig with his counterpart in the Argentine government and we thought *hopefully it will all be settled peacefully and diplomatically with no real cause for fighting.*

'Was there a moment when I realised it was getting serious? The first point was when we transferred to HMS *Fearless* to do the assault. They got us from the *Canberra* by landing craft. You climbed down ladders, which can open on the side of the *Canberra*, to the landing craft. From the marines' point of view, we are amongst family when we are dealing with landing craft because it's the Royal Marines that run them. Joe Bloggs knows Joe Smith, and Joe Smith knows Bob Brown and so on. We had to have a fairly calm sea and the South Atlantic was never calm, but we never lost anybody. It's kind of a tricky thing, as I recall, when you are trying to go down a rope ladder from the side of a huge cruise liner to a bobbing little landing craft. It's not something you would normally do unless you had to.

'Our company took over the officers' mess on HMS *Fearless* and to this day it is funny: I remember watching *Grease* on the video. I was sat there – we've gone from a cruise liner, which was nice and stable, nice accomodation, blah, blah, blah, to effectively a warship, HMS *Fearless* – which was a flat-bottomed landing craft ship, so we are getting all the effects of sea-sickness hitting us as well.

'We were accommodated in the officers' mess or lying down on the deck. I think even then it wasn't until about 4 o'clock in the morning we were given a brief of what we were going to do. We were given our ammunition and we did it at night time – the first guys ashore in San Carlos Water. San Carlos Water had been recce'ed [and found to be undefended]. At 4 we were loading up and getting into the landing craft. We were saying, "Right, this is it, let's rock 'n' roll." It was surreal because it's the middle of the night and we are going out.

'You get into the landing craft and the ship floods its backside, so to speak. Then the back gate of the ship opens. On two sides there are gangways that navy ratings stand on as the landing craft goes past them. I remember the navy guys saying, "Look after yourselves and we'll see you when you get back." I thought *oooh*. Not a word was said. We all looked at each other because we were camouflaged and ready. That is the most poignant memory I have, the navy guys saying, "Look after yourselves", because it meant we were going out to do some serious stuff. We had good intelligence: nothing was going to hit us, but we still weren't too sure about the initial landing.

'We had an army reconnaisance vehicle, a Scimitar,[1] in the landing craft with us, so we had to work our way round it: guys in front, guys at the side and guys at the back. We landed at San Carlos Blue Beach.[2] We knew we were among family members using the landing craft and they would do their jobs to the best of their abilites. The people operating the landing craft were part of the Royal Marines: the Royal Marines man and staff all the landing craft. I'm sure some navy guys get involved, but the Royal Marines all do the same training together, and from training we got into specialisations and the landing craft division, shall we call it, is one. They know exactly where to land us and how to land us, how to facilitate and accommodate us getting out.

'When we came in to land the doors went down, the guys in the front got out, but the army vehicle stayed where it was because you couldn't be sure how deep the water was. When the doors go down, that's when you're most vulnerable to anything coming in at you and we had to climb across this vehicle to get out of the landing craft. You're needing to get to a position you can defend more easily rather than getting shot at when that door goes down.

'I don't know if you've seen the film *Saving Private Ryan*. The opening scenes, which Spielberg did quite well, was the Second World War landing craft coming ashore. As soon as that front gate went down they had a rain of bullets ripping them apart. Ours was unopposed but you think just how horrendous it can be. You are confined in a small space and all the enemy directional fire can be coming at that. It can show you the true brutality of war and what it does.

'The defenders have got themselves set up. They know all the angles, they know where the threat's coming from and they've dug themselves in. If they've got any sense they've their main firepower coming down in those areas – but the Argentinians didn't have that kind of sense. Obviously, Blue Beach and all the other beaches at San Carlos Water and Port San Carlos were recce'ed by special forces prior to us going in, so we knew it was unopposed.

'We couldn't have been more than between 6 to 12 feet from the shore. I remember coming out and the water was only up to our thighs, but you were geared up to get off the landing craft and away from it as fast as possible. What concerned us was getting over this Scimitar. We scattered, we moved across the water and, as it happened, there was no opposition. Literally, from getting in to the landing craft to getting out was less than thirty minutes. Once we hit the beachhead we moved off as a company up to the hillside overlooking San Carlos. We started digging in ready for a counter-attack or whatever, we were basically getting ourselves defended should the enemy come back over and have a go. We knew they had been around because they'd run away from Port San Carlos. The Argentinians didn't know where we were going to land. I don't think they even second-guessed San Carlos. To land there, that far away from Stanley, was a no-brainer: they had no idea. We had an unopposed landing, which is always good for the landing force …

'We were digging in, and trust me if I say when you think they are coming back you don't need motivation to get yourself properly defended. You can dig very quickly.

'My memory of digging in was that it was very wet and you could only dig down 2 feet before you became waterlogged. We came to an understanding, certainly in our company: we dug until it became water-logged and then we built turf on the top to take the rounds of fire should they come our way. We made ourselves nice and cosy in there, actually.

'The first air attack we had from the Argentinian air force was in the morning. It was also the first time it had become *real* for me because what then happened, we lost our only person in the conflict. He was a guy called Marine McAndrews, part of the rear echelon brigade that supports the front guys. The Argentinian air force came over and started dropping what – because we were on the hillside and we were looking down on this – seemed to be little parachutes. *Oh look what they're dropping!* We were on the hill and so the aircraft had to climb to come back up over us and it was almost like a domino effect. When you saw the first ones drop you started feeling air bursts – they were air-burst bombs with a bigger spread to cause maximum injuries. We had the benefit of watching it begin to happen and then it was moving its way up the hill towards us. That's when ironically I thought *wow! This is NOT real.*

'Believe it or not, even with our expertise and marine training, most people stood up to look, not knowing what these parachutes were about. You looked up, the bomb burst and suddenly it was throwing shrapnel down at you to try and take you out. The realisation went from *aren't they pretty?* to *oh my word, get out of here NOW.* We were fortunate with that parachute display, as I call it, because seeing it happen from the start meant that by the time it got to us we were well covered.

'I watch war programmes and see things like that but you can't – how can I say? – you can't *interestingly* put over the realisation that death is staring you in the face. Right? To me it was *like* watching a film on TV. Everything happens in slow motion and even though you know death is coming towards you, it's as if it is happening s-l-o-w-l-y. I have experienced that in Northern Ireland as well. It's hard to try and put across how you feel when you're getting shot at. Certainly with these air-burst bombs I felt we were on a film set, which is strange. That might be a normal reaction but when you see the consequences the realisation kicks in.

'We were too far up the hill to see the guy get killed. We were notified. Across from San Carlos Water was Ajax Bay, where we had the medics as well. The helicopters were flying about all the time and, of course, we were still in the initial landing stage with people trying to bring everything in as fast as possible and getting everything stabilised.'

The word 'CONTACT' had been used, initiating a standard radio procedure.

'If "CONTACT!" is ever spoken all the call signs get off the net so that the person who is having the contact gets whatever he needs, because they are in a live situation with the enemy. It's what you can call a red-light word. Casevac was going on, too, so you know something was happening. He was dealt with quite swiftly, I understand – picked up by a helicopter and transferred across San Carlos Water to the medical facility.

'We consolidated there and the other units came on board: 3 Para. The first couple of days was getting everyone ashore before fanning out from San Carlos to move on. We were tasked to do other things like take an observation post up Sussex Mountain, which was overlooking Goose

Green. We spent a couple of nights there to cover the access. I came down with frostnip on Sussex Mountain. It was quite cold on top and although we had the Arctic kit with us not all of it was distributed at the right times so we were in what is known as GS kit – General Service. I remember having NBC boots – Nuclear, Biological, Chemical – that we tried putting over our feet to combat the water ingress and the very, very cold environment. I got my first touch of frontnip, but I was also conscious that the marines, the army, whoever marched on their feet and amongst your weapons the feet are the most important things. You had to look after them. We ensured that we always changed socks and talcum-powdered our feet.

'It was frostnip at the first stage. Basically, it's where your skin goes like white putty. It was OK. Frostnip is easily managed as long as you catch it in time. You can see it on your face to begin with as well. You take precautions: isolate it, cover it up, get it dry and make sure it gets warm before it goes into the next stage. I was able to do that.

'When I was on Sussex Mountain the Gurkhas, who had just landed, came through us. The Gurkhas – bless 'em! – had no end of motivation, but they had anti-tank weapons as big and as heavy as the man carrying it. When they were coming through our position, their unit was quite prepared to let the guys with heavy weights lag behind. I thought *hmmmm* because we would never, ever let that happen. As a fighting-strength force you have to stick together, you can't be spread out. I tried interacting with some of these Gurkhas asking, "How can you be left behind?" but they didn't understand English too well.

'We were de-tasked, we got back in the landing craft and went round to Port San Carlos where there was an Argentinian presence when we landed. That would be confirmed by the fact that some of our 3 Commando Brigade helicopters got shot [and one brought down]. That was another realisation that it wasn't a ball game and it wasn't the cinema. We were seeing things happening around us and we did some shooting in Port San Carlos.

'We dug in again, made defensive battle positions and waited. The countryside was sort of barren with the odd sheep shed and building.

The Falklands does not have any trees and you realise why. It's because of the prevailing wind and nothing with height can grow. So apart from the fact that you see settlements – a couple of settlements of houses – nine times out of ten they'll have a sheep shed with them because the main business of the Falkland Islands is sheep-shearing and sheep-producing. I remember the big sheep shed in San Carlos and a couple of settlement houses. I didn't see the helicopter crash – one of the Lynxes with some of our marine guys in it – but I knew there had been a contact with it because we were informed of that over the net.

'It was at that time we were given the disappointing news that we were staying as beachhead protection for the rest of the units to move through, so you had our other marine units, which were 42 and 45 Commandos, 1 Para and 2 Para, moving inland to reach their designated targets and take the fight to the enemy.

'To this day we have reunions on this. Our CO was a guy called Malcolm Hunt, Colonel Hunt, and the marines were in charge of this operation. We had successfully landed and got the beachhead secured and controlled. We were then held back in reserve and at any reunion I do you always hear how hacked off we all felt about that, even at our big twenty-fifth anniversary. Hunt went on to be a major general but he still brings it up in discussion. We couldn't quite get our head around it, the fact that the 3 Commando Brigade brigadier was Julian Thompson and he was a marine and he must have allocated the resources to go where – a marine, but keeping us back as beachhead protection.

'Everybody wanted to go. We were trained, we were brainwashed – if that's the right word – but that's what military training does to you. We were primed to getting in there and getting the job done. Now I can reflect and think I'm thankful we didn't. We were definitely up for it and there was a lot of resentment going about that. The story was that we had established the beachhead and if there was a counter-offensive they wanted a marine unit back on this area.

'We had an incident at Port San Carlos where we thought we saw a farmer coming towards us in the distance. We knew the Argentinians had a little force there when we landed and that's what took out the helicopters, but we didn't know they were still around. We were on guard just in case the counter-offensive was going to happen. Whilst we were sitting on our observation post we saw this farmer waving. We then scanned him with the binoculars and we saw he had the Argentinian uniform on.

'We started to go out and grab him. He was trying to wave a flag – a handkerchief, which in the distance you can't see. We weren't taking it as a threat to begin with and when we got up to him we realised he was Argentinian, one of the original Argentinians that had fled Port San Carlos when it was known we had landed. They were trying to make their way back to Stanley, where the main force was. Unfortunately for him, he and three or four of his fellow army guys suffered with trench foot. It's the rotting of the skin because you don't look after it.

'This guy was able to walk but he was obviously finding it very, very difficult. He couldn't speak any English but we had a navy guy who could understand the lingo. We brought the Argentinian back to our company lines where we'd dug in and we were trying to extract the information from him about what was going on. We had an intelligence officer with us in the unit.

'The crux of the matter was that he was one of four people holed up in a cave a certain distance away, so we thought *all right, OK, they are obviously the stragglers or they were left behind* – because they were a conscript army and were badly, badly treated. They had had it ingrained into them that should they be captured they would be killed. They put that fear into their own people: *if push comes to shove, you have to kill your way out or be killed yourself.* This guy had needed a lot of bravery to come to us against all he had been told. And here I was as a 19-year-old dealing with this, because I was one of the guys who picked him up.'

What happened then still troubles Golightly, even though it was in the context of war. They needed to know if the Argentinian was setting them up for an ambush when they went to get his comrades, who might be many more than three or four and might be anything but stragglers.

Golightly was told they needed to force 'the issue with this Argentinian to make sure he was telling the truth before we then bolted off after this group and came into an ambush'.

Golightly explains that as a young marine he was taking directions and 'when rank gives you directions you do it. In your own mind you're thinking *this is not right* but that's another matter. One of my poignant memories was this guy's reaction when he saw four or five of us approach him with weapons. Here was a 26-year-old guy, so a lot older than me, who was absolutely cacking himself. When he saw us with our weapons he clearly thought what he had been told in training was about to happen. He was crying out loud for his mother like you want to go back into your mother's womb. There was me and another couple of guys were uncomfortable with all of this. Here he was as a more mature man than myself but he was screaming at the top of his voice for his mother. I couldn't deal with the situation that I have got a grown man crying in front of me. What 19-year-old can? It's one of those things and it's always stayed with me.

'I did just a bit of growing up down there. The statement I used to use was *I went down as an 19-year-old and I came back as a 29-year-old a few weeks later.* I don't want to glorify this business because it's not a glorified situation. When you are killing each other, because all normal talking and communications have broken down, it's dog eat dog. It's the most horrific thing you can ever be involved with, it really is.

'Anyway, the validation of the information he gave us did not change.

'I went over to him and he was just a fumbling wreck, and rightly so. Let's be fair about this, war is not a nice place at the best of times. You either kill or be killed. It's as straightforward as that, but …

'I remember sitting next to him trying to calm him down. I remember giving him all the chocolates out of my ration pack and he didn't want to accept anything from me because he thought it was just another part of this thing that he was going to be killed anyway and here's your *last* bit of chocolate.

'We validated that information, then we flew off in a helicopter to go and get the rest of his friends and they were in a bad state. They offered no resistance. They weren't in a cave, it was a dug-out. They were cowering. Stupidly what they had done was tie plastic bags round their feet to keep them dry. Of course when you do that you have condensation and it gets worse. We took a troop with us because we didn't know how many of them there were. If you face one infantry you send six infantry to go and suppress it, if it's one unit you send ten units. It's all about the power of numbers. I don't know what had happened to their weapons, but they were totally defenceless.

'I am the 19-year-old looking at a conscript army much older than me thinking *how can you as an individual be so unprofessional?* But of course they were mis-managed, mis-informed, mis-controlled. With most of them their trench foot had gone on to the second or third stage of decay. They couldn't walk on their feet – perhaps that's why the first guy came, because he just about could. I kept thanking my lucky stars that a) we were a volunteer force, but b) we were a hundred times more professional than they could ever be. They were a conscript army and whether they wanted to serve or not, they were serving. What anybody thinks about Galtieri wanting to deflect the troubles at home by getting the Malvinas back, they were in the middle of it. Having said all that, I didn't feel pity for them. I didn't have time to feel pity for them, I had time to sort them out, check them over, get them on the helicopter, get them back to San Carlos and repatriated. That's how we were dealing with it. When we talked through our interpreter, they naturally thought we were there to kill them.

'They were treated very properly. Let's be clear about this; we're British, we play cricket and the reality is you can go in, hit hard and make a mess of things, but in my opinion we treated people the way they should have treated us if they had been in our position. All right, there was the odd nutter in the marines who thought he could take the mick and head-butt them or hit them with the butt of their weapon, and you will always have that in life: some individuals who think they can take the law into their own hands, and some people who are just stupid, but we treated them with mega-respect; we knew that we had to deal with information which was coming which was correct and was solid. Our lives may have depended on that.

'Whilst we were at Port San Carlos we heard of 2 Para taking Goose Green. In fact we heard of that before, because I remember being in San Carlos and being transferred across. And that's where we had the story about a journalist who blurted out what was happening on the world news and the attack hadn't even happened. We quickly learnt that you don't talk to these guys who are along with you, but it just shows you the power of communication. Needless to say, that speeded things up tenfold to make it happen.

'From there we heard about the surrender of the Argentinians at Port Stanley. It was a relief moment because in the intervening period we had had 5 Infantry Brigade join us. We'd dealt with another incident where we also picked up another load of stragglers. They were in a house settlement which was identified to us by an islander who said it wasn't occupied but, when we scanned it and took some observations, it had smoke coming out of the chimney. We made a tactical response. Because the islander said nobody lived there we put two and two together and obviously they were Argentinians who'd come from San Carlos.

'Luckily again, it didn't have to be resolved by weapons getting fired. By the time we were skirmishing – if that's the right word – well, we were dropped off by helicopter and skirmished up towards the house. They were obviously aware of our presence. I would say we were 300, 400 metres out we started to see white flags coming out of the settlement house. We knew knew it was enemy and we couldn't trust them with flags. Rightly or wrongly, until you've got the weapons off them you need to be untrusting. So we did a full contact.

'When we got round to the front of the building, and because we'd seen the flags, we knew they were in there. We had a troop of I guess thirty. I was the one standing next to the door and although I am by the door they hadn't come out. We are now preparing to go into a *hot* situation – we don't know what's in there. I had a guy either side of me and I did a really 19-year-old naïve thing. I turned round to the rest of the guys, who were backing us up, and I shouted for a grenade. As I shouted everybody in our troop – brainwashed, disciplined – went to cover. Initially I couldn't understand why they'd all gone down. *They* thought I had shouted, "Grenade!" and in training when you hear "Grenade!" you hit the deck and if you can dig with your fingernails you dig. Instinctively you know what to do. What I wanted was a grenade to take in first to quell any ambitions they might have had as we came in through the door. I remember we were so adrenalined up I burst out laughing!

'We went in and took about eight or ten prisoners. They offered no resistance. That was quite calmly done – I say quite calmly but we didn't know what to expect. We got the prisoners out and helicoptered back to Port San Carlos to be interviewed, questioned, whatever the word is. They were sent back on the *Canberra*, I believe.

'We were then lifted across to Port Howard in West Falkland to take the surrender of the Argentinian forces there so yes, we were getting around. We had a couple of non-starters. We tried go across by landing craft but the sea was too choppy so eventually we went by Wessex helicopter. We subsequently found out the main beach where we were going to land was mined, and in a sense it was a blessing we had had no intelligence on that and didn't know.

'It was just our company that took the surrender and I would say the Argentinian unit strength in Port Howard was about 750. They were a demoralised force and just wanted to go home, but you also had to comprehend the fact that they had professional forces at Port Howard, too. They were still highly tuned and were really disgruntled that, for whatever reason, Menéndez[3] – the Argentinian base commander – had given the surrender. You never know about the loose cannons who say, "I'm not going." It's like the Japanese in the Second World War still on some remote island fifty years later.

'Anyway, there was a famous photograph taken in Port Howard of the Royal Marines flag that had the Union Jack on and a guy kneeling – a PR photograph by the settlement houses. People thought it was taken in Stanley but it wasn't. That picture resonated quite a lot round the world.

'I remember processing Argentinians in a big line, taking weapons off them and throwing them down. I saw first-hand how the conscripts were treated by their professional special forces. In front of us and in clear light of day as we were taking weapons off people – we were making sure to get them in a line to get them shipped off – their special forces thought they were entitled to better treatment. They were treating their conscripts like dirt. We were going to treat them all fairly and it meant

I was determined to ensure that the special forces and their officers got the same treatment.

'They tried to tell us in their own way that they should be getting treated differently. For me, no. As a young marine, all right I was controlled by a section corporal, a troop sergeant and a troop commander, but I made an issue of that situation in front of all the rest of the Argentinian forces. I was making a point that *they may be conscripts but you certainly don't treat them like dogs*. They were doing this amongst themselves because their officers and their special forces thought they were above them as human beings.

'It's interesting. When we took the surrender in Port Howard they separated themselves, the officers and special forces from the conscripts. This is the thing about war: it is humanity at its lowest form of existence – but even so, to do that to your own men was too much, and after my experience at Port San Carlos I wasn't letting anybody get away with it. I had an affinity with these poor guys who were badly treated so when I saw that happen from their own guys I took exception to it, although I suppose in one way it was an easy get-out for me. I could deal with an enemy who were mistreating their own, I could stamp on it and squash it before they could do that. Needless to say, after I made an issue of it that did not happen again.'

Golightly came back on the *Canberra* and 'the good news was Julian Thompson arranged that the whole of the ship took 3 Commando Brigade, which was all the marines. We had a real blast. I'm 47 years old now and I have never known a stronger affinity than the Royal Marines family. When you're together, when you're in landing craft, you all know what's expected of you and professionally you know what you're doing. So when we were all coming back everybody respected each other because of what we'd done: 45 Commando and Two Sisters, 42 Commando and Mount Longdon. There was a respect amongst ourselves and we didn't have to interact with potentially explosive situations as we might have done if we'd been sharing with the army. Whoever made that call on the *Canberra* was fantastic: a nice sail back.

'That was like our de-stressing, de-pressurising, and again with our Royal Marines band on board. We had more beer this time! We were totally de-stressed, although people handled that in their own ways. Some went into themselves, some people bottled it up, some people were able to clearly and openly talk about their experiences.

'There have been more suicides from that conflict in the British armed forces than we actually lost in the conflict itself. That gathers and grips me, in the sense that I am lucky enough to be blessed: it never affected me in that way. What normally happens with PTSD is that people bottle it up for many years and then just explode. We're all youngsters, and that's the whole point about it. We know people who've been killed but we'd come though it. We'd had our own little experiences and episodes – either in the thick of it or being beachhead protection or whatever it was – but I was able to relate and de-stress. I wouldn't say open up, because I don't think I needed to.

'We were boys amongst boys, we were sharing a laugh, having a few beers. We had no serious fights or anything coming back. You think *well, you've come from a highly stressed environment of getting wound up, wound up and wound up, where does that spring coil come off?* We shared all the bars. We were amongst the marine family, which was great, and we came back like that.

'We heard a pipe over the intercom system that said one of the destroy-ers – maybe HMS *Glamorgan* or *Brilliant* – had caught up with us in mid-Atlantic and they were coming alongside. It was about 10 o'clock at night. We all went onto the starboard side where they had come along. When you're in the middle of the ocean and you've got nothing else around you, you think you are the only people on the planet, but this ship came blazing in, pulled right alongside us and the whole ship's crew started clapping us. I thought *wow, that's humbling and we should be doing it to you*. We started clapping them back ...

'What happens in the disarray of war is that you help yourself to what-ever weapons you want [as spoils]. Simply put, that's what goes on. A lot of the guys had the 9mm pistols the Argentinian officers carried. It was all common knowledge. I had an Argentinian bayonet: it has 'Argentina' blazoned on the blade itself. We even had Lynx aircraft coming off the destroyers to pick up some kit to take back to the ship!

'A poignant part of the story is that by the time we got back to Southampton Water – we were in the English Channel – it came over the tannoy system that we would be searched by Customs & Excise and, "Those of you who have goods that should be declared, please can you let your respective sergeant-majors know". That night over the side of the *Canberra* you kept on hearing plop! plop! plop! as people got rid of the weaponry and souvenirs. The English Channel must be full of stuff like that. The ironic thing was that we weren't searched. We came off the gangplank, we had a rose thrust into our mouths and we were reunited with our families. Then we were put on coaches to go to the unit, straightforward as that. So I got the bayonet through.'

Golightly left the services in 1992 for medical reasons. 'I became diabetic. I used to ski for the navy downhill team, my pancreas was hit and I became diabetic. I was given a desk job. You can imagine what a desk job in the marines was like and the sort of things people said to you. From there I was based with helicopter squadrons in Yeovilton, at the naval air station. I was restricted from going to the first Gulf War because of my medical condition. I thought *well, obviously I can't stay in. Whilst I am still hungry enough and young enough to pursue a career in civilian life I must.*

'I took a medical discharge at the age of 29 and from there I went into property management. I say property management: I started as the lowest of the low, working in the postroom of ICL – International Computers Limited – but Fujitsu took them over. Any military person applies themselves and they start climbing the ladder. I worked for ICL for the first four or five years, then I went on to a brewery company in Abingdon, Oxfordshire – always property, by the way – looking after their property interests. Then I worked for P&O and now I'm with Clarksons, a ship-broking company in central London, looking after their property interests.'

Golightly regrets that he's never been able to meet the terrified Argentinian with trench foot at San Carlos again. 'You can only imagine what he was going through. They were repatriated and I've never been able to get hold of that guy.'

Golightly still has the Argentinian bayonet. It's in his garage.

Notes

1. Scimitar: the Scimitar belongs to the family of full-track chassis and lightweight armoured military vehicles. It was designed and built in order to fulfill a wide range of military roles and saw its first deployment to the battlefield in 1970, primarily as an armoured reconnaissance tank. The Scimitar can be operated by a crew of three men and it can reach a top speed of almost 90km/h. The original vehicle was powered by the Jaguar gasoline engine and can be used in order to defeat small military vehicles and lightly armoured targets. The tank can be operated by the driver, the gunner and the commander. (www.armedforces-int.com/.../scimitar_armoured_tank.html)
2. Blue Beach: one of three landing sites around San Carlos Water, at San Carlos itself; the others were Red Beach at Ajax Bay and Green Beach at Port San Carlos. Fourteen of those who died during the conflict are buried in a military cemetery at Blue Beach.
3. Menéndez: Mario Menéndez, a general in the Argentine army and military governor of the Malvinas.

11

THE ISLANDER

Gary Clement is 'an ex-marine, and I was part of Commando Logistics Regiment, working in San Carlos Water. I was there when the bombing took place. I went on to Goose Green to help with booby-trap removal around Goose Green. I ended up in Stanley; I moved back to the Falklands about twenty years ago and I have been there ever since. I joined SAMA to replace Terry Peck. I was a marine.

'I was born in 1955 in Kent. My grandfather was a marine and my father was in the navy and that's it, really. My grandfather was the influence on me wanting to join the marines for sure. I don't know why, really. It was just something that I really fancied from a young age – I think I was about 9 years old when I first said that I wanted to join the marines. At least, that's what everybody seems to remember. The difference was that lots of kids of 9 say they want to be something, but I meant it.

'We moved to Cornwall when I was about 11 and I remember when I was about 14 – something like that – the marines sent a team round the schools drumming up business. I said, "I am interested" and within a couple of months – I must have been 15 – I went off to Poole in Dorset and had a weekend there with the marines. Next thing I knew I was in. I joined at 16.

'I was 27 when the Falklands blew up and I was just finishing, actually. I was due out that year – in the October of 1982.

'I knew where the Falklands were because I had been stationed there in 1977 for twelve months on that old Naval Party 8901.¹ That was absolutely fabulous. It was a very small group, about forty-two of us including officers and senior ranks, and it was more like a family. You became part and parcel of the whole island way of life. Interestingly I got married down there that year to a Falkland Islander: a girl born in San Carlos and who spent all her life in San Carlos growing up. That was interesting because we had had completely contrasting experiences. Quite funny. When I brought her back to the UK after we got married I hired a car from Heathrow Airport to drive home and – I hadn't even given it a thought – but she'd never, ever been in a car in her life before, only a jeep and Land Rovers doing about 5 miles an hour. We are now divorced, but she was called Jane.'

Did you ever think the Argentinians ever really would invade it?

'I'm not using the word invade.

'I wanted to go back very shortly after leaving the services, to be honest. In the early 1980s I wanted to go back but she wouldn't go. She did not want to go. What she was fearful of was the education system for our children and also the hospital system, because she'd lost her father very early on in life. The education system when she went through it offered nothing unless you were one of the lucky few that picked up a scholarship to go to Argentina; you had no paperwork at all. There was a whole generation of clever kids with no paperwork and it is proving a problem in the islands now.

'There was a vast life outside Stanley whereas nowadays two men are doing what forty used to do with modern methods. When I was first down there the settlements and the farms looked very smart and the upkeep was tremendous. Now they look quite run-down. There were foreign managers and farm managers and these were men you'd tip your hat to.

'I had just got home from Norway when it started to brew up. We received a letter from my mother-in-law, possibly in the last ten days before it happened, and I will always remember reading it. She said, "This is possibly my last letter." They definitely knew something was going on. We hadn't even gone on leave. We were still sort of sorting kit and getting ready to go on leave. This was in Plymouth. I went and saw my sergeant-major and I said, "Well, I've got to go, boss"' – go to the Falklands, not go on leave.

'Originally it was intended to go to the Falklands with one unit strength and I said, "I'll be your man." He said, "Right, OK, I'll put you forward." He came to me the next day and he said, "I've been thinking about that. Are you sure? – because it means your wife is going to be left here with kids, blah, blah, blah." I said, "No, no, I am sure, I need to go." But then, of course, it snowballed and became a big thing and the chances of one unit doing it were obviously gone. I went down on the *Sir Lancelot* as far as Ascension Island and then our job was to do all the stores and re-supplying. It was obvious that on leaving the UK things were just checked in to any hold that they could get and no-one really knew what was where or on what ship or anything. We were split up and put on different ships. There were three of us: me, a private and a staff sergeant. We moved to the Royal Fleet Auxiliary ship *Stromness*, which had 45 Commando on board. Our job was to go through the war stores which were on board there. That was a joke all by itself because we had stuff like old tin hats – we had Second World War stuff. We had spares for .303 rifles.[2] The whole thing was just a nonsense.

'Some of the stores that we had had obviously been locked up in some shed since the war and nobody had thought *oh my God, thirty-seven years have gone past since then*. We were literally throwing stuff over the side on a daily basis because it was absolutely useless and getting in the way. We were trying to sort the stuff on the basis of what needed to go to which ship. The staff sergeant was manifesting everything and someone would decide *right, this will go there*. We were pretty busy on there. It was at that time I remember the *Belgrano* was sunk and everybody on board was cheering and then of course the *Sheffield* was sunk and that was the day I think we all realised *hang on a minute, this isn't going to be sorted out diplomatically, we are going to war*. On our ship, anyway, the atmosphere changed totally. Everybody had been training and what-have-you all the way down but that day it got really serious and I think that was the turning point for us all.

'It was just such a shock that our modern ship could be sunk like that. It was an amazing thing really. It was full of technology and we couldn't work it out – and it made everybody feel vulnerable. There we were on a tin can with effectively no armament and no anything.

'To be honest, from that stage on I couldn't wait to get ashore. As a marine, that was my thing. Matelots seem to accept they are going to be locked down below and all that sort of thing, but I couldn't. I needed to be up on deck. I found it very difficult when they said, "OK, if there's an air-raid warning you are to stay down below" – very, very difficult. It was strange: the matelots found it very difficult when there wasn't a lock-down. It just shows you how you think differently as you are trained differently, I suppose.

'I went ashore in San Carlos Water. It's quite strange but I've got a total mental block. I can't remember how I got ashore, I can't remember to this day if I flew ashore or if I went on a landing craft. I couldn't possibly tell you. I've thought about it and I've asked that question lots of times and I really honestly can't. Anyway, I know I ended up ashore at Ajax Bay on the 21st so I was right in there. And thankfully I was, because there were air-raid warnings all day that day and I would not have been wanting to get locked-down then.

'It was just a madhouse. We obviously had to organise everything. We were the ordnance squadron so all armament, all food, everything that everybody needed was going through us. This was for the whole Task Force that was ashore. I can't recall our squadron strength but I suppose it would have been about forty to fifty men, absolute maximum. Mexi Floats would come ashore and we'd meet them, put food in the food pile, armament in the armament pile, depending on what it was. Also kit: that was the other thing that people didn't give credit to. It was one of the things that came out as the war went on – how much stuff was required to be reissued. If somebody died their equipment was coming in to us and going straight out for reissue. It was quite upsetting for some people – because we had some people arrive and say, "Oh, I've come for my mate's kit," and we'd say, "Sorry, it's already reissued." You were fighting a war and you can't worry about those things.

At the time it was *just get on with it* but now I realise we were working eighteen, twenty hours a day and that's when you make mistakes because you are just exhausted. For the first 4, 5, 6 days it was fine and of course every day you had this bloody air-raid warning, air-raid warning and the bombing of Ajax Bay, where the hospital got the bomb – that was on the fifth day, I think. That was just absolutely ridiculous in a way because, to be honest, people were starting to get a bit blasé. You get so many you think it'll be all right. The dinner queue was on and some people didn't leave the dinner queue. Unfortunately, that's what got hit – the galley. That's where I think about five people died. They probably kept their place in the queue and died for it. That was horrific and if I had a problem … well, I had a PTSD problem where I was reliving this bombing. I was on a gun and I fired off everything that was available to me on the gun. These two jets came across us and I watched and I could see it as plain as day: four bombs dropped off the bottom of this plane. I watched the parachutes open on the bombs and at that stage – I'd already fired off a belt of 200 rounds – I thought *I can't do any more* so I dived in a hole. Someody else dived on my back and I thought *thank God for that* – I've got some sort of protection. Then when the bomb went off …

'I was no more than 40 metres away from it.

'To be that close – there was a building between us, but even so it sucked every bit of air out of your lungs. An incredibly frightening thing. You sort of wait for the aftermath of it then you realise you can still move and all that sort of thing, and that's it, you're up and on the go again and trying to help wherever help was needed.

'The hospital was the very next building, no more than 20 metres – no more than 25. We were on the first bit of hard standing after the shoreline and then there was a very large Nissen hut and then right next to that – with an alleyway only wide enough to get a vehicle down – was the hospital. It was a pretty built-up area with lots of stonework. We were lucky, yes, but very lucky that all the bombs didn't go off. Two went off: one was fairly safe and out on the beach, one went into the roof of the hospital and stayed unexploded, one went straight through the wall into the hospital and sat for the remainder of the war in a cage that was in the hospital. I guess that the bomb-disposal people looked at it and decided *well, this is too dodgy to touch*. I know that in the hospital they continued right through to the end of the war with the bomb in the roof, right over the top of the operating theatre.

'From there, and for me it's a bit of a strange story, but I found like the head of a rocket or something embedded in a 105 casing. It had gone right through the box and embedded itself into the casing itself. I thought I'd better go and get the RAOC's equivalent of bomb disposal. He came up with me and I tried to describe this thing from about a hundred metres away and he wasn't having any of that so he made me come right up with him and he got hold of this thing and pulled it out of the box. I thought *oh my God*. Anyway the very next thing that happened then, 2 Para was having trouble at Goose Green with booby traps – things that had been left. The bomb-disposal guy was called and he said to my boss, "Right, I'll take him because he's really good at seeing things." He went with me and another marine. We cleared just about the whole of Goose Green between the three of us: all the hedgerows, all the beaches of everything that they'd left, and they'd left plenty. I wasn't at all trained to do this. It was quite funny because the first day he gave us a roll of white tape each and he said, "Right, anything you don't like put a circle of white tape round – otherwise have a go at it." By about an hour later I had used the whole roll of tape and I hadn't touched anything! I was told, "This is ridiculous – you're going to have to start looking." He gave us a bit more of a lesson on what we should be doing and that was it. The next day we probably used about a quarter of a roll of tape.

'This was just as Goose Green fell. It was at that time, when we were clearing all the weapons, that we were literally no more than about 25 metres away from where the armaments went up – booby-trapped – and the Argentinians were caught in the middle of it. They were moving their own stuff and all of a sudden that all went up. That was pretty horrific because you stood there knowing you couldn't get any closer and couldn't do anything for anybody that was there. These were prisoners who were basically moving their own stuff.'

I've heard at least one was so badly burned that he had to be shot.

'Nobody could do anything: it was just a mess. If it was only one I am surprised. It was that bad. I saw that. No, that did not give me nightmares, although the one thing that did was that all the way up the hedgerow. In Goose Green there was a big, big shed where all the prisoners were being kept and a hedgerow that ran away out of the settlement. Up there, that's where the bodies were being brought, all the Argentinian bodies. They were in such states of … death masks, if you like. They were in horrible positions, where they died in a hole, rigor mortis had set in and they were still in a sit-up position and all that kind of thing. I've got a really weird thing about dead bodies now. I can't stand them. Both my parents have died since and I couldn't have gone and seen them like some people go.

'I went back to San Carlos after we'd mopped up there and it was the big push and the work ethic then was so busy, it was amazing. Then we moved to Stanley once Stanley was taken.

'I did feel a sense of homecoming when I finally got to see my mother-in-law, yes. My immediate boss was a guy called Major Wilson and he was going to be running the resupply line in Stanley from the Hercules: come and do the drops from day one, more or less. He needed to be in there so we would have been among the first people into Stanley once it had fallen – because he didn't want to get there and find that everybody had moved in to these places and taken over. He wanted to find the best positions for us as a resupply unit to work from. He was adamant that we were first in there and we flew in very, very early. We landed on the playing field of what is now the school in Stanley, right next to the hospital, and funnily enough my wife's first cousin was playing around there on a motorbike – just a teenager. I didn't know who he was from Adam. I said, "Hey, d'you know Joan Middleton?" He said, "Joan Middleton? That's my auntie!" I said, "Well, go and tell her that Gary's arrived." And off he popped on his motorbike, one of the Argentinian motorbikes that had been claimed. Then when I got to see her that was the homecoming for me. And also I had a feeling we had done something really worthwhile. It was very, very strange, that, for a while. My boss decided we were going to live up on the side of Sapper's Hill and I managed to talk him round after the second day of freezing cold into going to live with mother-in-law. She put six of us up in the bedroom that she had in the loft.

'That was marvellous: much warmer than where we were.

'I left the service more or less on arriving back in the UK. We'd been in Norway and I was owed so much leave by the time we got back that they more or less said to me, "Well, do your leaving routine and you can go." So that's what I did. And that was it, really.

'I got into diving in the North Sea for nine years – in the oil game. My wife returned to the islands for her brother's wedding in 1989 and I'd been wanting to go back for four or five years. When she came back from her brother's wedding she realised that things had changed that much that it was probably OK to go, so we went back in the February of 1991. That's where I've been living ever since.

'When SAMA first started we all heard about it on the islands and I didn't get involved at all. I had pretty much given up on all that sort of thing. A good friend of mine was Terry Peck, the policeman. When I was stationed down there Terry and I played on the same football team. We were quite close friends. He tried to get me involved two or three times and I kept saying, "No, no, no." I ran The Globe tavern and hotel so I didn't have to get involved if I didn't want to. Terry got quite ill. I'd seen people come and go, he had people visit him, stayed with him and all that sort of thing. He'd done a bloomin' good job of getting this thing off and running, and also organising quite a bit of fundraising. I helped out where I could in a very, very small way – trying really not to get involved. I am one of those people who says yes and I follow it up. And no means no. I very rarely say no, that's the problem.

'There was the 20th-year pilgrimage, 2002. He asked me to get involved and I got quite heavily involved at that time. A group of us took over a big part of what he was supposed to be doing. I quite enjoyed it. I ended up as the mouthpiece and they started pushing me forward on the stage. "You talk to them, Gary, you know how to talk."

'Then Terry became very ill and he asked me if I'd stand in as chairman of SAMA for him whilst he was coming away – coming back to the UK for treatment. So I stepped in and took over whilst he was away. When he came back he'd been told to get out of it, he wasn't allowed to get involved, etc., etc., and Terry, God bless his soul, he couldn't say no to people and if people came down there needing his help he lived it with them. I think that's what got to him a lot in the end, and then he continued being friends with them when they left. He had a real network of people. So then the question was asked *would I take over?* I said yes, I would. The 25th-year pilgrimage was coming up – that was about two years off, I suppose.

'A lot of them had been on there right from the beginning so it was a chance to start afresh. I got a committee of real do-ers about me and we took it on. That 25-year pilgrimage was 250 people and it went as smoothly as you could wish, it really did. It was a pleasure to do. Lots of people say to me, "Why do you do it?" and it's nothing more than seeing the change on people's faces. Honestly, I have seen people arrive in absolute shock and horror, not knowing what's going to happen to them and will they be able to cope. I see them going back on the plane laughing and joking. I have seen total, total turnaround. I have had letters from people's wives saying, "Thank you for giving me my husband back" – the demons are the thing, and by no means is everybody suffering. Don't think that. But most are anxious when they are thinking about coming. I would say probably 80% of the people will write to you before they leave and say, "What about this, what about that?" You can tell that they are not completely sure, but of course as time's gone on now it's more word of mouth. People are saying, "Oh, don't worry, when you get down there Gary and his crew are going to look after you and the islanders will, too." That's the thing down there. The islanders will talk about it like it happened yesterday. So when the guys get in the pubs and places like that the islanders are more than happy to talk about it and the guys can't believe it – that there are people who want to talk about it.

'In the time I've been doing it – and I've probably helped well over a thousand people – I've known about three or four people that have gone home worse than when they arrived. That is extraordinary, it really is.

'Most of us who went down there had no idea what the islands were or what they were about or what they had to offer. We saw it at a time when it was drab, the weather was awful and to this day I think people in the UK still see the Falklands through those bleary eyes – as it was shown by the media at that time.

'If I say to people, "Oh, I live in the Falklands" they say, "Blimey, that cold, wet place" but nothing could be further from the truth. It's a fantastic place.

'I am the manager of the YMCA so I have had gainful employment all this time: never been out of work down there, no. And really it's through the YMCA that I have been lucky enough to hold down the position of chairman of SAMA, for which I have just been awarded the MBE. I have yet to collect it, but it has been announced [October 2010]. That's for the work I've done with SAMA and the veterans.

'Did I feel a bit sorry for the Argentinians? The older I've got, the more I realise we were probably the same. People talk about their youngsters and all that sort of thing – well, we had boys of 17 killed on Longdon, we had boys amongst us and they didn't know where the islands were before they went. Neither did more than half of the UK. The Argentinians were in the same boat as we were and I think that a lot of that is newspaper talk, if you like. It's something that's been built up and built up – a bad press on our part. I know the TV images of the wretched Argentinian conscripts, but we had people on mountain tops waiting and waiting and waiting for days with no sleeping bags, no nothing, in snow, so if you'd had pictures of those boys they would have looked wretched as well. I know the elements were against everybody but it was the same for us as it was for them. The difference, I think, was that we were a professional outfit looking after our own – let me be absolutely blunt with you: they weren't short of anything. Once Stanley fell and we started opening their containers they were not short of food, they were not short of warm clothing. It was all there. Their officers failed their men, that's for sure. If I felt sorry for anybody, it was the men that were failed by their officers.

'What stopped me really feeling sorry for them was what they did to islanders. They treated the islanders badly. If they went there to liberate them it's the worst kind of liberating you can imagine. They crapped on the floors in the middle of their living rooms. That kind of behaviour. And they weren't liberating it, not at all, no. They were there to seize it.'

Notes

1. Naval Party 8901: at the time of the Argentine invasion the islands were defended by Naval Party 8901 (NP 8901) which consisted of a Royal Marine garrison of about troop strength. It just so happened that NP 8901 was in the process of its annual rotation, with one troop arriving and one troop returning to the UK (a fact that Argentine intelligence did not know). Major Norman's troop of marines were being relieved by a troop commanded by Major Noott. This gave Rex Hunt, the governor, a total of sixty-seven Royal Marines to defend the Falklands. Major Norman, being the senior of the two majors, was placed in overall command and Noott was made military adviser to the governor. Twelve of Major Noott's troop had already sailed to South Georgia aboard HMS *Endurance* under the command of Lieutenant Keith Mills. They had been sent to keep an eye on some Argentinians at Leith. (www.britains-smallwars.com/Falklands/NP8901.html)
2. A .303 rifle: once the standard-issue rifle in the British armed forces, the venerable .303 had been obselete for many years by 1982.

PART TWO

'While I was serving I was hiding it through alcohol. When I came out the only job I could get was as a security guard. I was working long hours and Kirsty became ill, so I was concentrating on her then … when Kirsty had settled down and was getting better my body just gave up and said *that's it.*'

Mark Hiscutt, The Missile Man

'I'm still finding it difficult, quite frankly. I've never really settled down. I joined the Prison Service in March of 1983 and I have to say that is probably the biggest mistake I made.'

Brian Bilverstone, The Radio Operator

'I don't know why I haven't had PTSD. I've never been to see anybody. Whether it's just something I keep to myself and just get on with life or what, I don't know.'

Steve Wilkinson, The Marine Engineer

'I think the problems started in the mid-'90s when it struck me with feeling a little depressed. I got made redundant and I started to reflect on everything, trying to find a reason, but never really put it down to anything to do with the Falklands.'

David Buey, The Helicopter Expert

'PTSD? I'm all right. There's a lot of people got it. I think the missus might think I do have it sometimes because I lose my temper.'

Mario Reid, The Heavy Mover

'Half of it is the guilt of survival when your mates died. You'll be sat there watching something on telly and it will give you a flashback. You go from being a happy, self-confident, tough man and everything inside your body just turns round.'

Dave Brown, The Lucky Paratrooper

'I didn't have PTSD, not particularly, no. There were a lot of lads who did: you tend to find that the lads who suffer from it aren't the ones that get hurt. Most of the lads have what I think is called survivor guilt, it's the lads who think *well, why did I get away with it?* He got killed, he got hurt and I never got touched.'

Jimmy O'Connell, The Unlucky Paratrooper

'It hit me five years later. It doesn't happen straight away. Then all of a sudden I'd gone through a divorce, I couldn't hold a job down, the drinking kicked in and basically PTSD was not recognised in any way, shape or form. All the doctor did was prescribing me anti-depressants.'

William (Billy) Field, The Prisoner

'You are a coiled spring, but in a military environment you're well controlled. When you're in a civilian environment you're not, and that's when things go wrong.'

Graeme Golightly, The 29-Year-Old-Teenager

12

PERSONAL CONFLICTS

'The Post Traumatic Stress Disorder (PTSD)[1] is not difficult for me to speak about,' Mark Hiscutt says quietly. 'I left the services in 1988 and I actually broke down in 1999. While I was serving I was hiding it through alcohol, but it was there. When I came out the only job I could get was as a security guard. I was working long hours and [wife] Kirsty became ill so I was concentrating on her. Then what they believed happened was, come '99 when Kirsty had settled down and was getting better, my body just gave up and said *that's it*. Kirsty tells me I went downstairs one morning to go to work, stood at the bottom of the stairs and burst out crying.'

These are heavy words coming from a deep place and they demand a context. As I explained in the Introduction, each of the eleven interviewees volunteered to speak for this book and in each interview they inevitably reached the period after the conflict. They spoke quite naturally (and largely unprompted) about PTSD – whether they had had it, still had it or hadn't had it at all – as if it was simply a continuation of their stories, in much the same way as they spoke about their subsequent lives and careers. I do not mean the word *simply* to imply that they spoke carelessly about it, or they regarded it as in any way less than a very serious matter. I do mean *simply* to imply that, to those who had it, the PTSD was a natural continuation, an integral part.

As you might imagine, these brave men were unafraid to open themselves up, unafraid to bare themselves with astonishing candour and none were, I sensed, in the least bit embarrassed. That's a different kind of bravery, what Napoleon called '2 o'clock in the morning courage', where, whatever state you are in, you face yourself and find what you need.

There is another context. This chapter follows the sequence of the book, with each interviewee appearing in the order I spoke to them, rather than having a shape grafted onto it: hence, beginning with Hiscutt and finishing with Graeme Golightly. They say what they say and if there are repetitions, that's the way they are and that's what they say.

There is, also, a theme running through. PTSD is well known now and mercifully being treated, but was much less so in 1982 and arguably unknown in the long centuries of warfare before that. Dave Brown (The Lucky Paratrooper) gives his feelings on that full vent and he is probing a staggering question: how many thousands upon thousands of servicemen all down those long centuries suffered it, had their lives tormented by it, and had no idea what was happening or, if they cried out for help, nobody else had any idea what was happening?

In that sense the Falklands veterans are a bridge between then and now.

We left Hiscutt at the bottom of his stairs in tears. 'She phoned up the company I was working for. I wasn't a security officer any more, I was working for BP – a bit ironic in that they'd brought me back from the Falklands [on the commandeered *British Esk*]. She spoke to the occupational health adviser at work who she knew anyway. This lady was an American. Kirsty was telling her my symptoms. I have always had nightmares and I've struggled sleeping as well. That is all part of Post Traumatic Stress Disorder. Everybody has dreams, but in 1982 you had nightmares. The health adviser made a few phone calls and got in touch with an organisation called Combat Stress and spoke to someone on my behalf.'

This is how they describe themselves:

Combat Stress is the UK's leading military charity specialising in the care of veterans' mental health. We treat conditions such as Post Traumatic Stress Disorder, depression and anxiety disorders. Our services are free of charge to the veteran.

Since 2005 the number of ex-service men and women seeking our help has risen by 72% and we have a current caseload of more than

4,300 individuals. This already includes 102 veterans who have served in Afghanistan and 400 who served in Iraq.

In March 2010 our Patron, HRH The Prince of Wales, launched our major fundraising campaign – The Enemy Within Appeal. The £30 million, 3-year appeal is designed to help us treat the escalating number of psychologically injured veterans who are turning to us for help, by:

Establishing 14 Community Outreach Teams nationwide

Enhancing clinical treatment at our three short-stay treatment centres.[2] [Full contact details are given in the footnote.]

When Hiscutt 'went into work the following day I had a long chat with the American lady and she told me who'd she'd been in touch with and they'd be phoning me. That's how I got in touch with Combat Stress.

'One of the recurring dreams – nightmares, whatever you want to call it – is I'm inside the ship, it's smoke everywhere and there's banging on a door. I couldn't open it and I'm hearing screams. When I met up with *Bones* he was having the same nightmare and he goes to Combat Stress as well, now. I was telling one of the psychologists that it was strange we were having the same dreams and the psychologist said, "Well, was it really a dream or was it a memory?" I'm trying to keep it as a dream.

'I'm one of the fortunate ones with PTSD. I keep working and I've got a very understanding employer. The ones with real problems are the ones who it takes hold of to the point where you have to give up work.

'I don't like being in large crowds – like going into supermarkets. I don't socialise because that would mean going in to pubs. If I am going to a reunion that's different because I'm with people I know and can trust, guys off the *Sheffield*, for example.

'In 2004, I was struggling, really struggling with work because it was an open-plan office. There was lots of noise and I don't like noise. I asked if I could work from home and they said no, because there was no need, really. It was getting to the point where I might have had to give up working, but a job came up within BP that I applied for and I asked if I could work from home. They said yes. It's turned out nicely because

I work from home now. I do go to the office a couple of times a week and I can manage that. I'm on medication.

'I go to Combat Stress at the treatment centre in Leatherhead three times a year for two weeks. When you walk or drive into the place you relax, you feel like the weight is taken off you. You're leaving the baggage outside because it's only ex-service personnel in there. The nurses and the staff are civilians, but we trust them and because it's all ex-service – army, navy, air force – you get the banter and you get the jokes as well.

'The other thing is they have an activity centre so you can go in there and paint or whatever. It's surprising the talent of the people. I'd never painted but I paint now. I'd never even thought of it – because I can't draw I'd thought I can't paint. I do abstract and it only takes me 5–10 minutes to do one. In that 5–10 minutes my mind is blank. I'm not thinking about anything and that's a nice place to be. Combat Stress have had art shows and they've sold a couple of my paintings for me.

'What I'm having to deal with at the moment is that I look at three *mes*: there's the me that goes to work and I put an act on there; everybody sees Mark as a jolly guy who'd do anything for anybody. There's the me the painter to whom people say, "Yes, we like your paintings, we'll buy them." And there is the me at home, which people don't see. That's the one that the family sees. The wife notices as the anniversary – 4 May – gets closer and closer that I get more short tempered when I'm at home. I am not aware of it.

'My theory is that 1) it helps me but 2) it could also help someone else. That's why I've done interviews with Sky and ITN and so on: not to say, "Hey, look at me" but in the hope that perhaps someone will see it and say, "I recognise the signs in my partner" and understand there is help out there.

'The downside to PTSD is my nephew suffered with it. He was in the army in Bosnia. He took his life about five years ago, a couple of days before his second son's 1st birthday. He just couldn't cope any more with the negative side to PTSD. The effect it's had on my kids is that they keep looking at me and saying, "You all right, dad?" Those thoughts do come into your mind but then you have to cancel them.

'You know there's a chapel called the Falklands Memorial Chapel at Pangbourne? It's a beautiful, modern chapel – outside there are sculptures, someone has made some albatrosses and there's a cairn at the back which lads have brought stones back to make and then added to it. It is one of the most peaceful places I know. Inside there are kneelers which have the names of all the service personnel who died and all the ships that took part. Every year on liberation day, 14 June, a service is held. I go every 4 May and I pick up the kneelers. There are two people I always think about who never came home: Number One, because I never found him, and a bloke called Tony Marshall.

'Tony was the leading chef. I always think about Tony because while we were away in the Gulf we went down to Mombasa for a bit of R&R, and while we were there some of us went on a safari. I remember sharing a tent with Tony. One memory I have – although I don't know if it's true because my mind could be playing tricks with me – is that I'm pretty sure he said to me that his wife was expecting their first child when he got home. And he never got home.

'So whenever I go to Pangbourne I always look out for Number One and Tony's kneelers and just hold them at 2 o'clock. That was when we were hit. So at 2 o'clock I am always there with a couple of kneelers in my hands or sitting near them and having time to myself.'

Brian Bilverstone (The Radio Operator) answered the question *when you left, what did you do, because many people find this the most difficult part?* with: 'I'm still finding it difficult, quite frankly. I've never really settled down. I'm a bit of a doom-and-gloom merchant. It depends. I do suffer with depression from time to time and then I can be very down.

'I joined the prison service in March of 1983 and I have to say that is probably the biggest mistake I made in my life. I did that for three and a half years. Basically I thought it was like the services but not quite. Honestly, I didn't know myself very well back then, but I know now that I am not really suited to that type of life at all. I was 21 when I joined the prison service. Who does know themselves when they are 21? It seemed like safety and security, one uniform for another. I have often said since that if if I'd known then what I know now I'd have buggered off somewhere – gone to America or Australia or just *something*. They call it finding themselves nowadays, don't they? The gap year – but nobody had a gap year in our day.

'So I did that for three and a half years. I joined at Shepton Mallet, I spent just over two years at Wormwood Scrubs – I was at Wakefield Training College and they put out the preference forms of jails you wanted to go to. I wrote down Shepton Mallet and they said to me, "You're not married. Which London prison do you want?" That was it. I trained as a hospital officer while I was at Wormwood Scrubs, which is nursing. Then I went off to Wandsworth nick. The nursing I enjoyed, being a prison officer I didn't. I yanked it, I pulled the plug.

'What did I do after that? I've written a list. I left in August '86 and joined a company selling insurance. That was horrendous: cold-calling, and it's given me an innate dislike of the phone ever since. I don't like phoning people. If I can possibly contact them by text or email I will.

'In December of that year I joined a courier company because I had a motorbike, but that was in Guildford and I was married by that time living in Carshalton. They kept wanting me to go to the other side of the country and then to Guildford before going back to Carshalton, even if I'd had to come *through* Carshalton to get to Guildford. So I knocked that on the head. Then I was unemployed for a little while – in fact I've been unemployed a few times on and off.

'I worked for an agency doing security work and spent some time spraying oxygen cylinders. That was really interesting work! – some were black and some were orange. That, would you believe, was piece-work. I was paid on the number of oxygen cylinders I did. I worked for a firm doing security work and I always remember that because I was on multiple rates on Sundays, £2.75 an hour. I had a big falling out with the manager because those companies take the rise out of their employees.

'I left. I worked for a nursing service – I was a nursing auxiliary because the qualifications I'd got in Home Office employment didn't count in the NHS so I was a bed-pan operative working round nursing homes and hospitals in Surrey. It was all right but again I fell out with my employer – I have a history of doing this, unfortunately.

'Between 1987 and 1990 I went to Hamley's toy shop as a sales assistant, never having worked in a shop before, ended up as the manager of the Staines branch. I went back to Sutton where I'd started and managed that branch. We moved house out of the area so obviously I had to leave the toy shop. I was self-employed doing family history research before the days of the internet, when it was difficult to do. If people wanted it they had to have someone do the leg-work for them. I used to go up to London on the train and spend all day walking round the different record offices gathering information. I did that for five years, during which time I moved up to Clacton. Because I was further away from London it was more difficult to do.

'I did work for an ex-Royal Marine who was a private investigator – probate research for him, which was sort of related work [to the family histories], but in the end it just wasn't paying the bills. I got a job in a petrol station – desperate times because I had to pay the mortgage. I was there not quite a year but eventually I got work with Essex Rivers Healthcare Trust at Colchester Hospital. I trained as an orthopedic technician, qualified, and ended up a manager, but once again I had a falling out.

'In 2004 I started ABS Embroidery which is based at home. I do logo embroidery, a lot for the military – well, military people not *the* military. Mainly it means putting logos on shirts. When I came out of the navy I joined the Sea Cadet Corps and I was 23 years there [and am now back after a four-year break] so I have a lot of contacts and I do a lot of embroidery for them.

'I have always found it very difficult to get on with people. I get on with them for a little while or on a non-permanent basis, shall we say, but finding someone who will put up with my mood swings is quite difficult. I don't think there's a lot of doubt I've had PTSD but I've never had a diagnosis. I haven't been to the special clinics. I don't know why. I don't even know how to explain it, to be honest. I've always been a bit – what's the word? – sensitive. I took things a bit personally at times and I still do sometimes. I suppose that's part of it.

'The black depressions: I didn't used to get them. I get them now although not as much as in the past. That was very much post-Falklands and possibly induced by the Falklands. I don't know. I suppose I'm a bit worried about going in case I see someone and they tell me to buck my ideas up because there's nothing wrong with me. Or maybe they'll say there's a lot wrong with me and I may not want to know that, either. I've muddled through. I'm divorced but I've now got a partner who seems to be able to put up with me.

'There are things I have done in my life which I am not proud of and which I might not have done had it not been for the fact that I served in the Falklands, if you understand what I mean. It made me far more cynical – far more.'

How do you feel now with the thirtieth anniversary coming?

'I find that question quite interesting, actually, and I've been asked it before, as you can imagine. It's only thirty years, you know. I used to belong to the Naval Christian Fellowship because I was brought up in the Methodist Church. I hear people going on about how it reaffirmed their faith and all that. I could see myself thinking *well, what a lot of bollocks*. It opened my eyes to what a bunch of maniacs people really are and how religion and superstition and all that sort of thing is made up to suit people's agenda. Really, what is the basis of it all? I don't know how people can have that sort of faith, I really don't. I suppose they need it to make sense of things but how can someone stand there and look at a Royal Marine with his leg blown off and say, "Thank you for saving me, God."? How can they do that? I couldn't. I didn't.

'I saw some unpleasant things. I don't like to speak about them. I don't like crying.'

Steve Wilkinson (The Marine Engineer) 'left the services in 2000 so I did my twenty-two years'. Of the Falklands he remembers 'silly little bits and I miss big bits out. It's like the stress disorder. One of the guys off the *Exeter* has it – I knew him quite well – but I don't think I have. I've memories and a pile of slides but it doesn't worry me. I don't think it's ever coming back to bite me. Some of the boys have said, "You want to get yourself down there and put everything to rest," but it's only just now, as I'm getting a little bit older, that I'm thinking *I don't think I've got anything to put to rest.* That may be because my mind has excluded certain memories and that's the way that the brain has looked on to life. It can happen with the body, too: *I've had it, that's enough.* There are friends who haven't coped. [A full discussion of the problems of going back appears in the next chapter.]

'On the first Wednesday of every month veterans can go to a place in Portsmouth and see an Irish psychiatrist, Dermot. He's done a lot for the stress disorder. I spoke to him for a short time some time ago but I've never been to see anybody about what happened or anything else. Whether it's something I keep to myself and just get on with life or what I don't know, but it must take different people in different ways.

'How has it affected at least one of my friends and not affected me? Maybe a shrink can tell me if I sat down and talked to him for a couple of days. My friend has had his first set of treatment [summer 2010] after he'd been diagnosed following a review. He was saying he very rarely slept. He was on the same ship as me, and this is why I say what I say about taking different people in different ways. We were both in a similar environment. I see him now and again and he doesn't seem too bad when we meet up.'

Wilkinson didn't become involved in veterans' activities 'for a long time. It's only a few years ago that I started getting together with the others. I don't know why that was. Since I've come out of the services I've got remarried, bought the house that my wife was living in and it was a case of *you get a job, you keep the job and you finish work at 5.00 at night.* The last thing you want to do is go out and try and meet people you've not seen for years. You're trying to make your life where you live.

'I am associated with the South Atlantic Medal Association – there were almost 30,000 medals issued. The Association numbers only about 3,000 so where's the other 26–27,000? Maybe people aren't interested or don't want to be reminded. I've had to learn to drive. We have a caravan and the South Atlantic Medal Association wanted a volunteer secretary for the camping and caravaning branch. I thought *OK, I can do that* so I volunteered and they took me on.

'There is talk about getting more help for the veterans. That can be put down a lot to Iraq and Afghanistan, because the guys and girls are doing tour after tour. We just got hit once. The fact remains, however, that in our conflict more people have died at their own hand since the invasion than were killed during it so there has to be something which stimulates it, which sets somebody off.'

David Buey (The Helicopter Expert) 'had a few sleepless nights when I got back. I do recall one night when I was on the *British Tay*. Well, it was the early hours of the morning and not many people about. I couldn't sleep and I was walking down the side of the ship with my hands pressed against the bulkhead like you would if you were on a window ledge. I sat in silence with one of the cooks and when I did speak to him he didn't speak back. I looked to see where he'd gone and he'd gone back into the galley. I was out there on my own and I panicked because there I was out in the darkness again. This was within a week of it all happening. It freaked me out a bit.

'I've always felt that I was quite emotionally strong and even at 20 I'd still done a lot of things – I'd been skiing, had a motor bike, I'd lived a bit and now I'd lived a lot. I think the problems started in the mid-1990s when it struck me with feeling a little depressed. I was made redundant and I started to reflect on everything, trying to find a reason why I'd taken my eye off the ball, but never really put it down to anything to do with the Falklands. It didn't dawn on me that that potentially could have been the reason. It had been thirteen years before, after all.

'By this stage I'd heard that some of the people who'd been down there and I'd known had committed suicide or taken to drink and drugs and ended up in prison.

'In the late 1990s I went and had a series of treatments with a psycho-therapist to try and get me out of my depressions. That worked for a while and then about 2006 I went back and had additional treatment. I am currently taking anti-depressants. I think that anybody meeting me wouldn't know and to be fair it wasn't until the twenty-fifth celebrations that I actually felt that I was ready to go and get involved – I'd been back to the naval station at Yeovilton for the twentieth anniversary but it wasn't a celebration, just a get-together, really. A friend who was still serving invited me, I went along and I met a lot of people that I had served with. After that people were saying, "You ought to get involved in this" and, "You ought to get involved in that" and I didn't feel like I could or was prepared to.'

Mario Reid (The Heavy Mover) says, 'PTSD? I'm all right. There's a lot of people got it – I think the missus might sometimes think I have because I lose my temper.

'People like animals more than human beings – they think more of their pets – and I'm more of the other way round. It's ridiculous.'

Reid was referring to a truly astonishing story about a 66-year-old great-grandmother, Joan Higgins of Greater Manchester, who ran a pet shop and unwittingly sold a goldfish to a 14-year-old – by law you have to be 16. She was fined £1,000, curfewed and electronically tagged for two months.

'That's probably why I left the UK. I knew I wouldn't cope, I'd end up killing somebody. There's no respect. Having been institutionalised with the military it was difficult coming out. When I left, the ratio was 1 in 3 would die within five years. Why do they die? Different lifestyle. Could be heart attack, could be suicide, not coping with the change of lifestyle. How did I cope? I came out here to Spain! We've been here seven years now, nearly eight. The way of life is like when you grew up: your kid can go out on the streets and be looked after by everybody else, so it's totally different. You can leave your car unlocked and so on. I think that helped me because I immersed myself in re-forming the house I live in and life just went on from there.

'I went to the Gulf War but I wasn't anywhere special, once again moving stores, setting up camp, stuff like that. I got divorced after – she left me. I remarried quite quickly. We were both waiting for our divorce papers from the same judge. Mine went first, my missus Sarah's went second and we went off to St Lucia to get married.

'We live right down near Malaga in the countryside. I give guitar lessons and we've just set up a guitar outlet to try and get my daughter a job. She's due to finish school this year. My Spanish is good now.'

Dave Brown (The Lucky Paratrooper) 'got out in 1985. Discipline was going down, morale went down, alcohol problems started surfacing. The para regiments drink anyway but it was a different sort of drinking. Even the fights were getting really out of hand. This was the early sign of Post Traumatic Stress. Now we say Post Traumatic Stress because Post Traumatic Stress Disorder is when you've not been treated for it, you've had no help or support and it's been in your system that long it's a disorder. You can treat Post Traumatic Stress if it's captured and you get it out of your system.

'Our briefing when we got back was go home, get pissed for six weeks and forget about it, so it's no wonder that so many lads couldn't cope with it. When they were still in battalion they had their mates with them, they could talk with them, laugh and joke about it. When they hit civvy street and they were in a council flat on their own that's when the problems started hitting home. I know because I've been there.

'In World War One they called them cowards and shot them at dawn but for the officers they had a big hospital in Scotland. In World War Two with the RAF bomber crews they called it lack of moral fibre, they were srtipped of their ranks and sent to a special place near Chesterfield – a hospital – and kept there out of the way. And these were some of the bravest men: they'd flown like twenty-five missions, yet they were called cowards.

'The MoD say they weren't aware of it but they were. They knew all about the problems that could happen and would happen, and are going to happen now with Afghanistan and Iraq. I put it this way: they turned the light switch on but they forget to turn it off. You've got to find a way of turning that light switch off. That is difficult. For me? Yep.

'You can talk to a hundred different people from different units, even navy lads, and they'll tell you the same thing. Half of it is the guilt of survival when your mates died. You'll be sat there watching something on telly and it will give you a flashback, an incident that reminds you of when you were down there. You go from being a happy, self-confident, tough man ro everything inside your body turning round. You can't sleep and you don't care about anything.

'I got into a load of trouble – fighting, alcohol, you name it. Most of us have done it. I ended up being told to go and see Morgan O'Connell, who was one of the two Task Force psychologists sent down [Dr Morgan O'Connell of Spire Portsmouth Hospital]. He was Royal Navy. It meant people weren't treated as mental health patients, stuck on a ward and pumped full of drugs. I was booked on a course for four weeks – it didn't cure anything or solve anything but it did make me more aware of what I was living with and it answered a lot of questions to why my life had been **** for the last six years.

'Nowadays the Royal Marines have a system where every time they come back from operations they get all the corporals together, then they get all the lads together and they talk it through. *If you've got problems, talk to us about it.*'

By contrast: 'we were fighting-fit paratroopers and fair play – because I've talked to a few of them – the last thing you want in a regiment like that is to say you feel like a wimp. And you're worried you're going to be marked down and lose the chance of promotion and everything, so you keep it quiet. In a nutshell, you are trapped by your own macho. You think *I'm OK, I can handle this.*

'My main problem was of one my mates died and I was next to him when he died. We tried to keep him alive. When I came out into civvy street, if any of my mates were in trouble I'd stand up for them because I didn't want to see anyone else hurt. I ended up in a load of trouble, getting arrested quite a few times, because I just stepped forward thinking *to hell with it, it's happening again.*

'My PTSD is controllable. It's under control for one reason: I do therapy courses for other lads but in fairness that helps me. It's self-help, basically.

'If wives or girlfriends ring up and say they are slightly worried, I run through the symptoms and say, "Right, RAC – as in the Royal Automobile Club: Recognise I've got a problem, Admit I've got a problem – because when you deny it you shut it off – and Control the problem. Long term, PTSD is not curable, but it is controllable. That's what I try to say to them. You are never going to get rid of the bloody nightmares and flashbacks and panic attacks and everything else, but you can control it if you recognise it for what it is and know what it is. Do not go, "I'm a mental case, I'm written off." I say, "You could have been in a plane crash, you could have been on the *Herald of Free Enterprise* or in the Paddington train crash. That can cause Post Traumatic Stress.

'I get phone calls, sometimes at 3 o'clock in the morning, from wives saying, "He's lost it this time, he's going to kill himself" and things like that. I'll sit and talk to them all night long if I have to because I don't want another phone call saying, "He's just taken his own life."

'I don't sleep well at nights because I'm scared every time I go to bed I'm going to get flashbacks. I either take sleeping tablets when I'm tired and they knock you out completely or I'll sit up til daylight when I know it's safe. That refers back to what happened on the hill at Goose Green and that night. I can only unwind when I've seen daylight and I know I'm safe. That is going back to what it was *before* that night at Goose Green.

'The thing is, it isn't just with the Parachute Regiment, it's with the navy lads – everyone. It's like we are human time-bombs waiting to explode. I am seriously worried about Afghanistan. All right, we had a short sharp, brutal conflict over a couple of weeks period – maybe three, four – in the Falklands and that was it. These lads in Afghanistan are in firefights every day. Some of them have done three or four tours and now it's all IEDs [Improvised Explosive Devices] and suicide bombers. One minute they're talking to their mates, the next minute their mates are in pieces at the side of the road next to them. The problem with Afghanistan is you don't know who's who. One minute a man is shooting at you, the next minute he's shaking your hand …'

At least Dave Brown was spared that.

Jimmy O'Connell (The Unlucky Paratrooper) 'didn't have PTSD, not particularly, no. There were a lot of lads who did but, to be honest, you tend to find that the lads who suffer from it aren't the ones who were hurt. I know there are exceptions to the rule but most of the lads have what I think is called survivor guilt. It's the lads who think *well, why did I get away with it? He got killed, he got hurt and I never got touched.* I've heard that said before: it's the people who get away with it.

'It's just luck. When your number's up your number's up.'

William (Billy) Field (The Prisoner) says, 'my situation now is I'm still out of work. I can't hold a job down. I've had more jobs than the job centre. I just get very despondent with some things. I don't like being taken for a ride and some jobs might only be short term. I enjoy drifting, I enjoy picking a bit here and picking a bit there. I have tried many, many different jobs and been successful at most of them – very good with my hands. I am a clever person but I've never stuck at anything.

'I'm very restless and I think that might come from the Falklands: got to keep moving. If you start trying to explain to people how it was for you when you were in the services and how it is for you now, they haven't a clue. You go to the job centre and tell them exactly what you've gone through, what you've done and achieved, and they sort of just look at you.

'It's always the simple, trivial things that wind me up. Big things I can deal with, cope with straight away, but the smallest things send me over the edge. You're going into a war zone. Everbody on the lower deck had the use of metal trays to have their dinner off, because you can't have glass and china and crockery being thrown about – but the officers still had to have their plates, had to have their glasses, had to have their cups and they'd just leave them anywhere and everywhere: simple little things like that, and you think *hang on a minute, why do you have to eat separately? We were all going down there together so why can't we all eat out of one bloody bowl? Why are we having to have three bloody kitchens open when it can all be catered for in one?* I found that hard to take.

'As you're going towards a war zone, the first thing you're going to do on the ship is find stuff that burns and get it off. The lower rates have got to box everything, strap everything up, put this away, put that away – but the officers, no, no, no, they still kept their tables and their chairs and their carpets. They've still got to have their luxuries.

'The PTSD can hit you five years after, it will hit you later, it doesn't happen straight away – and then, all of a sudden, I'd gone through a divorce, I couldn't hold a job down, the drinking kicked in and, basically, PTSD was not recognised in any way, shape or form. All the doctor did was precribe me anti-depressants. Mixing them with alcohol made it worse. Then it really got totally out of hand. I went on a different road, I suppose. I was out every Friday and Saturday night drinking and fighting and that was my way of life then.

'I'm on a building site like fourteen storeys up, no scaffold, no harness, no nothing, totally off my face with drink. I was doing things like you wouldn't believe possible. It's been a constant drink ever since I left and every time you try to go forward you end up in hospital. I've been in hospital quite a few times. Bodily wise, I've come out of it quite well, but it has taken its toll. I've had so many broken bones and cuts and scars and everything else. That's all alcohol related, anyway.

'Then you have a prison record and that's another thing, see. You are on the ladder going down and, when you hit the "big time" and do something stupid, the judge looks down the list and he finds your record. I dealt with prison quite well, actually. It was very beneficial to me, to be honest. I had five years – I did eighteen months, I appealed my sentence. I was then released on bail for four months and the case was overturned, unsatisfactory verdict. I then went back to court, was found guilty again and sentenced to another five years.

'I went in for armed robbery on a post office on St Patrick's Day. I was absolutely off my head on medicated drugs – prescribed drugs – and alcohol and I walked into a post office and just asked for the money with a knife. The next day I realised. I crapped myself. I thought ****** *hell, what have you done?* I was with someone else, as well. The long and the short of it is, putting my hand on my heart, I did do it. I did deny it obviously: I don't want to go to prison – but you don't see any way out of it. Then the alcohol takes over even more.

'Prison was OK because, in many ways, it was like the army. I'm very regimented, even at home today. I still rolls my pants and socks up into little balls and put them in my drawer. I think it's a bit like OCD – Obsessive Compulsive Disorder – because you are forever putting things straight in your cupboards, in a straight line, that sort of thing. The remote controls for the television have got to be straight. That's why it is OCD.

'In prison I got a gold award for musical peformance. I played the narrator in *Blood Brothers*, played the Mikado, played Wilfred Shadbolt in *Yeoman of the Guard*, played Officer Murdoch in *Titanic*. Inside, I had my own drama group: plenty of things going on. Now, I write poetry, which I find is easy, very easy. I write short stories – in fact I've got a couple of stories in my head at the moment. There's a couple of books I want to write, too, and I think one will be called *From HMS to HMP* [From Her Majesty's Services to Her Majesty's Prisons]. I've always had a good sense of humour, I like joking, I like laughing.'

Graeme Golightly (The 29-Year-Old Teenager) has already said that 'you were youngsters, you all thought you were Schwarzenegger and you could take on anybody. The potential flashpoint was – and the paras must have thought the same, because I have spoken to many a para since – that any small reason we would have blown off.'

Reflecting, he says: 'To deal with this kind of explosion – when people come back from Afghanistan or wherever – they now have a decompression stage by stopping off in Cyprus and have some time out to talk about their experiences, whereas in our day you didn't get that. I think it's great it has been recognised that you do need a decompression stage when you come back to, effectively, spill out what your experiences were and how it affected you and so on. We have taken a great step forward.'

You could have been in the war, flown home and within twenty-four hours be in the pub on the corner.

'You are going from an unreal environment to a totally civilised and call it mundane but quiet environment. It needs a bit of getting your head round how you comprehend that change, especially if it happens very quickly. I was in Ireland getting shot at and, in less than a half-hour flight, I was back in the UK. I'm looking at TV and seeing the people who were trying to have a go at me, which is kind of surreal.

'We were lucky enough to be on the *Canberra* and when the Falklands conflict was over we had that sail-back to decompress. On the *Canberra* we all got chilled out and that was a great part of what went on. The sad state is – and it happens today as well – you are dealing with youngsters who have been highly trained to, let's cut to the chase, be vicious. They have been brainwashed so that when I say, "Jump" they say, "How high?" They will implicitly listen to an order of any kind from a senior rank and do it, and when you've got that control in a military environment you can manipulate it as you see fit. *I want you to start killing, I don't want you to stop until we get to that point.*

'When you are then brought back onto the civilian street and you are not directed, where does that focus of your training go? That's where sometimes people go straight to the bar, start drinking and then all of a sudden they think that they can do what they want.

'I'm lucky in my lifestyle because I saw at a very early age the differences between the coiled spring, which is controlled in a military environment, and the absence of control in a civilian environment. I look back on how my personality – my DNA – is built up and I can read my life now to see what went on, what I've come through and what I've moved on to. I understood it and that was very, very important. If you understand what you are dealing with, if you understand the complications, you can deal with it accordingly.

'There's many military personnel with a disgruntled family background who kind of keep themselves to themselves, so when they go through a stressful situation they don't let anybody else in on it, they you do the *Men are from Mars, Women are from Venus* thing. You go into your cave and you try to sort it out yourself, which is the worst thing you can do, because you are alone and knocking your head against the wall. Women talk openly about their problems and men don't.

'I recognised from an early stage that I had to talk about it rather than let it bottle up. I was lucky enough – and I do say I am lucky enough – that my DNA helped me to do that. Not everybody has this but I am lucky to have a sensible approach to how I dealt with pressure and with stressful situations and how I saw they were never transferred to civilian life. 'You could say, "Well, I must have hidden it" or, "I must have bottled it up and at some point it's going to come out", but I don't think I did.'

Notes

1. In 2010 the Associated Press reported that a 2-year-old German Shepherd called Gina, trained to sniff bombs, completed a tour of Iraq and after what she'd experienced returned home to Colorado 'cowering and fearful. When her handlers tried to take her into a building, she would stiffen her legs and resist.' A military vet diagnosed PTSD and insisted it could affect dogs in the same way as people, without meaning any disrespect whatsoever to servicemen and women. After a year, Gina was responding well to treatment.

2. Combat Stress (in their own words):
   Contact us:
   We would be delighted to hear from anyone who needs our help – or indeed from anyone who'd like to help us, perhaps by way of a donation, or as a volunteer fundraiser.
   If you need our support, or know someone who does, please click on the 'Need Help & Advice' button above [on www.combatstress.org.uk under the sub-heading 'Contact Us']. You will be directed to your local Community Outreach Support Desk. Also note: our services are free of charge.
   For general enquiries or if you wish to deal with Head Office, our contact details are as follows:
   Telephone: 01372 587000
   Email: contactus@combatstress.org.uk
   Postal address: The Chief Executive, Combat Stress, Tyrwhitt House, Oaklawn Road, Leatherhead, Surrey, KT22 0BX
   Audley Court, Shropshire: Combat Stress, Audley Court, Audley Avenue, Newport, Shropshire, TF10 7BP; Telephone: 01952 822700; Fax: 01952 822701
   Hollybush House, Ayrshire: Combat Stress, Hollybush House, Hollybush by Ayr, Ayrshire, KA6 7EA; Telephone: 01292 561300; Fax: 01292 561301.

13

TIME TRAVELLERS

Post Traumatic Stress Disorder is intertwined with another aspect of what war can do to the human mind. That is, going back and revisiting the scene or scenes of the conflict. Like PTSD, the idea of a return to the Falklands took different men in different ways. Some were unaffected and others suffered genuine agonies even contemplating it.

'I was finding it difficult,' Mark Hiscutt says. 'I went back on HMS *Manchester* at Christmas 1983/84 and when we got down there everybody was encouraged to go ashore, but I didn't. I saw the islands from the ship but I disobeyed orders. I was told by my boss to go and stretch my legs because otherwise I would have been at sea four or five months but the Falklands was a place I didn't want to go ashore at. I don't know why. There was something about it and I just couldn't do it. I think it was just too raw for me. It was only a year and a bit later and the memories were very fresh.'

Even long after, such difficulties did not necessarily diminish.

I propose to let two men set out the context. John Jones, a Welsh Guardsman, was a moving spirit at SAMA, organising visits in 2002 and 2007, and Alan Hamilton, an experienced *Times* hand, who reported the 2002 visit. When that's done I think you will appreciate what Mark Hiscutt and the others say more fully.

Jones was 'a Lance Sergeant, which is a rank peculiar to the Brigade of Guards. It's a corporal but with the privileges of the sergeants' mess. I served with the Welsh Guards in the Falklands. We went down on the *QE2* and then at South Georgia we trans-shipped to *Canberra*. From *Canberra* we disembarked at San Carlos. We all got back on to *Fearless* and

I landed from one of the landing craft at Yellow Beach by Fitzroy. Half the battalion went on board the *Sir Galahad*.

'I was ashore. It was a beautiful day, bright and sunny, cold, clear and blue. We got an AIR RED, the planes came over and we saw the ship hit. We didn't know the battalion was on there and I said to the guy who was with me, "Some poor bastards have copped a packet." It was our lot. Most of my platoon was killed or injured on the *Galahad*: thirty-four on board and seven got off unhurt.

'I was a mortar fire-controller and I was effectively redundant because I had nobody to speak to on the other end of the radio. The battalion was still active, however. I went to moving rations and ammunition – we'd pick it up from the dump and take it to the front line.

'After the war we were in Stanley and I was acting company clerk. I put myself on a detail to go to the airport to get some fresh air. We were supposed to clear the runway of snow and ice. They put up a Combat Air Patrol of Harriers and a Harrier fired both Sidewinders, the air-to-air mis-siles. One went straight down the runway on the far side and disappeared into the air. The one on our side hit the runway, broke up and eleven of us got hurt. I don't know what actually hit me but it took both legs off. I remember thinking *he's fired the Sidewinders* and next thing I'm on my back. I could hear somebody moaning next to me and I thought *Christ, somebody's hurt.* I tried to get up. My left leg came up minus the foot.'

You'd imagine that Jones would be an inevitable candidate for PTSD, but 'I haven't had any treatment for it because I don't think I have it. Yes, I have occasional nightmares, yes, I have occasional flashbacks, yes I get upset sometimes about things and sometimes a little depressed but that's normal, isn't it? I know a couple of guys who are suffering from it and I think I am very lucky not to.'

Approaching the 2002 return – marking the twentieth anniversary, of course – Jones faced a decision, because he had not been back before.

'I had this longing to go back, but I just didn't feel strong enough mentally to go on my own. I knew the secretary of SAMA and when the pilgrimage came up I said I'd do whatever I could to help. Funding was a big issue because it had to be self-funding. How do we get the money? Some were sponsored by Combat Stress, others paid their way. How do we choose who can go? Then there was the logistics of it all, and what about families – the relatives? In the end I did want to go on it, yes, because I thought here was an opportunity. We took about 180.

'We all met at Gatwick, which I think was a mistake. We didn't know who was coming and who wasn't. Everybody bomb-burst into the bar and threw *it* down their necks. I think that was the nervousness of seeing old friends and the nervousness over what we were about to do. There was a bit of tension.

'It was a hell of a journey. We went to Banjul in The Gambia then to Rio and then to Mount Pleasant on the Falklands. When we got off they took us all for breakfast in one of the messes and after that we got onto the transport so, at that point, if you like, we were back in to the service environment. It was like a comfort blanket but you could sense there was this nervousness and tension despite the fact that everybody was absolutely knackered. We got into Stanley, we met our hosts and they just couldn't do enough for us. I was staying with three other Welsh Guards with Jan and Tim Miller, who have been superb.

'Whatever you wanted to do you could do it. If you wanted to be by yourself you could do that. Some people did. There was a full programme of events but no pressure to attend them.

'I felt slightly humbled that people appreciated quite so much what we did and were prepared to do all this for us. Because I'd been on the committee I thought *thank God this has happened. It's worked!*

'I have been back to where I lost my legs. That was a bit ... spooky but I felt more comfortable in myself and that a chapter had almost closed. I can't speak for the others but I think everybody at the time felt *yes, wow, wasn't that something?* They'd renewed friendships, made new friendships and cemented friendships in the islands. Whether they were able to carry that on afterwards and were able to deal with it afterwards I'm not sure but I would say it certainly helped people to face their demons – and I think those that didn't recognise that they had demons found that they did and that they weren't the only ones. It was a long, exhausting flight back and we had trouble at Banjul with a burst tyre.'

We'll be meeting John Jones again in a moment.

Alan Hamilton has 'been to the Falklands a total of six times as a *Times* correspondent. That trip with the vets in 2002 was my fifth so, you know, I was the office Falklands hand because I knew the place. I didn't cover the war – in fact, my first visit was some months after the war finished, for the dedication of the war cemetery. For the first time ever, I think, Margaret Thatcher allowed anybody who wanted the body of a fallen serviceman brought back to be brought back. A few elected to have their husbands, brothers, whatever stay where they fell. There were, I think, sixteen in this war cemetery just above San Carlos Water. I went out to do that because it was a Ministry of Defence pool,[1] *The Times* drew the place for the broadsheets reporter and it fell to me. Ever since then, anything Falklands – "Alan!"

'It was difficult to say whether or not the veterans were apprehensive on the way out because they were all utterly pissed. The flight was a nightmare. There was a big drinking contest between them because roughly half of them were paras and the other half were Royal Marines – so a big rivalry there. I think they must have been apprehensive because they didn't know what they were going to find and they didn't know how they were going to feel. It was however many people an Airbus takes, roughly 200 I should think. They were all hoping to lay their demons by going back to the battlefields.

'When we got there they went to see the various battlefields where they'd been engaged in action – Tumbledown, San Carlos, Goose Green, wherever – and they were there for about five days. It seemed to have done them good, certainly in the short term. One of the things, of course, is that they were made extremely welcome by the local population, who regarded them all as heroes for having saved them from the Argies. They were offered tremendous hospitality.

'The other great thing was they had to collect souvenirs. In fact, on the flight home our aircraft was overloaded because it was carrying so many bits of metal picked off the ground. We were to refuel at Banjul in The Gambia and as it landed it burst a tyre. We were stuck there for hours while they got a new tyre. [They obtained a new tyre but the airport didn't have the equipment to blow it up. A Russian plane, which had just landed, did and for a bribe of two bottles of vodka, as John Jones says, the deed was done.]

'I was with a *Times* photographer and we were standing on a hillside somewhere outside Stanley. One of the chaps from our flight – a veteran – comes rushing up to us and says to the photographer, "Hey, you a photographer?" – a bit obvious, because he had cameras round his neck. The guy said, "I want you to take a picture of this." He had what for him was the perfect souvenir. He had been in the army catering corps and he'd found the remains of an Argentinian field kitchen. He was so excited by this.

'I think it did them good, in fact I'm fairly certain it did because on the flight back they were all quite subdued. That might also have been as a result of them being on the booze all week and they were just exhausted, no strength left, but I think it slew a few demons for them. I don't suffer from Post Traumatic Stress Disorder so I don't know but I expect it's very difficult to go back and face an actual physical spot where, perhaps, some of your comrades were killed or you were wounded. I am sure that is a very difficult thing to do. Whether it's a good thing to do will vary with the individuals.

'The one thing they were told was that under no circumstances were they to bring back any kind of live ammunition – especially on a plane. They were quite happy just with little 6-inch square bits of shattered aluminium which had been a helicopter.

'It was not as bad as they thought it was going to be. That was my own experience going back with the veterans, anyway.'

Jones was also involved in the twenty-fifth-anniversary visit and a lesson had been learnt by SAMA about meeting in a bar at an airport.

There were other, more important, problems.

'How do you select people? Anybody could go who hadn't been back before and you didn't even have to be a member of SAMA, you just had to be a medal holder.[2] There were some that the medical people wouldn't let go because they felt it would do more harm than good, but we said if there is a clinical need they can go. We gave ten seats to the Falklands Families Association so that bereaved relatives could go. We gave a hundred seats to Combat Stress. We had a hundred seats to fill and we said we'd do it on a draw basis, names in a hat.

'We booked the Union Jack Club, which is by Waterloo Station. It has around 300 rooms and is like a hotel. The Scots guys came down Friday, everybody else Saturday. That night we had a gala reception with Maggie Thatcher, a guy from the Lottery who had given us money and Julian Thompson. Overall, the atmosphere was not quite so boozy, although there was still a lot of tension – but everybody had met up at the club and got that out of the way. The approach was more chilled approach – perhaps controlled would be a better word.

'And we had families going down with us. For example, John Griffiths was with us. He could barely remember his dad [Guardsman Gareth M. Griffiths] so he was going to see his dad's grave for the first time. He was in company with people who knew his dad and could tell him what went on. There was still an awful lot of emotion there, an emotional tension, an anticipation but also trepidation. I think that's a fair way of putting it.'

Mark Hiscutt found himself back at the Falklands soon after the conflict. 'There were people on board who did go ashore and they'd been on the *Sheffield* or the *Coventry* but me, no. People came back and said, "It's great there" but I just couldn't do it.

'In the end, I made the decision in 2005 that I wanted to go back and I talked it through with Kirsty. Rather than doing it through SAMA and their pilgrimages I decided I didn't want to go round with a group, I wanted to go round with Kirsty. I contacted the Falkland Islands office in London. I was talking to a gentleman called Terry Peck,[3] an islander who was also in Combat Stress. He was the chief of police at the time of the invasion and he got out of Stanley and met up with the paras when they landed. He guided 3 Para across the Falklands.

'He arranged for me to have a bungalow, which meant we didn't have to stay with a family – I didn't want to burden anybody. It's normal practice to stay with families. We got funding from SSAFA [Soldiers', Sailors',

Airmen's and Families' Association]. I went to them and I said, "Look, we are going back and I need a hand." They kindly paid for myself and Kirsty to fly down. They were willing to pay for hotel accommodation but I said, "No – I just need the flights paying for" because we had the bungalow. I didn't want anything else out of them.

'I had letters from Morgan O'Connell and also from my therapist to say that Kirsty was my carer and I needed her to go with me. I wanted to be down there for 4 May 2005 – 4 May was our anniversary.

'We flew with the RAF from Brize Norton to a stop-over at Ascension and then carried on to Mount Pleasant, which is the RAF station in the Falklands. When we arrived we were met by a lady called Sue Bucket, who worked for the Falkland Islands Corporation, and she looked after us. They arranged a tour of the island for us, which was nice, a gentleman whose name I can't remember took us down to Bluff Cove and Blue Beach. We met some of the locals at their farms and then on 4 May I was picked up by the naval liaison officer on the Falklands and we were taken to Mount Pleasant, where we met the officer commanding the Falkland Islands, who flew us in his helicopter to Sea Lion Island. We laid some flowers and a plaque with poem engraved on it written by Smudge Smith, who was on the *Galahad*. We spent the rest of the time just looking round the island. We were given a Land Rover so we didn't have to walk everywhere.' (Of this, more in a moment – in the words of Kirsty.)

Sea Lion Island is:

one of the smallest in the Falklands archipelago (just 5 miles long and just over a mile wide at its widest point), and the most southerly inhabited island, but it is still a prime destination with the sheer abundance of wildlife in such a small area making it a must on any Falklands itinerary. Beautiful tussac plantations cover one-fifth of the island and provide a perfect habitat and protection for much of the islands' varied fauna, including elephant seals and sea lions. Besides the tussac, there are sand beaches, cliffs, fresh-water ponds and heath land, all with their own populations, and all within easy walking distance of the purpose-built lodge.[4]

Kirsty Hiscutt wrote about the trip and, with permission, I reproduce it with the lightest editing:

An Unforgettable Experience

My name is Kirsty and this is my account of my thoughts and feelings whilst accompanying my husband on a personal pilgrimage to the Falkland Islands in May 2005.

Mark (my husband) was diagnosed with PTSD approximately 6 years ago relating to his navy days – a trauma left unnecessarily undiagnosed for many years.

He served on board HMS *Sheffield* during the Falkland conflict in 1982.

Like others who fought in this conflict, it was suggested by Combat Stress (Morgan O' Connell) that as part of Mark's therapy he may find a visit to the Falklands beneficial. As his support I, too, was offered this opportunity.

SSAFA aided us with our funding and from there we proceeded with a year of planning for our trip.

Mark and I were married two and a half weeks after he landed back at Brize Norton 23 years ago – our original wedding cancelled due to the diversion of the *Sheffield* to the Falklands after a 5-month deployment.

As we approached our departure day we were filled with mixed feelings of emotion, trepidation, animosity (more on my part), apprehension and curiosity. I began to realise I was not only Mark's support, but I needed this experience too. I had many unresolved feelings for what happened all those years ago. It was time for both of us to face up to and talk about issues that we hadn't really been able to for 23 years.

Mark had experienced an awful trauma – the ship had been hit by an Exocet missile, killing some of the crew – and I, like many others, had been told the shocking news over a TV broadcast, the 9 o'clock news, having been shown previous pictures of a desolate-looking land with what seemed to be very few inhabitants, in a place called the Falklands (if we ever did it at school for geography I certainly don't recollect it). We had to wait until the next morning before we had news to confirm whether Mark's name was on the survivor's list or not. There was no sign of him to begin with.

As much as I told myself Mark was there because this was his job, I felt numb to the point of not recognising what I was feeling and bitterness for what this all seemed to be about.

Until 2004 I've not been able to look at it in any other way because there is nothing that can justify the deaths of our men, but when Mark asked me to accompany him to the Falklands as his support I began to develop a curiosity as to whether, by experiencing the islands first hand, would it alter my perspective on what it had all been about? It was time to find out.

We had brief contact with the Falkland Islands Government (London office) and the Falklands SAMA rep Gary Clement, who recently took over from Terry Peck (a courageous and lovely man I felt very privileged to meet) and Roger Spink from F.I.C. (Falkland Islands Corporation). We boarded our flight at Brize Norton.

Our first hurdle was the vivid memories we both shared from Mark's return with the rest of the survivors of HMS *Sheffield* all those years ago – and also being aware of the fact that yet another set of our troops were getting ready for their flight to take off to yet another war zone – Iraq – which meant more suffering just waiting to happen!

We proceeded to fly 18,000 miles across the world to a destination we knew nothing about, putting our trust in people we only knew by email and the address of our accommodation unknown. Needless to say there was a little apprehension on landing!

We landed, we were there and there was no turning back. The next plane out wasn't for another 5 days and we were there for 10!!!

We were met at Mount Pleasant Airport by a wonderful and caring lady named Sue Bucket from F.I.C. who drove us another 30–40 miles to Stanley, to where a bungalow had been provided for us. They'd thought of everything.

This is where our feelings – but not our thoughts – began to separate. This is where we found our memories of 1982 were totally different.

The islanders worked tirelessly in making us feel welcome, with endless invitations of transporting us to different destinations. They are very friendly, genuine people just wanting to show us their islands, so that we may appreciate them for what they are. In this respect it was very easy to do and to take in too much. We frequently needed to remind ourselves as to why we were there.

The initial reason was so that Mark could be on Sea Lion Island on 4 May – the anniversary for the *Sheffield*. This was his ultimate aim and he'd had a plaque made up with a very poignant poem, 'The Bravest of the Brave,' written by a good mate, *Smudge* (Steve Smith).

Although Sea Lion Island was closed for the winter, arrangements had still been made for us to fly over for a service in the helicopter belonging to the commander of the British Forces. We were well looked after.

By this time we were feeling very emotional, not only remembering the lads that died but also the ones back home and their partners. The bond was very strong.

The sea all around us was calm and peaceful. It was comforting to see these men were at peace – something I know Mark isn't. There was also a moment when some wildlife – small birds and a caracara bird – came to look approvingly. It was a good feeling. The caracara bird watching knowingly as we took off in the helicopter back towards Mount Pleasant Airport.

A unique experience I felt honoured to have been part of.

We continued to take in as much as we could, including the history of the islands pre-1982 and, of course, the conflict. Many refer to the conflict as a war. When you appreciate the scale of the islands and what took place, it is more appropriate to think: Britain sent 27,000 men and women – not all of them landed – to re-take the Falkland Islands after the invasion by Argentina, some as young as eighteen and nineteen. They went to a country with a population, then, of approximately 1,900 and a total land area of 12,173 sq km, approximately the size of Wales.

Some of the islanders proceeded to talk about 1982 as though it only happened yesterday. We gained insight into the expanse of devastation and the inhuman ways the Argentines treated the conscripts – their own people. Conscripts as young as sixteen were being taken off the streets of Argentina, inappropriately clothed for Falklands winter conditions, underfed, untrained and given weapons. Many weren't even wearing dog tags so they were unidentifiable when dead.

This widened our perspective greatly.

The memories of our troops and Task Force lost in this awful conflict will go on for many generations to come in the Falklands. There are many memorials, all beautiful and lovingly kept, and services are held at each one annually on each specific anniversary. This includes Memorial Wood, the most amazing place. There is a living tree for each man and the three islanders who died. This was quite the most comforting place of all.

The doubt in our minds as to what this had all been about slowly melted away. I could no longer hold a grudge. In my opinion these people are more British than I would ever confess to be, they know what community spirit really is, they have very little but are still contented with what they have, they have a passion for their home – more than I could ever imagine for myself – and a tireless determination to keep it this way.

The Falkland Islands are a beautiful, very peaceful place and although they have the same mod cons as us – including computers and PlayStations! – the environment and atmosphere makes you feel as though you have just stepped back 40 or 50 years. They have values much of our society lost sight of many years ago. They are very special people who deserve the right of British sovereignty and their freedom, though whether freedom is the right word, I'm not sure. Could freedom be the price we pay for war?

Most of all I have immense admiration and respect for all those who defended and protected the islands, those who gave their lives and who still are – who found themselves in what could have only been the most unimaginable conditions possible 23 years ago.

Without distraction, (including TV) Mark and I talked more in those 10 days than we'd ever been able to before. Our feelings became very different, but we had respect for each other's. Mark still has a lot to process and still has thoughts that are hard to come to terms with. I respect the fact that he will, in his own time, if and when he is ready, but on reflection I am so glad that we both had the courage to look – and – to share what we did.

Thank you everyone that aided us on our way to another step in our journey.

Kirsty Hiscutt
May 2005

As Kirsty mentioned, the Hiscutts visited Memorial Wood. The Cross of Sacrifice, Stanley Cemetery and Memorial Wood are:

at the eastern end of Stanley. The Cross of Sacrifice commerates both World Wars and a service is held here on Remembrance Sunday, in common with many other nations. Behind the cross is the cemetery. The inscriptions on some of the tombstones are a remarkable record of the spirit and courage of the early settlers. Just above the cemetery is the Memorial Wood … an area set aside to commemorate members of the British forces who served and died in the 1982 conflict. A tree is planted in memory of each British serviceman killed.[5]

Mark explains: 'There are no trees on the Falklands so Jan and Tim Miller planted a tree for each person who died during the conflict and had the person's name placed beside it. I found all the trees and I took photographs of all the names but the one I couldn't find was No 1. Kirsty found it – I'd been walking backwards and forwards and I'd walked past several times. That opened up a ghost because I thought *did I do that on the ship?* That really affected me. Was he that close to me when I was looking for him? *I couldn't find him then and I can't find him now.* But I'm glad I went and we are planning to go back. My youngest son, Corby, said he would like to go when he's 16 to see so we are planning to go back then.

'I think Kirsty put a lot of things to rest by going. For me it reinforced why we did it, because it was the right thing to do. They were British and as Kirsty said they are more British than we are. It will always be the right decision.'

Brian Bilverstone is 'a member of the South Atlantic Medal Association and they advertised at the end of 2006 that there was going to be the twenty-fifth anniversary pilgrimage. I thought *well, I don't know how I feel*. Over the years you build up certain things in your mind. I thought *do I want to go, don't I want to go?* I talked about it with Sue [his partner] and she said, "Well, if you apply you can always say no. If you don't apply you won't go anyway." So I applied and, not unexpectedly, I was told that I wasn't on the list and I wasn't on the reserve list.

'I thought *oh well, that's that*. I felt a little bit miffed and I took it a bit personally but life goes on. Then four weeks before it went I got a phone call saying, "There's been some drop-outs. Do you want to go?" and I should have gone *oh yes, put me down* but I heard myself saying to him, "I'm going to have to think about it." That must have been partly because I'm self-employed and you can't just drop everything but, I don't know, it was like something had hit me in the middle of the chest. He said, "Don't leave it too long, I need to know, I need to know."

'At the time we were having our loft converted and we had a carpenter here who was ex-Royal Marines. He was involved in the first Gulf War. He basically told me what he thought I'd be if I didn't go and Sue agreed with him. I said, "Well, all right, I'll go." I told them I'd go and I was *sort of* looking forward to it but I felt a bit apprehensive. I got more and more apprehensive and then, on the night before we all went to the Union Jack Club to muster, three times I phoned home. I was begging Sue to come and pick me up and take me home but she wouldn't.

'There were two lads who didn't go, for reasons which I can only imagine.

'We flew from Gatwick. We had a chartered Monarch Airlines plane – they helped us out and we had a Lottery grant. Two hundred and fifty of us went and we flew via Rio. All the way down I don't know how I felt but as soon as I got there I knew it was the right thing to do. *I knew.*

'And they treated us so well. They could not do enough for us. I laid a few ghosts, put it that way. I was confronting demons and some demons, I suppose, were real and others were perceived over a period of time and were in your mind. Seeing the fact that the islands are prosperous, they are full of happy people and clean now made an impact, too. You think to yourself *well, it must have been worth it because these people want to be here.* The family I stayed with had moved from St Helena in the intervening years and they had gone there by choice. I thought *well, that says something about the place, doesn't it?* It changed my perception completely, although I still remember how I felt before.

'The nasty part is a memory now, it doesn't sort of live with me. I do occasionally have dreams. Funnily enough, during that period just before I went down there I went through a period of treatment for the dreams, which helped. It's different now. I still have my moments, I still stand in front of war memorials and weep – all that sort of thing – but I don't see that as abnormal. I find I can live with it more now, although in fact, sometimes I'm almost ashamed of it – of having been involved in it and everything and – I still get embarassed about the weeping.'

When you look back on it now, 30 years later, what do you think about the conflict?

'I think a lot of things. My visit in 2007 made me decide once and for all that it was absolutely the right thing to do. It was a terrible waste on both sides but then any conflict is. However, you cannot let one country bully another country's possessions. The islanders were a small group of people who were entirely defenceless because a couple of handfuls of marines weren't a match for a full army.[6]

Steve Wilkinson hasn't 'been back. To be quite honest, it's only over the last couple of years that a few friends have said, "You want to go back, you'll lay some ghosts or whatever to rest." I'd never thought about it. As part of the Falklands Veterans Foundation[7] we did start raising a lot of money here in Gosport and the surrounding area towards the lodge down there, built so the veterans have some accomodation.

'I don't think there were any ghosts. I don't think in essence we'd been badly damaged – because of our skipper we'd come out of it quite well.

Nobody was mortally injured, we'd not had war damage to any extent and I'd like to think that, because of our prior training and the good skipper, we'd come through it well. So why is it that at least one friend of mine, if not more, have not come through so well even though they have had the same experiences?'

David Buey 'went back in 1983 for a short time on a tour of duty and I finally got onto the Falklands. I went to Stanley, albeit briefly. We landed on the lawn at Government House in a helicopter. It was nice to see the people. The brother-in-law of one of the lads on our flight was there and they took us scuba diving in Port Stanley harbour. It was bloody cold, I'll tell you that.

'We found a Pucara that had crashed into the hillside and hadn't been mapped. There was the pilot still in it. Our aircrewman took a bazooka and it was really strange because it was kind of an Argentinian blue. He took it on board the ship and we fired it off the back of the ship, which we weren't supposed to do. God, it made a bang before it disappeared over the horizon! We tossed the bazooka over the side and pretended it hadn't happened.

'We were supposed to be there for four months but the plans changed once we'd arrived. We spent two or three days and then went off around Cape Horn to Chile and Peru, up through the Panama Canal and back to the UK.'

Mario Reid went back. 'I was on a tour of duty, working, in 1983–84. All I did was road construction on night-time shifts so I didn't see anything. However, the Falkland Islanders have put me on a pilgrimage this year [November 2010] so I am going back. I have not been back since. I am quite honoured and I can't believe they have chosen me. They chose ten of us, I think.

'Going back that first time I didn't really know because I was so young – it was excitement, it was more like *well, you've already been there*. We flew to Ascension and when I got on the boat, for example, I'd been on that boat already because I came back on it. I knew my way round.

'I'm quite lucky because I'm not really mixed up, shall I say. I'm all right. It was just a job for me and I never saw any of the sights or anything like that. I put my head down and got on with it.

'This time I will go back and pay my respects to all the people we lost and for that I am truly honoured. To be honest, I'm quite chuffed because I didn't think I'd ever have a chance to do that. It's not just my respect I'll be paying but the respects of people I know, so I will be doing it on behalf of them. I've had someone staying and he talks about how they lost the lad next to him – but he was lucky. Talking about it between friends it's not a problem and they say PTSD doesn't come out until years later. A lot of people just don't talk about it.'

Dave Brown says that '80% who have gone back have benefitted from it. I think some of the others who went back went with the wrong attitude anyway and haven't done what they were meant to do down there, which is go out to the battlefields, spend time visiting other places, understanding what happened and why we did these things. The other category we were always worried about were single lads living on their own in a house or a flat. They get on one of these trips, meet all their mates again, go down the Falklands, manage to visit the graves and do understand. A couple of weeks later, when they're back in their flat on their own and they've got no wives, girlfriends, partners, parents, they go into a shutdown. They've had such a high experience going back and when they're sat on their own, no-one there to talk to them about it, and it opens up things they thought they'd left behind. It can work that way.

'I've run two official trips for the twentieth and the twenty-fifth and since then I've been back three times on holiday. I go for holiday now to take veretans back with us who haven't been back before. It's better if they go with lads who have been before. We know how to handle it and we also know where to take them, what mood they are in and when to take them.

'We explain they might go on a downer when they get back but we do it in a more positive way. We don't want to say, "When you get back you're going to hit the ★★★★" because 9 out of 10 don't. You speak to their little children and they'll say, "I've got my daddy back." Wives say, "I've got my husband back." We say *look, hope you benefit from it*. Say we go to Goose Green. The next day we'll go out fishing or something different to take their mind off it. We are always there when they get back, we stay in contact. We say, "You can ring anytime, you need to come over and have a couple of days with your mates, we're there for you."

'People don't take it badly on the islands, we've never had that problem on the island itself. I only know of maybe three or four people really who said it's had a negative effect on them and they don't want to go back again.

'The other point is we've had a couple of people who've gone down on these trips and all they wanted to do was get pissed up every night, which doesn't help the situation – because that's all they are doing in England. So they might as well stay in England and do it. They don't get out to meet people, they don't benefit.

'The people who go down, they have met people who were kids at the time and are now married with kids of their own. They are so appreciative, even the kids, for what we did for their daddy and mummy. That is the most important thing. I say to our lads, "The islanders are not overwhelming and they are not going to come up to you and shake hands and say thank you and all the rest. They appreciate what you did, they will leave you to your own privacy, but don't feel you have got to avoid them. They want to see you down there. They love you coming down."

'We organised the twentieth anniversary. I had not been back before 2002. I wanted to go because it was a five-year battle. We as a small group tried to get a trip down with the MoD and we were told for various reasons it wasn't feasible, they wouldn't do it, etc. SAMA said, "Right, we're going to take a plane back." I was on the plane from Gatwick.

'I was so over-hyped looking forward to it that I couldn't wait to get there. Obviously we had a couple of moments when we went up to Goose Green.'

Jimmy O'Connell says, 'I'll go as many times as they'll let me. I was there in March and I am going back in October [2010]. I first went back in 2007, so that was still a fair time afterwards. It was so long because I never got the opportunity, otherwise I would have gone before. No, no, I wasn't worried about confronting anything; I just wanted to go back.

'I had no demons to face. I just wanted to go and walk round just to have a look. I know lots of friends who weren't hurt and who suffer more than people like me who were hurt. I've got friends – I won't mention their names – who are in an awful state. I have been told it's a thing called "survivor's guilt" because they come away from it unhurt, whereas people who got hurt … well, it's happened; it's one of those things. I am not a psychologist but it's never bothered me.

'It was dark when I got hurt and as soon as I got hurt I had shell dressings put on my face, which is like putting a bag on your head. The round had entered my eye and come out the side of my face. I had two shell dressings covering my entire face so I was like blind. In the daylight – I was there until the next day because they couldn't get the casualties out – it was the same, so I never really see the place. So when I went back it was all new to me, and that's why I wanted to go back: to see what I hadn't seen the time before, to have a walk round and see the place, to say, "Ah, that's what it looks like."'

William Field has 'never been given the opportunity. I have never been informed of anything, really, since I left the navy, and my financial position wouldn't have been able to take me back, plus I had commitments and the other things that have happened in my life. You'd always love a trip down memory lane, I suppose. The idea is to confront the demons and I think it is a good thing if you can confront them. You can put things to sleep then – you see it in a different light on a different day. I would go back if I had the chance, yes.'

Graeme Golightly hasn't been back. 'I was due to go in 2010 and for a number of family reason I couldn't fit it into my programme, because I'm doing quite a few things this year. It's just the way it happened. I already had my accommodation sorted at Port Stanley. It's nothing military orientated. I have had no qualms about going back, none whatsoever. It's not a question I've been asked before, but certainly when I was thinking about it, it's something I would like to put closure on as a youngster that I was at the time – because really what I went through with the friends I now keep in contact with, that experience then governed the rest of our lives, whether we like it or not. Some suffered from PTSD, some didn't. Some went on to better things, some didn't. But from our young-ster days of being trained Royal Marines that then governed how we lived the rest of our lives.

'I have heard many a time that many people found it difficult to go back and unfortunately I can't vouch for that because I have never expe-rienced it myself. Maybe this is the way our DNA is built up, but from my point of view I would like to go back for the pure reason of closure and also the places, the times, the smells could be put all into the one bucket and then I can put the lid on it, so to speak.'

There has to be a natural curiosity over what it looks like because all you've got is fleeting memories from thirty years ago.

'It is. It's interesting. I am still in contact with a number of the guys I served with down there. Of our company I am aware of one individual who came from, as I am led to believe, a fairly structured family and from the experience in the Falklands came back and went on the road and has been ever since. No matter what has been done and said, not matter what organisations have tried to do, he just never wants to come back into the fold of the military again.

'I am so lucky in my DNA, or my profile, my upbringing, which was very traumatic in itself, put me on the right track to be constructive and use the situation as almost an outsider looking in, saying *yep, bad situation, I can take the good bits from that and then move on.* Maybe clinically that's how I coped with what went on down there and, touch wood, it didn't really affect me that much.'

Alan Hamilton says, 'I have in my time done a lot of interviews with First World War veterans – very old chaps who were at the Somme and places like that, anniversary stories really about the seventieth or the eighti-eth anniversary of the Somme, etc. You have to be very patient with old gentlemen because they get tired very easily and a bit confused. You say,

"What was it like on the Somme?" and they describe it, the mud and so on, but I was never sure whether they were telling me what they remembered or whether they were telling me what they'd read about it since.'

Looking back nearly thirty years on, what do I think? I think it was something that only Margaret Thatcher would have attempted. I'm not necessarily a fan of Margaret Thatcher in every way, but I think it was the last blast of British grit and determination. It would be physically impossible now to mount such an operation. You couldn't get that Task Force together and I don't think there would be the will to do it in this country. That's possibly to do with our experiences in Iraq and Afghanistan.

Notes

1. A newspaper pool is, literally, what is says: journalists pool their material and it is sent out to everyone. Hence you sometimes see, rather than a by-line on a story, 'Pooled Despatch'.
2. The South Atlantic Medal was awarded to British military personnel and civilians who served in the Falklands. A total of 29,700 have been issued. The South Atlantic Medal Association was formed in 1997.
3. 'Terry Peck, who has died aged 68, played a dashing role in the Falklands War when he first spied on the enemy in Port Stanley, then escaped to become a scout for the 3rd Battalion, Parachute Regiment, with which he fought at the Battle of Mount Longdon.
   'A rumbustious member of the legislative council as well as a former head of the police force, he puzzled locals after the Argentines arrived on April 2 1982 by walking round Stanley with a length of drainpipe. This concealed a Russian camera with a telephoto lens with which he took pictures of enemy anti-aircraft missile sites. They were taken to army intelligence in London by returning contract workers. When told that he was about to be arrested, Peck made a hasty exit on a motorcycle.' (www.telegraph.co.uk/news/obituaries/1538660/Terry-Peck.html)
4. www.ladatco.com/fk-sli.htm
5. www.falklandislands.com/contents/view/178
6. Bilverstone's joke: 'Heard the one about the marine on the hill? Silly joke, really. I can't remember which hill was involved and it doesn't matter. The Argentines were trying to storm it and the commander sent up a reconnaissance of ten men. These men disappeared and a lone marine

appeared standing on top of the hill making V-signs and swearing – "Is that the best you can do?" So the commander sent a hundred men up, same thing. So the commander committed his whole force and there was an enormous fight on the other side of the ridge. Eventually a few bedraggled Argentines staggered back down the hill and the commander said, "What the hell happened?" "It was a trap – there were two of them ...'"

7. The Falklands Veterans Foundation incorporates Liberty Lodge www.falklandsveterans.org.uk

About Liberty Lodge:

'The Falkland Island Government leased the land at Rowlands Rise to the Falklands Veterans Foundation (FVF) at a "peppercorn" rent to enable them to build a place of residence in Stanley, the capital of the Falkland Islands, for Veterans of the Falklands War of 1982, their families and present day service personnel serving in the South Atlantic when the Lodge is not in use by Veterans and their families.'

'Just to let anybody know who hasn't yet taken advantage of the indulgence system, it is a great way to go and visit the Islands. Had a great time down there, which at times was very emotional. Things I had forgotten came to light and memories came flooding back.

'The Lodge is amazing ... It is Sanctuary, it is warm, comfortable and well looked after. I don't know if it was the Lodge or the fact that I was in the Falklands but for the first time in years I managed to sleep without nightmares. I would just like to thank everyone involved in making my journey and stay such a memorable part of my life.'

A/B(M) RFA *Sir Percival* 1982

14

JOKING, CRYING AND DYING

'It is difficult to be exact about how soldiers and marines cope when the weather is freezing them, the enemy is killing them and the odds are against them. Perhaps it is because they don't look at life the same way civilians do. Most of us can get out of the cold, rarely see death and often think the odds are against us when, really, they are not.

'And we civilians have the privilege of debate. We can argue an issue hoping to win over others, like friends or superiors at work for example, to our point of view. Soldiers and marines do not have this facility. They are trained to be fit, to obey orders without question and to fight to win.

'So they must be androids.

'Not really.

'They are as able as any civilian to stand their ground intellectually, but you cannot have a battle where the boys are arguing the toss for hours on end over which hill to assault. That would tend to give the enemy an edge. So they do what they are ordered to do and, sometimes, bicker about it afterwards.

'To that end, British forces are highly trained to do their job, to watch out for each other and to be fully committed to the task before them. In this case the job was to turf out the Argentinian trespassers and hand back the Falkland Islands to those who lived there and had the right to decide their own destiny.

'Their training, which now as then makes them the best in the world, is the key to how they coped. Weld that to a positive attitude and a sense of humour as uniquely British as it is black and you have a formula for survival and success that is second to none. It was that way for a very long time before the Falklands and today, as the heroism and sacrifice go on, I doubt anything has changed.

'And so it began for them and me in the drizzle over the South Coast ports of Southampton, Portsmouth and Marchwood, a baptism of satire and loathing for the journalists and for some of them, their first experience of the human form of Rottweiler. Moaning, groaning under the weight of their weapons and Bergens, taking a rise out of anyone in sight and muttering with disdain about those who were not a part of their particular unit, the paras and marines I was with boarded their ships in the opening days of April 1982, frequently addressing each other by first names and nicknames.

'The Airborne is fairly free with uncomplimentary epithets and, because I was to be attached to 3 Para, it was not long before they gave me a few which, if I had a maiden aunt, she would not approve of. Taking the mick is all part of the coping game and, as it was explained to me bluntly: "If you can't stand a joke you shouldn't have joined."

'Paras and marines formed the bulk of 3 Commando Brigade, to which I was attached. The Guards and Gurkhas made up 5 Brigade and I had little contact with them. So my not saying anything about them does not mean I think their achievements were any less important. It just means I did not know anything about them at the time.

'From the outset, if any of 3 Commando Brigade thought they were on a winner being ordered to embark aboard a cruise liner they were soon gravely disappointed. *Canberra*'s decks were crammed with everything from ration packs to medical supplies to ammunition. Tall men walking from one area to another had to stoop because the height between decks had been reduced by boxes of supplies 2 feet deep or more. Accommodation was cramped, so much so that one resourceful soldier had made his bed in a bookcase, books and all.

'Inter-unit rivalry was rife. Paras disliked marines and the feeling was mutual. Although marines are part of the Royal Navy they, along with the paras, didn't much care for the Senior Service and the navy returned such sentiments with bells on.

'*Canberra* had a Royal Navy captain and crew along with a P&O one and the first episode of eye-balling came when the navy insisted that the bar used by officers of all units must be known as the wardroom, as is the navy custom. It was not to be. With their legendary reputation for tact and diplomacy, the paras encouraged all present to refer to the bar as the officers' mess, which is the army custom.

'As the Task Force sailed south and equipment on the wrong ships was gradually cross-decked to the right ones, paras and marines trained harder on each passing day. If marines jogged round the promenade deck in PT kit, paras would do it in full combat gear. If paras then ran carrying their Bergens, marines would do that and carry a mate across their shoulders as well. And so it went on, units constantly trying to outdo each other, even in the 35°C heat around Ascension Island. One marine lieutenant aboard the logistics landing ship *Sir Lancelot* ran a full marathon distance up and down the little ship's sea deck as she headed south. No-one topped that.

'Morale was high, letters from home regularly reached the men, beer was on tap, rationed to two cans a day, although not everyone could count. The humour became blacker, Cliff Richard's hit *Summer Holiday* was given new words and there were many renditions of a little ditty containing the words "God is Airborne".

'The main body of the Task Force had sailed on 5 April and on 2 May I listened as I did several times a day to the BBC's World Service news. I taped what I heard and took the recording to the Meridian Room aboard *Canberra*, otherwise known as the sergeants' mess. That the sergeants allowed me to use their mess was a considerable honour for any other rank, let alone a civilian.

'We were still nowhere near the Falklands but the carrier force was way ahead of us and in striking distance, and their Harriers and the RAF's Vulcans had been bombing Stanley airport. There had been no reports of fatalities.

'All that now changed. I played the tape to a room full of silence.

'Outside the 200-mile Total Exclusion Zone around the Falklands the British nuclear fleet submarine *Conquerer* had fired a pattern of torpedoes into the Argentinian cruiser *General Belgrano*, sending it to the bottom with the loss of 323 lives. The paras and marines did not rejoice at the news. Instead, the mood was almost sullen, a realization that they were on their way to a war in which the dying had begun.

'Irrepressible as ever, it was not long before the humour returned and the fighting men got on with the inter-service sledging, general micky-taking and even compiling what they called *Essential Phrases to be Used in the Event of Capture*. Advice such as, "You are trespassing," "Can we talk this over?," "Is this Guernsey?" and "My sister's Spanish." There were others not as polite. And so it was to be until the war ended: high times of elation and humour followed by the lows of exhaustion and grief.

'All too soon we all learned that a British Harrier had been brought down and the pilot lost. That World Service report was followed by another revealing that the destroyer HMS *Sheffield* had been hit by an Exocet missile, killing twenty of her crew and injuring many others.

'It was 4 May 1982 and the day the British joined the ranks of the fallen. Some navy men aboard *Canberra* knew men aboard *Sheffield*. Their distress was almost tangible. Sorrow now had a face.

'The training intensified, the collective attitude grew ever more positive. The men were being psyched up, psyching up each other and reaching levels of aggression which impressed their officers while making many of us glad they were on our side. As one company commander said, "They're ready for a brawl. Right now I really wouldn't want to be an Argie."

'And on it went, from the landings of 21 May in San Carlos to the white flag over Stanley on 14 June: wise-cracking and joking, crying and dying, all the Task Force men, and some women, struggled dangerously close to defeat to win their battles ashore, in the air and in defence of their ships, and claim victory. They coped and won because they believed what they were doing was right. They stayed flexible when plans went wrong, as plans often do. They stubbornly refused to let the appalling weather, the inhospitable terrain and a larger enemy force overwhelm them. Being comedians didn't hurt, either.

'How was I picked by the *Daily Express* to go? That is best answered by those who picked me. Apart from that, I know that one of the reasons would have been my constant lobbying of the news editor, the editor and everyone else on the paper who I thought might put a good word in for me. I had also recently shared the British Press Awards Reporter of the Year gong and had covered a few wars, sieges and Northern Ireland, so I considered myself to have the necessary credentials. I was convinced there was going to be a serious difference of opinion once Argentina had raised its flag over South Georgia and I campaigned in the office to go to the Falklands to be in position should there be an invasion.

'I was not convincing enough and was not sent, and threw all my toys out of the pram when *The Daily Telegraph*, the *Sun* and the *Times* were. When I was finally ordered by the office to go with the Task Force, it was certainly not because I was the best the paper had, but more likely because I asked first.

'What do I think now, gazing back? I think that Britain would almost certainly not have the resources to mount a similar operation now, in terms of ships, aircraft, equipment and supply. Mind you, that is exactly what I said in early 1982, but I do not doubt for a second that it has the personnel, probably even better trained now than back then, who are just as professional and with a sense of humour just as wicked. Whatever, that is for the men and women still involved, and for other military and political experts, to debate. I have moved into the dinosaur period of my life where I'm usually asked such questions by the pub piss-taker who doesn't really want to know the answer. So when he corners me at the bar I bore him with anecdotal drivel until he falls into a coma. Even so, I remain very aware of what thousands of our young people are still doing, in Afghanistan and elsewhere, and hope they will always get everything they need to do the job they were sent to do. And all of our support.

'What mattered to me in the Falklands, and still matters, is that I was able to do my job at foot-soldier level because I had been lucky enough to have been accepted by them, trained by them, "educated" by them and on several occasions, almost certainly saved from death or injury by them. It was also a relatively unique experience in that the journalists with the Task Force who I was with were, for many weeks, confined with the troops in cramped conditions aboard the ships. Soldiers and marines did not need to make any particular effort to get on with us while we had to earn what little respect we could from them. We could not sulk off as in other wars to the pub, or back to the hotel – there was no pub or hotel – any more than they could. We were trapped together in tin cans for seven weeks and regularly in trenches for almost another five in the rain and snow and had to make the best of it. I might not have survived without their support, given willingly while they had far more important things to do.

'Personally, I still feel privileged to have been in their company and to have experienced the camaraderie that comes from people thrown together, learning much about each other and being there when all of us were scared, and when the dying and the hurt began to worsen by the day. Sadly, I also look back and remember that in less than twenty years after the Falklands fighting had ended, more men had taken their lives than given them there. As a grim comment on Post Traumatic Stress Disorder and any other post-war factor that may have been overlooked, I can think of nothing more tragically eloquent than that. I do hope things have changed. And it is, perhaps, worth pointing out that a golden rule of journalism is that you must not get personally involved. It's a good rule. It keeps one dispassionate. It encourages the necessity to tell both sides of the story, impartially.

'As far as my journalistic coverage was concerned, all I can say is that a huge snag when covering a war is that one cannot always, if ever, canvas both sides. Attempting to do so would be extremely foolish and deeply frowned upon by the people one is with.

'So you stay with the people you are with. You get to know them and they you. Therefore, it CAN get casually personal. That is journalistically wrong and realistically unavoidable. I don't care. I had the absolute good fortune to spend three months with some of the finest people anyone could be lucky enough to meet. Hidden in there are memories which last a lifetime.'

APPENDIX

MEN AND SHIPS

Pte Richard J. Absolon, POAEM(L) Michael J. Adcock, AEM(R)1 Adrian U. Anslow, MEM(M)1 Frank O. Armes, AB Derek D. Armstrong, A/Cpl Raymound E. Armstrong, A/Sgt J.L. Arthy, A/WO1 Malcolm Atkinson.

Staff Sgt John I. Baker, Lt-Cdr David I. Balfour, Lt-Cdr Richard W. Banfield, AB Andrew R. Barr, Lt James A. Barry, Lt-Cdr Gordon W.J. Batt, A/Cpl William Begley, L/Cpl Gary D. Bingley, AB(R) Ian M. Boldy, POMEM(M) David R. Briggs, POAEM(M) Peter Brouard, Cpl J.G. Browning, Pte Gerald Bull, L/Cpl Barry C. Bullers, A/Sgt Paul A. Bunker, L/Cpl Anthony Burke, A/Cpl Robert Burns, Private Jason S. Burt.

ACWEA John D.L. Caddy, Marine Paul D. Callan, MEM(M) Paul B. Callus, L/Sgt James R. Carlyle, POACMN Kevin S. Casey, Elect. Fitter Dis Leung Chau, Merchant Navy, Bosun Yu Sik Chee, Merchant Navy, L/Cpl Simon J. Cockton, Pte Albert M. Connett, Catering Assistant Darryl Cope, L/Cpl Anthony Cork, Pte Jonathan D. Crow, Sgt Philip P. Currass, Lt William A. Curtis.

Guardsman Ian A. Dale, A/Sgt Sid A.I. Davidson, Marine Colin Davison, APOCA Stephen R. Dawson, Guardsman D.J. Denholm, Capt. Christopher Dent, Pte Stephen J. Dixon, AWEM(R) John K. Dobson, Bosun John Dobson, Merchant Navy, Pte Mark S. Dodsworth, Cook Richard J. S. Dunkerley, Guardsman Michael J. Dunphy.

Cook Brian Easton, Guardsman Peter Edwards, WEA1 Anthony C. Eggington, Sgt Clifford Elley, Sub-Lt Richard C. Emly, Sgt Roger Enefer, Sgt Andrew P. Evans, Cpl Kenneth Evans, Lt-Cdr John E. Eyton-Jones.

PO Robert Fagan, Butcher Dis Sung Yuk Fai, Merchant Navy, L/Cpl Ian R. Farrell, C/Sgt Gordon P.M. Findlay, Cpl Peter R. Fitton,

CPOWTR Edmund Flanagan, Pte Mark W. Fletcher, A/Ldg Cook Michael P. Foote, MEM(M)2 Stephen H. Ford, Maj. Michael L. Forge, Mechanic Frank Foulkes, Merchant Navy, PO(S) Michael G. Fowler, Lt Kenneth D. Francis.

WO2 Laurence Gallagher, Sapper Pradeep K. Ghandi, Guardsman Mark Gibby, L/Cpl Brett P. Giffin, Cook Neil A. Goodall, Guardsman Glenn C. Grace, Guardsman Paul Green, Pte Anthony D. Greenwood, S/Sgt Christopher A. Griffen, Marine Robert D. Griffin, Guardsman Gareth M. Griffiths, Pte Neil Grose.

3rd Eng. Officer Christopher Hailwood, Merchant Navy, WEM(O)1 Ian P. Hall, Capt. Gavin J. Hamilton, 3rd Eng. C. Hailwood, A/Steward Shaun Hanson, Cpl David Hardman, A/Sgt William C. Hatton, Std David Hawkins, Merchant Navy, Flt Lt Garth W. Hawkins, AB Sean K. Hayward, Lt Rodney R. Heath, Pte Peter J. Hedicker, AEM(M) Mark Henderson, 2nd Eng. Paul Henry, AB(EW) Stephen Heyes, L/Cpl P.D. Higgs, AEM(R)1 Brian P. Hinge, Pte Mark Holman-Smith, 1st Radio Officer Ronald R. Hoole, Cpl Stephen Hope, Guardsman Denis N. Hughes, Mechanic James Hughes, Merchant Navy, Guardsman Gareth Hughes, A/Sgt William Hughes, A/Sgt Ian N. Hunt.

Pte Stephen Illingsworth.

MEA(P) Alexander S. James, Guardsman Brian Jasper, Pte Timothy R Jenkins, C/Sgt Brian R. Johnston, Sapper Christopher A. Jones, Pte Craig D. Jones, Pte Michael A. Jones, Lt-Col. Herbert ('H') Jones, A/Sgt Philip Jones.

Yeung Swi Kami, Merchant Navy, Guardsman Anthony Keeble, L/Sgt Kevin Keoghane, Laundryman Lai Chi Keung, Merchant Navy, LMEM(M) Allan J Knowles, Laundryman Kye Ben Kwo, Merchant Navy.

Private Stewart I. Laing, WEM(R)1 Simon J. Lawson, LACAEMN David Lee, Sgt Robert A. Leeming, MEM(M)2 Alistair R. Leighton, L/Cpl Paul Lightfoot, L/Cpl Budhaparsad Limbu, Corporal Michael D. Love, L/Cpl Christopher K. Lovett.

Marine Stephen G. McAndrews, AEMN(I) Allan McAuley, Cpl Keith J. McCarthy, AEA(M)2 Kelvin I. McCallum, Cpl Douglas F. MacCormack, A/Cpl Michael McHugh, C/Sgt Ian J. McKay, L/Cpl Peter B. Mckay,

Cpl Stewart P.F. McLaughlin, Cpl Andrew G. McIlvenny, Marine Gordon C. MacPherson, Cook Brian J. Malcolm, Guardsman David Malcolmson, Guardsman Michael J. Marks, NA(AH)1 Brian Marsden, Ldg Cook A. Marshall, Pte Thomas Mechan, Cpl Michael Melia, Private P.W. Middlewick, ALMEM(M) David Miller, L/Sgt Clark Mitchell, Guardsman Christopher Mordecai, 3rd Eng. Off. Andrew Morris, A/LS(R) Michael S. Mullen, L/Cpl James H. Murdoch, Lt Brian Murphy.

LPT Gary T. Nelson, L/Cpl Stephen J. Newbury, A/Cpl John Newton, Guardsman Gareth D. Nicholson, POWEM Anthony R. Norman, Capt. Ian North, Merchant Navy, Marine Michael J. Nowak, Lt Richard J. Nunn, Maj. Roger Nutbeem.

A/WO2 Patrick O'Connor, Cook David E. Osborne, AWEM(N)1 David J.A. Ozbirn.

APOWEM(R) Andrew K. Palmer, Pte David A. Parr, Guardsman Colin C. Parsons, L/Cpl John B. Pashley, MEM(M)2 Terence W. Perkins, Guardsman Eirwyn J. Phillips, Marine Keith Phillips, Seaman Ng Por, Merchant Navy, Guardsman Gareth W. Poole, Staff Sgt James Prescott, Pte Kenneth Preston, Cpl Stephen R. Prior, LAEM(L) Donald L. Pryce.

Guardsman James B.C. Reynolds, Cook John R. Roberts, Lt-Cdr Glen S. Robinson-Moltke, Craftsman Mark W. Rollins, Sgt Ronald J. Rotherham, Guardsman Nigel A. Rowberry, Marine Anthony J. Rundle.

L/Cook Mark Sambles, L/Cpl David E. Scott, Pte Ian P. Scrivens, Lt-Cdr John M. Sephton, Craftsman Alexander Shaw, Seaman Chan Chai Sing, Merchant Navy, L/Cook Anthony E. Sillence, Sgt John Simeon, Pte Francis Slough, Cpl Jeremy Smith, L/Cpl Nigel R. Smith, Cpl Ian F. Spencer, Steward Mark R. Stephens, L/RO(W) Bernard J. Still, Guardsman Archibald G. Stirling, MEA2 Geoffrey L.J. Stockwell, L/Cpl Anthony R. Streatfield, A/Weap. Eng. Art. David A. Strickland, Steward John Stroud, S(M) Matthew J. Stuart, WEA1 Kevin Sullivan, Cpl P.S. Sullivan, Cook Andrew C. Swallow, L/Cpl Philip A. Sweet, AAB(EW) Adrian D. Sunderland, Cpl Paul Sullivan, Cpl Stephen J.G. Sykes.

Sapper Wayne D. Tarbard, Guardsman Ronald Tanbini, Lt N. Taylor, Guardsman Christopher C. Thomas, Guardsman Glyn K. Thomas, L/Cpl Nicholas D.M. Thomas, Guardsman Raymound G. Thomas, ACWEMN

Michael Till, Lt David H.R. Tinker, MEM(M)2 Stephen Tonkin, A/Cook Ian E. Turnbull.

Cpl Andrew B. Uren.

POACMN Collin P. Vickers, Mechanic Ernest Vickers, Merchant Navy.

Guardsman Andrew Walker, WEMN2 Barry J. Wallis, Cpl Edward T. Walpole, L/Cpl Christopher F. Ward, Corporal L.G. Watts, Cpl Laurence Watts, Guardsman James F. Weaver, Master-at-Arms Brian Welsh, Ldg Cook Adrian K. Wellstead, Private Philip A. West, AWEA2 Philip P. White, ALMEM(M) Stephen J. White, ALMEM(L) Garry Whitford, WO2 Daniel Wight, Sgt Malcolm Wigley, Guardsman David R. Williams, MEM(M)1 Gilbert S. Williams, WEA/APP Ian R. Williams, Cook Kevin J. Williams, Marine David Wilson, Cpl Scott Wilson, Capt. David A. Wood, Lt-Cdr John S. Woodhead.

Doreen Bonner, Mary Goodwin, Susan Whitley.

www.britains-smallwars.com/Falklands/roh.html

Royal Navy: HMS *Active, Alacrity, Ambuscade, Andromeda, Antelope, Antrim, Ardent, Argonaut, Arrow, Avenger, Brilliant, Bristol, Broadsword, Cardiff, Conqueror, Cordella, Courageous, Coventry, Dumbarton Castle, Endurance, Exeter, Farnella, Fearless, Glamorgan, Glasgow, Hecla, Herald, Hermes, Hydra, Intrepid, Invincible, Junella, Leeds Castle, Minerva, Northella, Penelope, Pict, Plymouth, Onyx, Sheffield, Spartan, Splendid, Valiant, Yarmouth.*

Royal Maritime Auxiliary Service: *Goosander, Typhoon.*

Royal Fleet Auxiliary: *Appleleaf, Bayleaf, Blue Rover, Brambleleaf, Engadine, Fort Austin, Fort Grange, Olmeda, Olna, Pearleaf, Plumleaf, Regent, Resource, Sir Bedivere, Sir Galahad, Sir Geraint, Sir Lancelot, Sir Percivale, Sir Tristram, Stromness, Tidepool, Tidespring.*

Ships taken up from trade: (liners) SS *Canberra,* SS *Uganda,* RMS *Queen Elizabeth 2*; (tankers) MV *Alvega,* MV *Anco Charger,* MV *Balder London,* MV *British Avon,* MV *British Dart,* MV *British Esk,* MV *British Tamar,* MV *British Tay,* MV *British Test,* MV *British Trent,* MV *British Wye,* MV *Fort*

Toronto, MV *G. A. Walker*, MV *Scottish Eagle*, MV *Shell Eburna*; (roll-on, roll-off general cargo) SS *Atlantic Causeway*, SS *Atlantic Conveyor*, MV *Baltic Ferry*, MV *Contender Bezant*, MV *Elk*, MV *Europic Ferry*, MV *Nordic Ferry*, MV *Tor Caledonia*; (container ship) MV *Astronomer*; (passenger/ general cargo) MV *Norland*, TEV *Rangatira*, MV *Saint Edmund*, RMS *Saint Helena*; (general cargo) MV *Avelona Star*, MV *Geestport*, MV *Laertes*, MV *Lycaon*, MV *Saxonia*, MV *Strathewe*; (offshore support vessels) MV *British Enterprise III*, MV *Stena Inspector*, MV *Stena Seaspread*, MV *Wimpey Seahorse*; (tugs) MT *Irishman*, MR *Salvageman*, MT *Yorkshireman*; (cable ship) CS *Iris*.

INDEX

Other titles published by The History Press

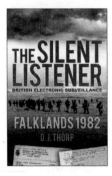

The Silent Listener: Falklands 1982: British Electronic Surveillance

MAJOR D.J. THORP

On 2 April 1982 Argentina launched Operation *Rosario*, the invasion of the Falklands. The British, caught off guard, responded with Operation *Corporate*. Deployed alongside the rest of the British army was a small specialist intelligence unit, whose very existence was unknown to many commanders and whose activities were cloaked in the Official Secrets Act. Trained during the years of the Cold War, the OC of the unit, D.J. Thorp, recounts their story.

9780752460291

Don't You Know There's a War On?

JONATHAN CROALL

Gathering together the personal stories of thirty-five people, drawn from all walks of life, this book evokes the reality of life in Britain during the Second World War. Here is a personal portrait of a nation at war, with contemporary photographs, diaries, letters, poems, and other memorabilia belonging to the men and women whose wartime lives are featured.

9780750936996

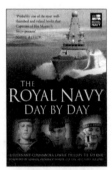

Royal Navy Day by Day

LIEUTENANT-COMMANDER LAWRENCE PHILLIPS

The Royal Navy Day-by-Day recounts all major events during the Royal Navy's rich heritage from 1 January to 31 December throughout history. The fourth edition of this much-admired book is fully revised with stunning new illustrations, bringing the history of the Royal Navy up to the present day. From the battle of Trafalgar through the First and Second World Wars, the Falklands, Gulf Wars and modern conflicts, including Libya and peacekeeping missions – this is the only book to detail Britain's extraordinary maritime history.

9780752461779

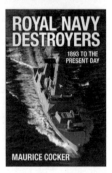

Royal Navy Destroyers: 1893 to the Present Day

MAURICE COCKER

The Torpedo Boat Destroyer became indispensable to the navies of the world and in two world wars its importance both as an offensive and defensive weapon for fleet and convoy escort duties showed that no task at sea was too much for the destroyer. The post-war Royal Navy has seen cutbacks and increased sophistication. The destroyer – now larger and armed with guided missiles – has seen both, and in this revised and updated second edition Maurice Cocker charts its history, providing much new information and a comprehensive record of the history and appearance of each class.

9780752461595

Visit our website and discover thousands of other History Press books.

www.thehistorypress.co.uk